"In this challenging book, graceful writing meets grace-full theology. The wounds of the world cry out in poetry and poignancy; the call to care crushes complacency; places below rise to expose suffering and healing in the depths; darkness shines upon light, transforming Word and world in reading, hearing and doing."
—PHYLLIS TRIBLE, Baldwin Professor Emerita of Sacred Literature, Union Theological Seminary, New York City and author of *Texts of Terror* and *God and Rhetoric of Sexuality: Overtures to Biblical Theology*.

"This is a beautiful book and a true book, proving again that they are the same thing! You will get to the essentials quickly here, and in a way that will change you both painlessly and painfully."
—[FR.] RICHARD ROHR, O.F.M., Center for Action and Contemplation, Albuquerque, New Mexico and author of *Everything Belongs: The Gift of Contemplative Prayer* and *The Naked Now: Learning to See as the Mystics See*.

"In *Geography of Grace* you will be exposed to some of the first fruits of a really novel insight into Christian faith and living. What a rich understanding of how Jesus steps into our shame and holds it in tenderness so that we can really learn to love! And how much clearer, now, that this, which we have so easily missed, goes to the core of the Gospel."
—JAMES ALISON, Priest and Theologian, Sao Paulo, Brazil and author of *On Being Liked, The Joy of Being Wrong* and *Broken Hearts and New Creations - Intimations of a Great Reversal*.

"This book smells like Jesus. It gives us permission to stop racing towards the top and take a plunge with Jesus to the bottom."
—SHANE CLAIBORNE, Author, Activist, and Recovering Sinner, Philadelphia, Pennsylvania and author of *The Irresistible Revo¹ ⁿ: Living as an Ordinary Radical*.

"Kris Rocke and Joel Van Dyke demonstrate in these r
for, find, and effectively live out Good News in som
places. Like the Jesus they follow, they show a wi'   ₁
with the transgressors, choosing to stand with   ₁an the
law-enforcers, the excluded rather than the ₅   growing
violence that makes many's hearts grow c   ₂s food
that will help people endure, making a ₅   ₁owards a
desperately-needed upgrade in street theo.
—BOB EKBLAD, author of *Reading the Bible wi.*   ₁.

"As thousands of street-level people-lovers all over the world already know, my brothers Kris and Joel are the best kind of Jesus people—kind, wise, and soulful. As you are about to find out, they are also first class thinkers. This isn't a joint memoir, or a how-to ministry book, or a polemic against selfish materialism . . . this is a seriously biblical, thoroughly Christian, 'from the gutter' reflection on the nature of God's relationship with humankind."
—BART CAMPOLO, Communicator, Pastor, and Activist, Cincinnati, Ohio.

"I had the same emotions reading this book as I had watching the first human being descend alone 7 miles to the bottom of the deepest ocean on the planet. Tantalizingly few photos have appeared to-date, but enough to know that the entire planet looks different from below, and how ironic that we know more about outer space today, than this subterranean geography. Kris and Joel explore the contours of doing theology from eerie and marginal places, yet in community. They do theology in ways that connect hopefully, but gently with powerful images and stories for those locked into unimaginable terror, in and outside prisons."
—RAY BAKKE, Urban Missiologist, Founder of Bakke Graduate University, Bakken, Washington and author of *A Theology As Big As the City* and *The Urban Christian*.

"Geography of Grace is written from the fringes but it hits at the center of where the world meets the Word. We hope to introduce these sometimes unorthodox and slightly irreverent reflections to the thousands of church planters we train, who often work on the front lines of human pain and suffering. I have personally been stretched and challenged by intersecting with their writing and ministry, and I trust them because they hang out with the Shepherd and smell like sheep."
—JUAN WAGENVELD, President—Multiplication Network and author of *Iglecrecimiento Integral* and *Sembremos Iglesias Saludables*.

"Grace is shared abundantly in the poetic beauty of this book: a grace located in the deepest trenches of human suffering and global urban fractures; a disarming grace, meeting you on every page, robed in profanity, steeped in the incarnation, erupting in surprising, awe-inspiring transformations. It is a guide book for opening us up to the poetry and profanity of God's beautiful grace, a grace more than able to make us over, and also the cities in which we live."
—STEPHAN DE BEER, CEO—Tshwane Leadership Foundation, Pretoria, South Africa.

"Searing in its exploration of troubling texts in Scripture as well as the painful journeys of people pressed to the bottom by society's superstructure of privilege, *Geography of Grace* reminds us God doesn't miss a footprint of those sacred journeys. Simultaneously, it illuminates the crawl spaces of our own lives pushed down by the weight of our own egos. This is the most helpful book I have read in years—and I have lived and worked with people in poverty for thirty years."
—JOHN HAYES, Founder and President of InnerCHANGE, London, England, and author of *Submerged: Living Deep in a Shallow World—Service, Justice and Contemplation Among the World's Poor.*

"Reading *Geography of Grace* provides a unique opportunity to eavesdrop on a dynamic, on-going conversation between the Word and the world. The protagonists in this conversation are people who live and minister in some of the hardest places of our world. I can personally attest to the transformative power this conversation has had among grassroots leaders and their communities in Central America and the Caribbean. Don't read this book expecting to agree with everything. But do expect to be challenged and moved."
—JOEL HUYSER, Founding Director—Nehemiah Center for Transformation, Managua, Nicaragua.

"This is a remarkable book. Remarkable for its accessibility, its creativity, its humanity, and its methodology. Engaging with a range of marginalized contexts, the authors and the communal project of which they are a part develop a jazz-like theological method that inhabits the interface between the prophetic biblical text and 'abandoned' communities. The narrative style they adopt allows the dangerous memories of scripture and marginalized community to weave their way into our stories and journeys."
—GERALD WEST, Professor—Ujamaa Centre for Community Development & Research and School of Religion, Philosophy, and Classics, University of KwaZulu-Natal, Pietermaritzburg, South Africa and author of *Reading Otherwise: Socially Engaged Biblical Scholars Reading with Their Local Communities.*

"Whether you've been a faithful believer since a child, threatened to walk away from it all or new to a life with Christ, your mind, soul and body will be engaged and transformed as you read this. Don't miss a word!"
—DR. NANCY MURPHY, LMHC, Executive Director, Northwest Family Life and educator, advocate, supervisor, Seattle, Washington.

"The single most important issue that we face is how to meaningfully undergo and demonstrate the grace of God in tangible ways to those in difficult places. It is through the mystery of the incarnation that we can touch both a spiritualized church and a materialized world with equal integrity. *Geography of Grace* embodies this mystery and distills its essence without denaturing it. The outcome of this work is that it allows the reader to traverse this vast landscape in intelligible ways that is so critical in the 21st century."
—DAVE HILLIS, President, Leadership Foundations, Tacoma, Washington.

"I'm always on the lookout for resources to help sustain the lives of ministry teams in our lower-income, higher-risk urban settings. This book is precisely what I've been looking for. I'm confident that *Geography of Grace* will become one of the primary texts we'll use for training, and for developing a common theological language to help our team make sense of continuous suffering and constant change within our context."
—JEFF JOHNSEN, D.Min., Executive Director, Mile High Ministries, Denver, Colorado.

"Too often we read books that confirm our thoughts by giving words to what we were already thinking. *Geography of Grace* opens up whole new thoughts and disrupts many old ones. It is a prophetic journey of the soul. It will make you laugh and cry. It will make you feel stupid and humble, angry, and frustrated, unsettled and full of hope. A book like this deserves to read in the same way it was written—in community. Do not read *Geography of Grace* alone."
—BRAD SMITH, President – Bakke Graduate University, Dallas , Texas.

"Kris and Joel take us on a vision trip, recounting their own joy and surprise as they have read the Bible with vulnerable people in vulnerable places. They weave Bible stories, mission experiences, poetry, and theology together to re-imagine a 'sustainable missional theology' for people who have been 'crushed by life.' They call us all to see the movement of God's grace in these places, knowing it will change how we see God at work in our own lives. Their stories will stir your heart and draw you into God's hope for the world."
—JO-ANN BADLEY, Ph.D., Professor, New Testament, The Seattle School of Theology & Psychology, Seattle, Washington.

Geography
of Grace
Doing Theology From Below

Geography
of Grace
Doing Theology From Below

Kris Rocke & Joel Van Dyke

Street Psalms Press

For more information on Center for Transforming Mission or to
contact Kris or Joel please go to www.CTMnet.org

ISBN: 978-0-9852334-0-2

Library of Congress Cataloging-in-Publication Data is available upon
request.

Published in association with Samizdat Creative:
samizdatcreative.com

Cover design: Jeff Hostetter

Cover photo: Tim Merrill

To grassroots leaders
who teach and preach good news
in hard places.

contents

introduction   17

section 1—descending

1   blue note   29

2   reading the word   45

3   reading the world   59

4   radical presence   71

5   beautiful questions   78

6   holy ground   89

section two—hovering

7   symbolic universe   99

8   insiders and outsiders   124

9   drama of embrace   139

10   unbounded spirit   149

11   riddles of grace   169

section 3—hanging

12	cruciform mission	179
13	the poetry of truth telling	202
14	voices from below	212
15	ministry of memory	221
16	cruciform community	230

section four—ascending

17	seeing a new thing	255
18	the new normal	261
19	the god who sees	280
20	community of desire	287
conclusion (or lack thereof)		306

appendix	308
bibliography	311
endnotes	326

acknowledgments

Today we begin the long journey to Easter by way of the cross. We have made this journey many times before, but never exactly this journey because each year things are different. Circumstances change, lives unfold. We've been here before, but never exactly right here and so we journey on.

It is fitting that we should wrap up this book today, Ash Wednesday. This is a book about the journey to Easter by way of the Cross and such a journey cannot be made alone. It requires a community—a community of the cross, and this is what we have been gifted with. Each companion in our lives brings the journey to life in ways that only they can, and so we write from within a community who has shaped us deeply and irrevocably. It's silly to try and qualify all the contributions of those who have made this book possible and grounded its contents in the reality we seek to honor. We simply want to say thanks and trust that what is left unsaid about the people we love most will make room for the Spirit to do what the Spirit does best—call forth life.

Joel: I would like to thank my wife Marilyn and children Joel and Sofia who have displayed an unbelievable amount of patience with me during the two years or so of this project. They are, for me, God's daily smile of scandalous grace.

Kris: I would like to thank my wife Lana who is one of the most grounded people I know and whose experience of the incarnation has given me the courage to trust what I have seen and heard. And my sons, Grant and Mitchell who still let me bless them each night.

We both want to thank the Street Psalms Community and the ministry staff with whom we have served. They have provided us with a home filled with friends who have helped us act, reflect and discern like Jesus. Their collective fingerprints are all over this manuscript.

We'd also like to thank Scott Dewey for giving this book, and many more to come, a home at Street Psalms Press.

Finally, we want to thank the grassroots leaders we serve and the communities that they love, most of whom will never in a million years read this book and don't need to! What a gift.

—Ash Wednesday, 2012

I know nothing, except what everyone knows
if there when Grace dances, I should dance.
—W. H. Auden

introduction

WHEN IT COMES to grace, geography matters. This book is a conversation about what it means to teach and preach good news in hard places. It is *theology from below.* It is a biblical conversation set in the underbelly of a global, urban, and postmodern world. It is a conversation especially suited for those who serve high-risk youth and families in hard places.

In this book, we'll explore the geography of grace with and for those who have been labeled the "least, last, and the lost." It was written from the crucible of deep personal struggle among a community of leaders that has spent many years "doing" grassroots theology.[1] So, we are not writing in isolation as "keepers of truth" or "insightful innovators"; rather, we are attempting to give voice to a conversation that we have been engaged in for 20-plus years. A conversation rooted in our growing love for both the Word and the world.

This community of urban leaders has gelled into a sort of ragtag religious order, called "Street Psalms: A Community of the Incarnation," and part of what has pulled us together is that we have come to see Scripture as God's declaration of love

for the "least." So, we as a Community hope this book will encourage, challenge, provoke, disturb, and raise questions among
grassroots leaders who have sometimes given up finding good
news in the Bible that can be heard and received in their context.
As we've said, we wrote this book out of love for God's creative work among those who live at the margins of society. But
we also wrote it out of a holy discontent for the gospel that is
nurtured and proclaimed within the mainstream church—a
gospel that can unwittingly sows seeds of violence and despair
among society's most vulnerable members, a gospel that has
been and still is being exported from North America to hurting
people around the world. We confess our own participation in
the spread of such a gospel, but it remains our prayer that both
love and holy discontent will inflame in us a desire to take greater responsibility for the gospel we proclaim and the social loca-
tions from which we proclaim it.

Our exploration of the geography of grace, will test two
assumptions:

1. *Grace is like water—it flows downhill and pools up in the
lowest places.* This is our basic thesis. It begs the question of
whether or not there is indeed a "geography" of grace. Could it
be that the deepest reservoirs of God's grace are located in the
lowest places? If we seek to experience deeper levels of God's
grace, shouldn't we take a swim in the places where God's grace
pools up? Do the people and places most marginalized and os-
tracized by the mainstream society and the church actually hold
a prophetic vision *for* us all? We will engage these questions as
we explore the limits and boundaries of God's grace on behalf of
those who feel damned and disinherited by God.

2. *If we are going to test the limits of grace, we must be willing to be wrong.* It is incumbent upon all of us, especially those

of us who are leaders to risk our power and privilege on behalf of the powerless, learning to embrace not only the possibility, but the very distinct *probability* that we have been wrong about a great many things that have seemed so central to our faith. This is especially true of white, male leaders (like ourselves) who share in and benefit from the dominant culture. Our proclamation of the gospel is often a product of the power and privileges we enjoy. Therefore, if we are to teach and preach good news to the poor who live at the mercy of the dominant culture, and who endure the theological categories we produce, we must be willing to take great risks. The gospel of Jesus' liberating word invites us not only to examine, but also to challenge and even subvert, if necessary, "orthodoxy" as it is defined and practiced by the mainstream church. In other words, we are invited to reclaim the Bible's liberating Word for the world and risk being wrong about unexamined assumptions and long-held beliefs that in reality do great harm in the name of being "right."

At the risk of sounding dramatic, perhaps a classic literary quotation will make this point clearer, a bit of spiritual wisdom from a patron saint of our work, Saint Huckleberry Finn:

"All right, then, I'll go to hell."

In Mark Twain's American classic novel *Huckleberry Finn*, Huck is a 13-year-old white boy growing up in the pre-Civil War American South, who helps a runaway slave named "Nigger Jim" escape to freedom. Huck's declaration is the moral center of the story. The 1850 Fugitive Slave Law made it illegal to aid or abet a runaway slave and required that every U.S. citizen assist in the capture of runaways. Huck deeply and genuinely believes (as he was taught) that by helping Jim he will not only suffer the wrath of the law, but also the wrath of God Himself. Huck is convinced that he will be sent to hell for helping Jim escape slavery.

Suffering under the weight of this moral dilemma, Huck writes a letter to Jim's owner, Miss Watson, to turn him in, thus freeing his conscience and his soul from eternal damnation. After writing the letter, Huck reflects on his relationship with Jim, their journey together down the Mississippi river, and the deep friendship they had formed along the way. Huck realizes something for which his upbringing, culture, theology, and even his God had not prepared him for—that "Nigger Jim" was a human being. Huck is completely undone by Jim. He tears up the letter, convinced that by doing so he is condemning himself to hell. This is where Huck's adventure takes a huge turn. He is undergoing grace—the kind that empowers us to risk it all for the sake of those we love.

All right, then, I'll go to hell.[2]

Salvation has come—to both Huck and Jim. They are of one piece. Their salvation is bound together and inseparable. These fugitives become symbols of freedom.

This is a beautiful picture of what it means to do "theology from below" in the context of high-risk communities. We in the Street Psalms Community have within our network many Hucks and even more Jims. Our salvation is bound together and costly to both.

In his poem "dive for dreams," e.e. cummings writes, "trust your heart/if the seas catch fire/(and live by love/though the stars walk backward)."[3] The gospel invites us to follow love even when our theology, our culture, and yes even if what we take for god says otherwise. What courage, what humility, what generosity! Like Huck, our friends within the Street Psalms network have been mapping the geography of grace and even celebrating what theologian James Alison calls the "joy of being wrong."[4] We invite you to join the celebration.

THE GROUND ON WHICH WE STAND

Our reflections on God's grace and its meaning for the mission of the Church are grounded in the concrete realities we have experienced in the low places of the world. For example, we live and work with leaders in cities throughout the United States, Central America, the Caribbean, Africa, Thailand, and Romania who serve some of the most vulnerable youth and families in the most challenging communities. We look for what God is doing in places of pain and shame among the world's poor where poverty and violence are the daily realities. We want to understand the gospel among the least by removing the stained glass from Scripture and learning to "do" theology from below.

We believe that God's voice, like the voice of Abel—whose very name means "vapor" or "breath"—is speaking through the bloodstained ground of the people and places where suffering and death is a way of life.[5] In fact, it is our hunch that God's voice is clearest and most strikingly Godlike in these places. In this sense, *theology from below* is to the Church as research and development is to business—when we learn to hear the voice of God in the vaporous holes of the world, we learn how to make sense of His voice, and perhaps even to occupy one or two of the holes we stumble into.

To avoid unseemly places is to avoid God's grace in its most abundant and often scandalous form. Phyllis Trible puts it more forcefully in her book *Texts of Terror* when she insists that to avoid the low places is not only to avoid the theological challenges they present, but to "falsify faith"—the very faith that claims to give meaning and hope to those who have been crushed by life.[6]

Trible's challenge will function as a guide, especially through the most difficult parts of the conversation that follows. The meditations of this text are something of an Augustinian statement of faith in that if they accurately represent faith at all, it is "faith in search of understanding."[7] We do not pretend to claim any mastery of what we have come to believe. We as a community are growing into our faith—slowly and sometimes with great resistance. In fact, another patron saint who represents our collective voice might very well be the father of the sick child who said to Jesus, "I believe Lord, help my unbelief."[8]

Above all, this book is a conversation between two passions that have shaped our collective calling over the past twenty years: The Word and the World. We are in love with both. It is not a particularly new or innovative conversation for those who are accustomed to such things. But it is a conversation that has occupied, consumed, disoriented, frustrated, shattered, and transformed us in our daily lives as ministers of the gospel of Jesus Christ in hard places. It is both unapologetically personal and also uncontrollably public. It has made us and unmade us many times over, and we suspect it will continue to do so as long as we have breath.

At its core, this conversation is a dialogue between Scripture and the street. Karl Barth taught that if Christians are to preach good news, they must learn to hold the Bible in one hand and the newspaper in the other—and do so with equal integrity.[9] We take this to mean that if our gospel is to be good news, it must speak *in, to, with,* and even *from* the reality of daily life and the concrete contexts in which people live. To sever the Word from the world is to do violence to both. If Christians are to preach and teach good news, text and context must greet one another with a holy kiss. Even when the romance is stormy, as it is so often, they must at least be on speaking terms with one another.

Therefore, with the help of our contemplative brothers and sisters, we are learning how to pray the Word and the World in the same breath. We are learning how to fall head over heels in love with both the Word that creates and sustains the world, and also the world which is the very cradle of the Word.

A WORD ABOUT OUR METHOD

Another hope we have for this book is that it will accompany a series of courses we use with grassroots leaders around the world called the Street Psalms Intensives. (For a description, see pages 308-310.) We employ a highly dialogical approach in the Intensives—one that is hard to replicate in book form. Therefore, it is important to say something about the methodology that informs this text.

When we talk about doing "theology from below," we are making a very practical statement. We are talking about reading Scripture with and for vulnerable people and vulnerable places. Our use of the term "theology from below" does not dismiss important insights to be gleaned "from above"; for instance, it does not deny the academy its place in the conversation nor does it dismiss the contributions of scholarship. Doing theology from below makes room for all these gifts, but they are not the only voices and they are no longer the most privileged ones. As Bob Ekblad suggests in the title of his book, our work is about *Reading the Bible With The Damned.*[10] Dietrich Bonhoeffer puts it this way,

> We have learned to see for once the great events of world history from below—through the perspective of the barred, the suspects, the badly treated, the powerless, the oppressed, the scoffed—in short the perspective of those who suffer—we see that

personal suffering is a more suitable key, a more
fruitful principle, than is personal good fortune for
exploring the world by observation and action.[11]

It helps to remember that most, if not all, of Scripture was written within the context of oppression and suffering. God used a
minority voice to speak within the dominant culture. Almost
all of the people we read Scripture with are amazed and comforted to find in its pages stories that match their own experiences. Such is the gift of doing theology from below.

In our search for a methodology of reading Scripture that
works among hurting people, we have also had the good fortune of discovering that the Spirit delights to not only move
within us, but the Spirit also moves *between* us. In fact, we have
come to believe that the space *between* relating partners is the
space in which the Spirit is most fully revealed and most fully
at home. Many of us have been taught that the Spirit takes up
residence within us, as if this were the Spirit's primary home.
We are discovering that the Spirit does not merely take up residence within us but also delights in moving between us, occupying the space between relating partners, making it possible
for real connection that is otherwise impossible. Martin Buber
went so far as to say, "All real living is meeting."[12] Buber believed
that a true, encounter between people is holy ground and the
basis of life itself. He called it the I-THOU relation. Paul Tillich
called it the realm of the "really real."[13] C. S. Lewis noticed the
same thing in his foundational prayer: "May it be the real I who
speaks. May it be the real Thou that I speak to."[14] There is nothing more fundamental, mysterious, freeing, or life-giving than
when the real "I" meets the real "Thou." A face-to-face meeting with anyone, especially God, is the momentary glimpse of
all that is real. In that moment, all that is false grows strangely

dim and ultimately dies in the face of the really real. It is in this space that we encounter both the mystery and power of what we call conversational theology—the very substance of our communal work with leaders pouring out their lives on the margins of society.

Our approach keeps us from staking out some privileged dogmatic claim where there is only one right answer. As others have noticed, our style is more jazz than classical, more narrative than prose, more informal than formal, more communal than individual. We enter the conversation from the margins to influence the center. We enjoy lyrical, poetic, and playful language. We love questions that tease, provoke, and sometimes confuse. We can be slightly irreverent—and it might be important to state that from the outset. There is movement and direction to our work, but it is not linear. We readily admit that our approach is not without risk. We borrow the words of Phyllis Trible, who once warned her readers, "In joining this venture the reader assumes its risks."[15]

As we've said, our method has a jazz-like quality to it. It really is true, and we make much of the jazz metaphor in our training. Doing theology from below means all participants have a voice and stake in the conversation, even those with whom we disagree. All voices are featured—sometimes most especially the ones that are hardest to listen to. Listening well is part of what makes jazz work. In keeping with the jazz metaphor, we often refer to these voices as the "blue notes."

The blue note is the note that puts the *jazz* in jazz—it is the unique contribution of the genre. There are three "blue notes" in jazz—the flatted 3rd, flatted 5th, and flatted 7th. The flatted 5th is the bluest of the blue notes. Jazz invented that strange and elusive note to give voice to pain. It is the note that disrupts and creates dissonance. It resists resolve. It disorients and sometimes irritates, but when blended with the larger score, it gives voice to the ache and longing associated with pain. Kathleen O' Connor writes, "The first condition for healing is to bring the pain and suffering into view."[16] For the jazz connoisseur, it is known as music that heals in part because the flatted 5th is the note that brings pain and suffering into view. To that end, our hope is that this book gives voice not only to those on the margins, but also to those for whom pain is a way of life.

This adventure will bring us into conversation with Central American gang members in maximum security prisons, with street youth in Central America's largest city, with prostitutes on the streets of Santo Domingo, scavengers in city garbage dumps, orphans in Eastern Europe, tribal conflicts in Kenya, and the extreme poor in some of the largest slums in the world. These are just a few of the "meeting spaces" of the grassroots leaders we serve.

Authentic encounters within the realm of the really real are fleeting at best. As T.S. Eliot says, "Humankind cannot bear very much reality."[17] We know this to be true. We will not ask the reader to bear too much reality. However, we do hope to honor the Spirit at work in the low places. We pray that it honors our colleagues who serve there. Most importantly, we pray that it honors those who swim in the deepest pools of God's grace, who have taught us to hold the Word in one hand and the world in the other with great affection and hope.

—*section one*—
descending

And the Word became flesh and lived among us.
John 1:14

The hint half guessed, the gift half-understood,
is Incarnation.
T.S. Eliot, "The Dry Salvages"[18]

1

blue note

Consider it, take counsel and speak out.
Judges 19:30

The journey is solitary and intense. In joining this
venture the reader assumes its risks.
Phyllis Trible[19]

THE STREET PSALMS network regularly hosts groups of North
Americans on what we call "vision trips" in hard places
around the world. In contrast to a "mission trip," which centers
on what an outsider comes to "do" in a foreign country or another culture, a vision trip focuses on the invitation for an outsider to come and "see" what God is doing through grassroots
leaders serving their own people. Well-crafted encounters and
targeted theological reflection enable visitors to re-imagine and
broaden their understanding of life and mission—they become

students of God's activity in a foreign country or another culture. Vision trips liberate "mission" from incarceration to the limitations of a program or the responsibility of a select committee in a church. The goal is for mission to become a lifestyle. These vision trip experiences, when rooted in the correct geography of grace, help make that happen.

In Guatemala City, every vision trip group will at some point make its way to the national cemetery that overlooks the *basurero* (municipal garbage dump) where hundreds of families sustain themselves by digging through the daily trash looking for discarded treasure amid the filth. There among broken tombstones, dead trees, and swarming vultures, we read and reflect upon Judges 19.

Why Judges 19? And why read it in the place of the dead beside the largest garbage dump in Latin America? It could be said that this chapter is perhaps the lowest point in Scripture, except for the crucifixion of Jesus. If we are to hear the Word with equal force in our sacred text and in our own challenging context, we must have the courage to listen from the furthest reaches of each—even in the depths. We must resist our inevitable urge to quicken our pace, to hurry past horror. We have learned to linger in the stench of death as we wait for a word of life. And so we linger here, in these pages, at the outset of our theological work—not passively, but attentively, with the *basurero* and the pages of an appalling story spread before us.

This largely unread chapter of the Hebrew Scriptures tells the gruesome story of an unnamed sex slave who is gang-raped, beaten within an inch of her life, and then murdered by dismemberment by the one who said he loved her. Her death sparks a civil war in which thousands of other innocent men, women, and children are brutally killed. To top it off, another six hundred young and unsuspecting virgins are forced into "marriage" and turned into sex slaves as a result. To add insult to injury, this woman is never given the dignity of a name, neither is she allowed to speak for herself. Apparently, all of this happens because, "In those days there was no king in Israel; all the people did what was right in their own eyes" (Judges 21:25).

The unnamed woman at the center of the narrative is the sex slave of a Levite, a member of the priestly tribe of Israel, who lives in the remote parts of the hill country of Ephraim. The fact that he lives in the remote hill country is an important detail in the story, because we know that a good Levite should reside in or near one of the forty-eight Levitical cities that God had set aside when he parceled out land to the twelve tribes of Israel. All the other tribes got tracts of land, but the Levites were given cities since their job was to be God's priestly presence in the public squares. For whatever reason, this Levite lives in a remote hill country with his concubine.

The Levite and the concubine have a fight, and the concubine is moved to anger. She becomes so angry that she leaves the hill country to return to her father's house. A sex slave with no rights does not take matters into her own hands, so she must have been deeply provoked to shame her master in this way and expose her shame to her father's house. It is a risky move on her part. Something has gone dreadfully wrong.

Ironically, her departure awakens something unexpected in the Levite. Her insolence gives rise to feelings of concern, and for a moment he becomes almost human. It seems that he remembers that he loves her. He decides to go after her to "speak tenderly to her, and bring her back." This beautiful and poetic phrasing in the text connotes deep affection. It is the language of love. It is the same language God uses toward Israel many years later after Israel's return from exile in Babylon. "Comfort, O comfort my people, says your God. Speak tenderly to Jerusalem . . . " (Isaiah 40:1). So the Levite sets off to win back the sex slave he loves, and it is clear from the narration that we are to believe his motives.

The Levite arrives and is greeted with warm hospitality by the concubine's father. Given the circumstances, this seems a strange welcome by the father, even by Middle Eastern standards where hospitality is highly valued. There is no mention of the concubine, no words of tenderness. In fact, the Levite never speaks a word to the woman at all, let alone speaks to her heart. Instead, the Levite and the woman's father launch into a four-day party. Each day, when the Levite gets up to leave the father insists that they eat and drink more. In fact, the text says that he "made" him stay. We are not witnessing simple Middle Eastern hospitality here. We are more likely witnessing the wild binge of a raging alcoholic. Perhaps he drinks like this to live with himself for what he has done or failed to do with his daughter. There is no mention of the father's spouse. We are left to speculate whether she is dead or has fled the house because she can't take any more of her husband's binging, or perhaps she remains in the house but has fallen silent to protect herself.

On the fifth day the Levite is determined to leave with his concubine, whom he has still not talked to, but her father convinces the Levite to have a few more for the road. Finally, after another full day of drinking, the Levite shakes himself loose of the father and leaves with his still-unnamed woman, his "property." Even now there is still no sign that the Levite has spoken tenderly to her heart. Perhaps the party has dulled his memory and quieted his longing for reconciliation.

The Levite and his sex slave have gotten such a late start

on their journey home that they spend the night among the Benjamites in Gibeah. Ironically, the only one who offers to put them up for the night is not a Benjamite, but an outsider. This small detail foreshadows the peril that follows. Some of the boys in town, who are described as a "perverse lot," hear about the visitors and come knocking. The text says that, while these men are "enjoying themselves," (a wildly suggestive image open to all kinds of lewd possibilities) the host answers the door. They ask if they can have sex with the Levite. Shocked and deeply offended at the idea of such a wicked and vile thing being done to his male guest, the host angrily refuses. However, he offers as an alternative his own unnamed virgin daughter to do with whatever they want. The host's response is even more shocking than the original request. The men, however, persist in their desire for the Levite. Fearing for his life, the Levite violently "seizes" his concubine and throws her out to the mob—as Trible writes, the woman is cruelly "betrayed into the hands of sinners."[20] Angered by this rebuff, they gang rape her throughout the night. The next morning, when the Levite awakes (amazingly, it seems he had a good night's sleep), he opens the door to go back home and finds his concubine's body barely alive, with her hands on the threshold of the door. Here we get the clear impression that the Levite is on his way out the door not to rescue his love and speak tenderly to her heart, but rather to cut his losses and head home. Apparently he has decided that the concubine had been defiled and is of no more value to him, but he can't leave because she's lying at the threshold of the door. She is quite literally in his way.

Then we finally hear the Levite speak his first and only words to her. They are not words of tenderness spoken to her heart. He does not confess his fear and weakness, nor does he reassure her of his love, as she lies at the threshold of death itself. Instead he says, "Get up! We are going." But she can't get up. She has been beaten and gang-raped all night long. It is a miracle that she made it back to the threshold of the door. "Behold, I stand at the door and knock"—the irony here is brutal and heartbreaking. After a torturous night of abuse, she crawls back to the one who fed her to her abusers.

"Get up!" he yells. She can't get up, or even respond. So, the Levite throws her on the donkey, much like he threw her out of the house the night before, and quite literally decides to cut his losses. The Levite "grasps" his sex slave and cuts her "limb by limb" into twelve parts. He then mails the pieces to the tribes of Israel. (The text gets fuzzy on whether or not the concubine is alive or dead when the Levite dismembers her, but as Trible suggests, there is textual evidence that she was still alive.)

At this point in the text there is a break in the action, and we hear what sounds like a new voice. Some argue it is the Levite himself, but given the half-truths he later tells the twelve tribes about what happened with the concubine, it doesn't seem likely to be him. Trible points out that it may be the real voice of the narrator interrupting the story, having had enough of the Levite's carnage. But who is this mysterious narrator?

The voice says, "Thus shall you say to all the Israelites, 'Has such a thing ever happened since the day that the Israelites came up from the land of Egypt to this day?'" It is a rhetorical question to which the only possible answer is an emphatic "NO!"

The voice continues and offers a three-step plan for redemption: *Consider it. Take counsel. Speak out.* We will look at each of these in turn.

Consider it. Trible points out that this first imperative is actually the Hebrew idiom "direct your heart to her," which parallels the Levite's initial intentions toward the concubine when he set out to bring her back. The voice is asking Israel to do the one thing that the Levite himself could not bring himself to do.

Take counsel. The voice instructs Israel to reflect on the heart of the one who has been raped and dismembered. The voice pleads with Israel to build a council that will consider her and reflect on her heart tenderly.

Speak out. Having considered her heart tenderly, and having built a council that does the same, then and only then does the voice urge Israel to speak out.

Notice the order of the commands. The voice knows the danger of speaking without reflecting—of acting without thinking. Had Israel listened and done what the Levite failed to do, perhaps things would have unfolded differently. Unfortunately the tribes didn't listen. Civil war breaks out and the other eleven tribes crush the Benjamites, killing 25,000 men and *all* of the women and children. They even killed all the Benjamite "beasts," perhaps the most innocent of all the victims. Only 600 Benjamite men survived.

What started out as the story of one man failing to direct his heart and speak tenderly to his lover, becomes the story of a nation that fails to direct its heart to one of its most violently abused victims and speak tenderly to them. What started as the death of one unnamed woman escalates into the death of thousands of unnamed men, women, and children. The ultimate betrayal is that Israel pulls God into the sordid mess by projecting her lust for vengeance into God's mouth. What started as the brutal rape of one sex slave becomes the brutal rape and enslavement of 600 innocent women, allegedly sanctioned by God himself. We are in radically dangerous geography.

When the Israelites fail to direct their hearts to the unnamed woman, they go on a rampage to exact vengeance from the tribe of Benjamin. The indignation of the heinous crime galvanized the community's self-righteous thirst for revenge and gave them a scapegoat that would satisfy and justify their own brutality. In disregarding the prayers of the mysterious voice, they disregard their own humanity.

In a final and absurd act of violence, the eleven tribes agree that they cannot leave their cousins, the 600 Benjamite male survivors, without wives to replenish their tribe lest they die out and be lost forever. So they decide to attack Jabesh-Gilead, killing all but four hundred virgins. These four hundred virgins are given to the 600 Benjamite men. But that is bad math, leaving 200 Benjamite men without any female companionship to satisfy their needs. The elders gather one more time, now turning their attention to the daughters of Shiloh. At the annual praise festival where the women would be worshipping the Lord through dance, the tribal elders instructed the 200 remaining Benjamite men to hide in the bushes and seize whichever virgins caught their fancy. That day, an additional 200 virgins are turned into sex slaves— they are taken against their will and forced to have sex with "husbands" that they do not know or love. Order is restored and the tribe of Benjamin survives.

WHY JUDGES 19 AND WHY IN A CEMETERY?

So we return to the question with which we began this chapter. "Sad stories," writes Trible, "yield new beginnings."[21] This strange hope gives us courage to sift through the carnage of this haunting story and test the limits of the gospel we teach and preach. It is an extraordinarily difficult blue note to hear, but to stop our ears to it is to abandon not only the unnamed sex slave in her already abandoned state, but also countless modern day victims for whom this story is a present reality.

When a group of North American Christians stand on the precipice of a cliff in Guatemala overlooking hundreds of garbage-pickers in squalor, the immediate impulse is to demonize the Guatemalan church for being so blind to these deplorable conditions in the middle of their own city. However, the journey into the narrative of Judges 19 (if peered into long enough), eventually leads North Americans to consider the *basureros* full of isolated and marginalized people groups in their own cities that they had overlooked. That's when we encourage them to consider the words of the anonymous narrator in Judges 19— to consider, take counsel, and speak out on behalf of the least, last, and lost; to seek what might be a tender word for the dismembered and nameless concubines of their own communities. This disorientating and painful reorientation has borne much fruit, as our vision team visitors return to the "mission fields" of their daily lives. After leaving Guatemala from his first visit there, Henri Nouwen wrote, "We had traveled between two worlds and found them one."[22] In the same way, reflecting on Judges 19 enables us all to realize that the terrible texts we suppress even in our own Scriptures are not so far removed from the worlds we encounter

Texts of terror are daily being written in the ghettoes, slums, *favelas*, and *barrios* around the world. They are what Paul might have called "living epistles," but these epistles are horrifying tales of abandonment, brutality, violence, and despair for which there seems to be no gospel. These present-day texts of terror are daily life for the more than one billion people worldwide who live in slum communities and know the unspeakable horror that abject poverty breeds.[23]

This terrible story is not fiction for the orphans abandoned in Eastern European institutions who are beaten, sexually assaulted, and pimped on a regular basis, according to one of our Street Psalms friends. It is not a distant tale for the millions of modern-day sex slaves in Thailand, or for the gangs of North and Central America. These Scriptural narratives of chaos and terror are familiar, their plots and characters ring true. They plumb the depths of God's goodness in the face of evil. They are also routinely hidden, suppressed, denied, and dismissed by those of us who steward power in the North American church as we decide which stories are permitted in the daily lexicon of life and from our pulpits on Sunday mornings.

It is an evil that these stories exist at all, but it is twice as evil when they are virtually expunged from the church's sacred book. As Martin Marty writes, "Refusing to hear or tell the story of suffering is brutalizing."[24] Scripture itself bears witness to this truth. We need only to remember that over one third of the Psalms are written from the perspective of abandonment. Scripture gives piercing voice to pain. It is brutally honest about the failures, shortcomings, misery, and suffering of its many flawed characters. Abraham, Isaac, and Jacob were both victims and victimizers. Moses, David, and Solomon were oppressed as well as oppressors. Scripture does not spare us the sordid details of their lives, nor does it begrudge us the flatted fifth of pain that emanates from them.

The rejected "daughter Zion" in Lamentations cries out in her broken and abused state at the side of the road, "Look at me, Look at me!" to any passerby who will dare to stop and hear her story of abandonment (Lam. 2:18). She cries out to strangers (and us) believing that God has long since turned a deaf ear to her misery. And Job, the patron saint of suffering, screams for God's attention and insists on telling his story.

René Girard argues that one of the things that makes the

Bible unique is that it is the only sacred literature in history to tell the story of the victim *from the perspective of the victim* and to see and uphold her innocence.[25] Scripture gives voice to the voiceless and declares God's solidarity with the victim, yet this is the very thing that is in such danger of being lost within the North American church with our penchant for feel-good stories that uplift and inspire.

The Bible's insistence on giving voice to the victimized, unnamed sex slave, regardless of who it implicates, mirrors what we have seen and heard in the dark alleys and crowded streets from Nairobi to Guatemala City. The voice of the voiceless is God's megaphone calling us to reexamine the gospel that we teach and the theology that gives it meaning so that it becomes tangible *good news* for people who have been crushed by life.

Elie Weisel, in his autobiographical Holocaust novel *Night*, tells of the hanging of two adults and a young boy who were caught stealing a piece of bread in the concentration camp. It is a brutal story that ends without mercy. Apparently, the young boy did not weigh enough to be hung properly and ensure a quick death. Weisel and the rest of the camp watch the boy die a slow and agonizing death. One man asks, "Where is God now?"

"Right here," replies another. "Right here."[26]

This question of God's whereabouts is precisely the question that Judges 19 raises. Where is God for the unnamed woman? The only immediate and acceptable response seems to be silence. It is the same response God the Father gives when Jesus cries out on the cross. And if God responds with the sacrament of silence in the presence of his Son's agony, perhaps there is wisdom in doing the same when confronted with the reality of another's pain—to hold and be held by the pain of another long enough to be transformed by it. If this is true, how then shall we proceed? Can we say anything at all when confronted by stories like these?

Risky as it seems, we must proceed. The wisdom of silence in the presence of another's pain is not a license to avoid the faith challenge such stories place on us. There is a way to speak from within silence. We must not shy away from the theological challenges that these stories present lest we "falsify faith," as Trible says.

Liberation theologian Gustavo Gutiérrez argues, "The theme of the book of Job is not precisely suffering—that impenetrable human mystery—but rather how to speak of God in the midst of suffering," and to consider what it means "to talk to God in view of the suffering of the innocent."[27] How will Job speak to God? Even about Him? Will Job curse Him or not? This is of course the wager Satan makes with God¯the outcome of which depends on whether or not Job caves into the dominant theology of the day represented by Job's comforters. Job's comforters insist that Job deserves what he is getting, and that God is punishing Job for his sin. God blesses the righteous and punishes the sinner, right? No other explanation is possible. But Job stands firm in the midst of his pain, refusing to accept this "transactional theology" that has been used throughout history to re-victimize victims. God acknowledges Job's refusal, saying that Job has "spoken correctly of me" in Job 42.

To speak authentically and with authority of God while we stand on "the harsh demanding ground" of human suffering is precisely our task at hand.[28] It is a dangerous and difficult road that forces us into a geography of grace—a place that can be excruciating to enter and navigate. This is not only the challenge of Job, but also the challenge of Judges 19—where is God in the story of the dismembered woman, and how should we speak of divine presence in the place of the dead? So we will play a kind of Russian roulette with Scripture, using Judges 19 to test the limits of God's solidarity with the least.

THE HINT HALF-GUESSED

As we've seen, the interpretive center of Judges 19 is found in the three commands: *Consider it. Take counsel. Speak out.* We are asked to *consider* the heart of the unnamed woman in a way that the Levite failed to. Why? What does the voice expect us to find there? We are also asked to consider her heart in the context of community—to *take counsel* together, doing collectively what we should have done personally. Again, what does the voice expect us to see? We are invited to *speak out* only after considering the unnamed woman's heart tenderly and building a council that does the same. But what does the voice expect us to say when we finally speak?

To get at these questions we need to recognize that, of all the tragic characters in Scripture (and probably in our world today), this unnamed sex slave is at the bottom of the rubbish heap— even Job was given a name and the dignity of telling his own story. The sex slave is the least in every way imaginable. On the rare occasion that we can hold the gaze of the unnamed woman long enough to reflect on her heart, we might even hear the words of Jesus in Matthew 25 faintly in the background, "Just as you did it to one of the least of these who are members of my family, you did it to me."

This sort of re-imagination is essential to our jazz methodology of reading Scripture—you might call it *lyrical imagination*, listening for and trying out syncopated rhythms and strange harmonies amid dissonant notes. There is something strangely discomforting in hearing Jesus' words when reflecting on the heart of the unnamed woman. Is it possible that God is really Immanuel to an unnamed sex slave that is gang-raped and dismembered? If we reflect long enough and look deeply into her heart, we discover the unthinkable. Or to be more precise, we are discovered by it. There is one very small detail in this story that gives us the courage to believe what we are suggesting.

As it turns out, this unnamed woman was born in an insignificant town called Bethlehem. This key, mentioned no less than four times, turns and liberates our imagination. Jesus was not only born in Bethlehem, but on the night that he was betrayed and abandoned into the hands of his enemies, he broke the bread, which was his body, and gave it to the twelve disciples. He asked his disciples to remember him in this meal. Jesus' body was broken and his blood was shed for the nation of Israel—a group of people that wanted him dead.

When reading Judges 19 with a sanctified imagination, it is as if we become the disciples of Jesus on the road to Emmaus in Luke 24. This passage tells of the disciples' long walk with the stranger who is suddenly revealed as Jesus when he reenacts that meal on the night that he was betrayed. Just as the stranger is revealed to be Jesus in the breaking of the bread, so too is the unnamed woman revealed to be Jesus in the breaking of her body. "Just as you have done it to the least of these . . . "

If we reflect long enough on the heart of the unnamed woman, we will come to know not only her heart, but her name as well. We will dare to give her the dignity of a name that she has been denied for more than three thousand years. We will even dare to name her the name above all others.

As grace flows downhill and pools up in Judges 19, we are confronted with what looks like a cesspool. It is offensive and scandalous beyond words, but if we can hold our gaze long

enough and reflect on the woman, she teaches us a hard but liberating truth—that she was not alone in her abandonment. She
was not alone when she was handed over to the mob. She was
not alone when she was gang-raped and beaten that night. She
alone was not cut into twelve pieces and handed out to Israel.
God was with her that night. God too was abused, beaten, raped,
and dismembered. Where is God? God is with us, particularly
among the least. Immanuel.

Now this may not seem like very much good news, but we
suspect that is because we are not nameless sex slaves. In the
Street Psalms Community we have come to believe that the last
and final question in the hearts of those who have been crushed
by life, is not the great "Why" question, though it is undoubtedly and rightfully asked by all who have ever felt forsaken. There
is an even deeper question that lurks beneath the surface of human pain. It forms itself in the deepest waters of our chaos. It
is the question too hard to put to words, too scary to mention.
The most wrenching of all questions we demand of God in our
greatest moment of need is, "Where are you? Are you with me?
Or am I utterly alone?" Nobody wants to die alone, especially a
nameless, faceless, sex slave who is being dismembered for the
sins of others. When all hope is lost, the crushed want to know
that God is with them, and if God is with them, then in what
way? As witness? Judge? If the story of the unnamed woman is
any indication of the way God is present in our suffering, it is as
One who suffers with us. And what may take an eternity to fully
comprehend is that God suffers with us during our most terrifying powerless times. This is what the Gospel dares to suggest.

This is precisely the story that Jesus came to tell when he
left his Father's house and "moved into the neighborhood," as
Eugene Peterson says.[29] When we read Scripture in light of

Judges 19, the incarnation is not just an abstract theological idea whose sole purpose is to fix the problem of sin. It becomes the concrete expression of something that has always been true. Jesus moves into the neighborhood to reveal something that has been true since the beginning—God is with us, radically so. Of course, there is more to the story of transformation than just God's presence, but this is where we begin. Trible reminds us, "As we leave the land of terror, we limp."[30] And so, as we leave the shadow and fog of Judges 19, we continue our journey, limping deeper into the geography of grace.

2

reading the word

Teacher, which commandment in the law is the
greatest?
Matthew 22:36

If you're not willing to undress,
don't enter into the stream of Truth.
Rumi[31]

I T MAY BE helpful to pause here and explore more about our
method. In this chapter, we try to make explicit what is im-
plicit throughout the rest of the book—that is, how we are learning to read both the Word and the world.

In our experience, retelling the story of Judges 19 raises all
kinds of questions about the way people approach Scripture and
see the world. Many folks have never even heard of the story of
Judges 19, let alone heard it preached in their church. It appears

that the story of the unnamed sex slave has been almost completely expunged. Hearing it for the first time in a classroom is
hard enough. Hearing it for the first time in a cemetery overlooking a garbage dump can be radically disorienting.

In Barth-like fashion, our hope is to hold the Word in one
hand and the world in the other, engaging them both in a long
conversation. But this language is misleading, for whose hands
are big enough to hold the Word or the world, much less both at
the same time, or which of us, in our fearful attempts to coerce
and control them, will not do violence to both? So, to be more
precise, our hope is to *behold* the Word and the world. Or, to
be even more precise, we want to be *held* by the Word and the
world—cradled by both with full confidence that there is a kind
of goodness and mercy at the base of it all. This grace allows
us to relax and trust that all is well. It is from this place of primal trust that we discover playful freedom even in the midst of
very difficult terrain. For some, our playfulness can be misunderstood for a lack of reverence. For others the freedom, while
deeply inviting, can also be disorienting and confusing. But,
such playful freedom does not dismiss or demean the value of
doctrinal certitude, neither is it held captive by it. We want to
engage in a challenging conversation that does not coerce us toward one point of view or another. We are concerned with *meeting* in the space between, not mind control.

Karl Rahner, the architect of the Second Vatican Council,
said what the mind wants most is *communion*, not *explanation*.
Unfortunately, communion rarely happens in a culture that feels
compelled to explain and defend almost everything, particularly our faith. It is interesting that Jesus rarely explained anything.
Richard Rohr points out that Jesus was asked 183 questions in
the Gospels,[32] but he only answered three of them directly: one

concerning his authority, another about being a king, and the third about how to pray. Jesus reframed questions into stories, riddles, dramatic theater, or he simply remained silent, but did not feel compelled to offer answers. We are convinced that Jesus wanted to subvert our human addiction to explanations wherever possible, opening us up to the possibility of communion with the Father and the promise of transformation that such communion holds for us all.

Bob Ekblad, director of Tierra Nueva and The People's Seminary in Burlington, Washington, has worked extensively with migrant farm workers and prison inmates in the United States and Central America for more than 25 years. He has been both a mentor and a friend to many of us who are learning how to read Scripture with people in the margins of mainstream society. As a result of years of trial and error, Bob has identified at least seven barriers that keep wounded people from experiencing the liberating Word of God in Scripture. He deals with some of these "common pitfalls" in his book *Reading the Bible With the Damned*, and we will explore several more.

Strangely, these pitfalls are not experienced as such by most of mainstream Christianity in North America. In fact, if they are seen at all, they are interpreted as trusted guides and guardians of orthodoxy, which is why they are so powerful and dangerous. They are like lenses that are hardly noticed or questioned and serve as unintentional and largely unconscious tools of the status quo. The net effect is twofold: First, God's Word is used to justify and reinforce the values and position of privileged insiders. Second, it becomes a tool of condemnation and judgment for those on the margins. Ekblad identifies the following barriers to reading Scripture for good news, which we have adapted from our experience as a community:

Hyper-Personalism, or *It's All About Me*. We have a tendency to fuse personal experience with Scripture in a way that prevents us from experiencing the otherness and distance of the Word. We need to respect and honor the voices in the text and let the text do the work of engaging, challenging, encouraging, unmaking, and remaking us. In a sense, we need to dumb ourselves down as humble learners before the text, letting the text speak its liberating Word of life, without grasping too tightly our fixed categories and interpretative strategies. We must recognize that premature closeness leads to false intimacy with Scripture.[33]

Domestification, or *Taming the Wild Beast*. This reflects our tendency to tame Scripture and make it safe. While we desire to encounter Scripture on its own terms and allow it to speak its liberating word into our lives, very often we (consciously or unconsciously) work to control it. Because of our fears, real or imagined, we de-claw and domesticate it, with the effect of walling ourselves off from its transforming power. These safe and self-absorbed interpretations come almost automatically.[34] In order to combat them, we must learn to reflect on Scripture from a place of active listening, humble unknowing, respect for the other, and a place of weakness. Reading the Bible (Old and New Testaments) means that we keep in mind the New Testament writers' claim about Jesus as the most complete revelation of God (Col.1:15). Reading the Bible from the perspective of faith in the untamed Jesus unlocks the Scriptures and releases its liberating power.

Reductionism, or *Bumper Sticker Bibles*. People of faith often reduce the complex realities of life into simple spiritual formulas, giving way to overly simplistic thinking. We are uneasy with mystery. We like to compartmentalize the world in artificial and rigid categories of right and wrong. So much of Scripture calls us away from our hard categories into mystery and paradox. It resists simplicity. Instead, Scripture often "complexifies" things and asks us to be willing to do the same. Behind this resistance to mystery and our desire to over-simplify things lies our need for control. True understanding involves a willingness to explore the complexities of Scripture and live with the tensions and ambiguities they create.

Isolationism, or *Just Me and My Tribe*. We tend to think of everything from the perspective of our own small world. This adversely affects our reading of Scripture, because Scripture casts a wide net. It is most powerfully liberating when read in the context of a broad and diverse community, especially among those who most intensely long for liberation. The more closed our community within rigid boundaries, the more likely is our temptation to engage in a closed and rigid reading of Scripture. In that case, we easily smuggle our political, cultural, and ideological leanings into our interpretation of the text without even knowing it, gutting the text of its power to transform. Just as we explored Judges 19 in the cemetery with the *basurero* laid out before us, we must not only learn how to read Scripture from the margins, but also to read Scripture in its whole canonical context, not just our favorite passages. We most profitably read in communion with the saints who have preceded us, with the lenses of diverse theological approaches (i.e. Protestant, Catholic, Mainline, Orthodox, Pentecostal), in active dialogue with the social sciences (psychology, sociology, political science), and even in active dialogue with the "powers" (courts, police, immigration, politicians).

Heroism, or *Superheroes and Villains*. Hero worship stems from a deep desire to "clean up" humanity, and a mistrust of human complexity. We desperately want unsullied heroes to inspire our imagination. To that end, we dangerously elevate certain biblical characters as models to emulate (Abraham, Jacob, David). But creating biblical heroes is often a way of escaping through the backdoor the scandalous nature of God's grace. This hero worship tempts us to imagine personal growth and even salvation as a magical phenomenon rather a messy process of transformation. Ironically, heroism also serves as a twisted attempt to rescue God as well as ourselves from the reality of the cross. Literary critics observe that the biblical narrative has only one hero—God—and even God as revealed in Jesus Christ was subject to great turmoil as he was "made perfect by the things that he suffered" (Hebrews 5:8). The honest reader will search the Bible in vain for model characters. We must avoid minimizing the failings of biblical personalities and resist cleaning them up even for the youngest crowd. Children and youth understand failure better than we think. Rather than touting simple virtue or superhuman success, an honest reading of scripture helps us recognize human failure as a vehicle for God's overwhelming and sometimes outrageous grace. Our children (as well as we ourselves) need to have the freedom to struggle and fail.

Moralism, or *God's Little Instruction Book*. Very often we come to the Bible as though it were a rule book primarily concerned with correcting our behavior. People of faith often search the Bible looking for information about what to do in a given situation. Like the rich young ruler in Acts 6, we want to know, "What must I do to be saved?" But the Bible is not constructed to manage our every action; even if it were so, it proves to be exceptionally difficult to find clear advice for every sort of circumstance (an index might be helpful!). Rather, the Bible tells the story of a God who saves by grace.[35] Moralism turns us away from grace and makes monitoring our activity the focus of Scripture rather than participating joyfully in God's activity. For example, the parable of the prodigal son doesn't provide a recipe for how we should stop sinning and return to God so much as it portrays the overwhelming love of God toward those who are lost. It should perhaps be more properly referred to as the story of the "Prodigal Father" with his wanton love and appalling generosity (the word "prodigal" means reckless, extravagant, and wasteful spending).[36] We must consciously ask the question, "What does this Scripture tell us about who God is and what God has done for us? What part do humans play or not play? Who is really the subject of the passage?"

Dualism, or *Split Personalities*. Robert McAfee Brown calls dualism the "Great Fallacy."[37] It is the tendency to "disincarnate" the Word by artificially dividing reality into two realms—spiritual and material. With this worldview we are tempted to regard the spiritual realm as good and the material realm as bad. This "Gnostic" way of thinking goes back to the earliest days of Christianity—the biblical writers and the earliest church leaders fought against it for important reasons. When applied to the interpretation of Scripture, it disengages divine activity from human and historical context, leading to a disembodied faith of free-floating and abstract principles. On the contrary, the vital Scriptural notion of incarnation should nudge us as readers ever deeper into our own flesh and the flesh of others.

Leaving these barriers behind will ultimately lead us to the mystery of the Incarnation—God's journey deep into humanity. This is why we must always seek to understand the real-life context in which Scripture was written, refusing to jump over the realities of the human condition to get at the "spiritual truth" of the passage. The reader must acknowledge and bring his or her own real life context into dialogue with the text, not allowing the text to become a disembodied abstraction.

Bob Ekblad and his colleague, Chris Hoke, came to Guatemala City several years ago to guide us through a process of reading the Bible with the damned, in this case gang members in maximum security prisons. In his written correspondence about the experience, Ekblad demonstrates just how important it is to not be saddled with the weight of the pitfalls listed above, so that the transforming power of Scripture can be unleashed in even the harshest and most oppressive environments:

> The guards opened the doors and left us off in the midst of 180 young men, many with tattoos covering their faces and upper bodies. Unlike our local jail, marijuana smoke, cell phone calls, a prostitute, and a dispute over a woman made it hard to get people's attention for the Bible study. I asked permission to lay hands on each one and pray for God's Presence to heal, fill, and bless them. I could sense that each hardened guy softened as Joel and I prayed with them, but the men had to be careful not to express outwardly that they were being positively affected.
>
> I then led a reflection on the call of Matthew in what turned out to be a breakthrough Bible study. I described how Matthew was a tax-collector—a member of a notorious class of people that nearly everyone hated. "Who might fit the description of tax-collectors today?" I asked. Gangs in Guatemala are accused of extorting businesses in their

territories to pay "protection taxes" [from themselves] and taxi/bus drivers to pay "circulation taxes." The men smiled and looked at each other, acknowledging that they fit the description.

"So, what was Matthew doing when Jesus called him?" I ask. The men look surprised when they note that he wasn't following any rules, seeking God or doing anything religious, but practicing his despised trade when Jesus showed up on the street and chose him.

"Let's see if Jesus made Matthew leave his gang to be a Christian," I suggest, and people look closely at the next verse. There Jesus is eating at Matthew's house with other tax-collectors and sinners and the disciples.

"So, who followed whom?" I ask, excited to see people's reaction. The men could see that Jesus had apparently followed gangster Matthew into his barrio and joined his homies for a meal as opposed to the idea of Matthew immediately leaving his "family" and joining Jesus in church.

"What do you think, you guys? Would you let Jesus join your gang?" I ask, looking directly to the two chiefs of the gang. They both had big smiles as we looked at Jesus' reaction to the Pharisees' disdain.

"Those who are well have no need of a physician, but

only those who are sick." I ask them if they are at
all offended to think of themselves as sick—and
they don't seem to be at all. I've got their attention
and Jesus' final word to the religious insiders hits
these guys like a spray of spiritual bullets from a
drive-by: "Go and learn what this means, 'I desire
mercy, not sacrifice.' For I have come to call not the
righteous but sinners." I knew from experience that
they were letting Jesus inside and hearing his call
to follow. Last Thursday, back in our local jail, two
groups of ten inmates all welcomed Jesus into their
cells and into their lives after talking through this
same Scripture with them.

But that day we still had to leave the prison. On
our way out, I wonder about the warden just as
Joel suggests we thank him. We step into his office and shake hands. I acknowledge that he has a
very complicated job needing lots of wisdom and
ask if we can pray for him and bless him. "Bueno,"
he says, and I ask if we can lay hands on him. He
accepts, but just as we begin praying he suddenly
pulls out his handgun, takes out the clip, and empties his pockets of other clips. "This is more proper!" he says, placing his gun and ammunition atop
his file cabinet. He receives our blessing and we
offer to pray for healing for an injury related to a
machete fight that left his arm, shoulder, and chest
with shooting pain. "All the pain is gone," he tells
us with a grin after we pray. We leave amazed by
the truly special unique Spirit who disarms and

loves both gangsters and warden.[38]

When we remove the barriers that blind us to the liberating power of God's Word and practice reading Scripture from below with those who have been damned by society, the text comes alive in fresh ways. We begin to see contemporary equivalents to ancient realities with striking regularity. People and places that have historically been excluded from the text find their voice, and so do we. That which seemed hidden before becomes obvious. It takes practice, but eventually text and context begin to speak with one another in radically liberating ways. We have gleaned much from people like Bob Ekblad, Gerald West, Ray Bakke, and others who make it a habit to read the Scriptures contextually. For example, when we look at the life of Jesus from below, here a few of his traits that scholars, as well as our friends from marginalized contexts, have helped us identify.

Asian-born. Jesus was an Asian-born baby. It is often overlooked but the Middle East is Asiatic and we are mindful that nearly 60% of the world is Asian born.

Mixed-race heritage. The genealogy of Jesus in the Gospel of Matthew includes four non-Jewish women. They are the only non-Jews in the line-up: Tamar and Rahab are Canaanites, which is the African side of Jesus. Ruth is a Moabite and Bathsheba is a Hititte. These "grandmothers of Christmas," as Professor Ray Bakke likes to call them, make Jesus a mestizo savior. One of the fastest growing racial groups in North America is "multi-racial."

Scandalous past. The grandmothers of Christmas have particularly colorful stories and Matthew wants us to include their stories as part of salvation history. Tamar and Rahab were prostitutes, which is bad enough, but Ruth's story is even more scandalous. Ruth was a Moabite—a group of people who were regarded in ancient Israel as the product of Lot's incest with his daughters after fleeing Sodom and Gomorrah. Because of this, the Moabites were considered perhaps the most scandalous people group of the Middle East. The last grandmother of Christmas, Bathsheba, was caught in an adulterous affair with King David that resulted in the murder of her husband, Uriah. In light of the fact that Bathsheba was a woman and a foreigner, she was likely a powerless pawn of royal abuse. Today, nearly a million women and children are trafficked as victims of the sex trade worldwide each year—an industry worth billions of dollars.[39] The grandmothers of Jesus give voice and hope to these women and children.

Teenage mother. Mary was likely as young as 13 years old when she gave birth to Jesus. Worldwide, some 14 million teenagers give birth each year.[40]

Shameful birth. There was scandal concerning Mary's conception. Joseph was tempted to quietly divorce her. It is likely that the story of Jesus' birth was some topic of concern among the community. Today, ninety-nine percent of births to teenagers under 15-years-old in the United States are outside marriage, resulting in children that some still slur as "bastards."[41]

Poor. The meager temple offering that Joseph and Mary gave at the temple was the offering of the "poor." Today, more than one billion people live in slums worldwide, a number that is expected to double in twenty years.[42]

Political refugee. Jesus' family fled to Egypt to escape Herod's persecution. Today, more than fifty million people worldwide have been forced to flee their homes in the last five years due to conflict, persecution, and political unrest.[43]

Immigrant. Jesus' family returns to Israel and quietly settles in Nazareth. Today, over ten million undocumented immigrants currently reside in the United States.[44]

Drunkard and glutton. Jesus was frequently labeled a drunkard and glutton. His first miracle of 120 gallons of good wine (6 stone jars) could not have helped his reputation in this regard. These days, the average American consumes over 25 gallons of beer, 2 gallons of wine, and 1.5 gallons of distilled spirits each year.[45]

Mentally ill. At least for a while, Jesus' own family thought that he was "out of his mind." In the United States, twenty percent of adults experienced mental illness this past year and five percent suffer from serious mental illness.[46]

Outlaw. Jesus broke Sabbath laws. The United States today has more than 1.5 million people in prison for also breaking laws.[47]

Despised and rejected. In the end, Jesus was rejected by everyone and was even thought to be cursed by God. In the United States, the leading motivations for hate crimes are race (48%), religion (19%), and sexual orientation (18%), revealing who our most despised and rejected people are.[48]

Innocent victim. Jesus was the archetypal innocent victim. Speaking of innocent victims, more than 700,000 children are confirmed by Child Protective Services each year in the United States as being abused or neglected, which represents only a fraction of those who suffer abuse.[49]

Forsaken by father. Scripture tells us that Jesus cried out, "My God, my God, why have you forsaken me?" Scholars point out that this is the only time in the New Testament that Jesus does not refer to God as Father. Fatherlessness is not unknown to us either—almost one third of all children in the United States live without their father; 50% of these are African-American.[50]

Murdered. Jesus was a victim of homicide. Today, violence is among the leading causes of death for people aged 15–44 years and affects certain populations disproportionately. For example, in the United States, African-American males aged 14-24 make up one percent of the overall population, but 30% of all homicide victims.[51]

Resurrected as wounded healer. The resurrected Christ bears the scars of his death. Some of the early church fathers believed the Church was born out of the wounds in Jesus side much like Eve came from the side of Adam. We live in a culture of the walking wounded. Over 100 million Americans suffer from chronic pain.[52]

These are just a few examples of what it means for text and context to speak with one another. Jesus occupies the shame of first century Israel with incredible ease and grace, just as he does the same with the 21st century world. Robert Capon was onto something when he suggested, "Shamelessness is the supreme virtue of the incarnation."[53] To read Scripture from below requires a certain kind of shamelessness, something that is hard to acquire for those of us who still burn with the fear of shame.

3

reading the world

God so loved the world, that he gave his only son.
John 3:16

I saw paradise in the dust of the streets.
Denise Levertov, "City Psalm"[54]

W E ARE BEGINNING to discover the thrill of two conver-
sions—one with the Word, as we have just described;
the other with the world, which we'll explore more fully in this
chapter. Each conversion invites and ignites a greater capacity to
love the Other. If learning to read the Word from below is challenging and liberating to our faith in God, learning how to read
the world from below is challenging and liberating to our faith
in humanity.

Our students are invariably interested in hearing more about
ways to see beauty in the world while looking at the grinding,

disfiguring poverty and violence that is a daily reality for so many. There is no easy path to this way of seeing. We almost always must lose our sight before we find it. Acquiring such vision has a paradoxical quality that is deeply felt but hard to parse. On the one hand, new sight almost always seems to "just happen"—arriving as a moment of unbidden insight. It is pure gift. We call it revelation.

On the other hand, new sight also almost always comes to us through pain and what at times feels like an endless journey. The disorientation associated with this process can be terrifying, but in the end it makes room for a new way of seeing. Old Testament scholar Walter Brueggemann identifies a similar pattern of transformation in the history of Israel in which biblical writers reveal a constant process of orientation, disorientation, and reorientation. It is Israel's rhythm of life with God. Regardless of whether new sight happens in moment or throughout a lifetime, the pattern is the same. This in a nutshell is the process of transformation.

The poem "City Psalm" by Denise Levertov describes a way of seeing the world that is infused with gospel insight—one that truly celebrates good news in hard places:

> The killings continue, each second
> pain and misfortune extend themselves
> in the genetic chain, injustice is done knowingly, and the air
> bears the dust of decayed hopes,
> yet breathing those fumes, walking the thronged
> pavements among crippled lives, jackhammers
> raging, a parking lot painfully agleam
> in the May sun, I have seen
> not behind but within, within the

dull grief, blown grit, hideous
concrete facades, another grief, a gleam
as of dew, an abode of mercy,
have heard not behind but within noise
a humming that drifted into a quiet smile.
Nothing was changed, all was revealed otherwise;
not that horror was not, not that killings did not continue,
but that as if transparent all disclosed
an otherness that was blessed, that was bliss.
I saw Paradise in the dust of the street.[55]

Like Levertov, we too are learning to see "paradise in the dust of the street." We are learning to see not "behind but within the dull grief and blown grit." We are learning to see an "abode of mercy" at the center of it all, even when that center is buried in layers of hurt. It is a new way of seeing that requires no small amount of practice, patience, imagination, and faith. As Isaiah writes, "I am about to do a new thing, now it springs forth, do you not perceive it?" (43:19).

There is nothing romantic or sentimental about seeing like this. It requires raw and relentless honesty about ourselves and the world—not the kind of honesty that is veiled in self-hatred or displaced anger, but the kind of honesty that is born from a deep desire for what is true. The "abode of mercy" that Levertov speaks of in her poem does not deny the horror. It does not deny the killings. Nor does it justify the carnage. It invites us to take another look—to consider this world in all its flaws and to do so without judgment—to hold and be held by the gaze of brutal affliction longer than we'd like. In our experience, it takes at least two doses of gratitude in one's heart and at least one dose of revolutionary courage to see this way.

The promise of the gospel is that God does not stand behind the world in some remote or veiled way. We don't have to look past this world and her afflictions to find hope. We do not have to convert the world before we console it. God is here now, active and present—or as Paul says with breathtaking freedom, "Christ is all and in all" (Col. 3:11). In other words, Christ is within all things, bringing forth life with the promise that we will one day see it for what it is. In this sense, the Gospel invites us to take a second look, at God, yes, but also at the world, particularly its most difficult aspects—to hold and be held by the gaze of the unnamed woman until another face emerges.

The poet Yeats declared, "Things fall apart; the center cannot hold."[56] Levertov catches a glimpse of what Yeats couldn't and calls it mercy. What a sight! What a home! Perhaps this is why Jesus wept over Jerusalem, saying, "I desire mercy, not sacrifice." The radical claim of Jesus (one that is so chronically misunderstood by our timid souls) is that within all this dust sits paradise at work, an abode of mercy that will one day be fully disclosed, even as it is disclosing itself now. This is the gospel.

The way we see sets parameters on our actions. If we cannot see paradise in the dust of the streets, it is nearly impossible to participate in it—we find it hard to celebrate life in the midst of great suffering. Judgment and bitterness threaten to overwhelm us. But, if we can see paradise in the dust of the streets, we find within ourselves a growing generosity and courage to celebrate life even in the face of suffering. To see this way can be heartwrenching, but when practiced over time, we fall more deeply in love with this world. We begin to engage it not as enemy territory whose occupants need to be evacuated to a better place, but as our home in need of healing.

But even if we do see paradise in the dust, we see only its

faint outline. Thankfully, even the traces are enough to fill our hearts with joy. It frees us to give and receive mercy, the very thing that God desires. To say it again, gospel sight does not look *beyond* the suffering of this world—it dares to look *within* it and declare that in some crazy way, notwithstanding all the pain and suffering of this world, we are already in an "abode of mercy." We are convinced that this is what Jesus came to help the blind see. To see the presence of God's kingdom at work is to be set free to practice it now.

This vision, or something very much like it, is what sustains us in our work. We call it radical realism—that is, realism grounded in the concrete experience of hope. Gospel hope dares to cut through the fog and call things what they are. It dares to suggest that within both beauty and affliction there is the real presence of a loving God. This, in fact, is reality; it is the deepest reality. We will share many stories to illustrate this hope, but for now we simply want to describe its basic shape.

Hope is changing the language we use to talk about the urban communities that we serve. We are discovering ways of speaking about our work that recognize the challenges without caving into them. We work to honor God's presence without denying the pain of the least. We are learning to see the cities of our communities in three practical ways—as *classroom, parish,* and *playground.*

City as Classroom

Jesus went throughout the cities of Galilee teaching and preaching the Gospel (Matt. 4:23). Paul moved throughout cities to bear witness to the gospel. These are examples of what it means to engage the city as a classroom. To be clear, we are not talking simply about urban ministry as a strategy to change the world.

We are talking about the fact that cities have within them all the riches of the kingdom of God if we can only see it. Our job is to pay attention to what already exists—to pray for the eyes to see and the ears to hear what God is up to in a given place.

The city is a living, breathing, and growing library of wisdom that functions in real time and is always accessible to those who are willing to sit at her feet and learn. This is because the city functions as both a *magnet* and a *magnifier* of culture, as Ray Bakke suggests.[57] It is a magnet in that people are streaming to the cities fleeing oppression and seeking opportunity. Cities continue to grow throughout the world because of this magnetic pull. In fact, more than 50% of the world is now urban. Some experts expect that number to grow to 60% by the year 2050.[58] With that growth comes the cultural richness and wisdom of people groups who in many cases have survived against great odds. Their stories deserve to be heard.

The city also functions as a magnifier—it magnifies the concentration of urban culture and exports it to the world through modern tools of communication as well as the natural relocation of people over time.

There are huge implications of this dynamic that are beyond the scope of this book, but we simply want to note here that this dynamic is at play—it is real and growing. Amid the many challenges it generates, the magnetic pull and the magnifying push of urban reality create an incredibly dynamic learning environment. The city is a living laboratory that is perhaps the most affordable and accessible graduate school in the world. Many in North America's educational system from primary to post-graduate school are beginning to recognize the limits of the traditional academic model—sequestering themselves behind the walls of a physical classroom, acquiring knowledge through objective distance from the world. The traditional model has enabled great scientific and technological advancements, but it is beset by blind spots in applying those advancements to real life—in our case, to life on the streets. Thankfully this is changing.

Brazilian educator, Paulo Freire, encourages us to create learning environments where the teachers are students, and the students are also teachers.[59] He also encourages us to consider the context in which learning takes place, beginning with concrete local questions and drawing from others' ideas, challenges, and opportunities to inform the learning process. The Street Psalms network continues to explore what this means for leaders serving in hard places and we are developing practical tools that encourage students and teachers to engage the city as a classroom.

Our basic approach is a threefold commitment to know the *hurt, hope,* and *heart* of a particular place and we use this framework in two ways—to map the external realities of that place and to map the internal realities of the leaders there.

Mapping the Hurt. The sacred center of any community is its pain and there are many ways to map it. One method is what we call "Moments of Blessing." It is a public liturgy designed for victims of violent homicide. A faith-based group called Associated Ministries in Tacoma, Washington, has been practicing this for more than twelve years. Every time there is a homicide in Tacoma, a small group of clergy and lay people gather at the site of the event to offer a fifteen minute public liturgy that acknowledges the violent act and reclaims the space as sacred and holy ground. After twelve years of standing on the bloodstained ground of every homicide in that city, acknowledging the pain and grieving with neighbors, one begins to understand the wounds of their own city.

The internal work of mapping our own wounds is equally important. This tends to be more private than public of course, but it is equally significant. Many of us pray a version of the Examen (from St. Ignatius) daily—confessing our wounds and longings as well as our gratitude. Many of our leaders also find the practice of lament a valuable way to map their own pain. Each year as a network we enter into a time of *lament* over the season of Lent, learning to give room and voice to the wounds we carry.

Mapping the Hope. Hope is always particular—it is never generic. Each community expresses its hope uniquely and it deserves to be seen uniquely. We have already mentioned one method of mapping hope: "Vision Trips." These trips function as pilgrimages, intentional journeys in search of God's healing presence that we trust has preceded us. We also search for external signs of hope in local contexts, signs that may be clearly visible or deeply hidden. And we pay great attention to our own internal geography of grace—the work of mapping our own hopes and dreams. Many of our exercises with local leaders require memory work, looking back over their lives to discover and recover their own aspirations for their context and their own lives.

Mapping the Heart. Knowing the heart of a place is the most elusive part of the mapping process because it is more than just the sum of its hurts and hopes. Mapping the heart requires what the Christian tradition calls discernment, and discernment is the domain of the Spirit. The Church has employed many forms of spiritual practice throughout history to help pay attention to the Spirit's movement and all of them have their place. One very practical method of mapping the heart of a community is through the regular discipline of prayer walks. Prayer walks involve walking in a neighborhood with the eyes of our heart wide open, reflecting on the hurts and hopes of the people who live there, paying attention to God's heart for that place as well as our own.

The internal work of mapping our own heart works much the same way. The key word to pay attention to when mapping the heart is "desire." We are formed in and through desire. Jesus put it this way, "For where your treasure is, there your heart will be also." (Matt. 6:21). Mapping our heart, and the heart of God, is the life long process of knowing not only God's desire, but ours as well.

CITY AS PARISH

John Wesley declared, "The world is my parish." In that same spirit, we are learning to see the city as our parish. John Stahl-Wert of the Pittsburgh Leadership Foundation has written extensively on this.[60] Parish is an old word that has been lost in many Protestant circles, but it is making a comeback. It describes the geographical community surrounding a local church. Before the spread of suburbs in North America, people typically worshipped in the neighborhood in which they lived. Parish ministry meant that a local church would exist to serve not only those who attended Sunday morning worship services, but also those who lived within their geographical area. In this model, a pastor's responsibility is to care for the community, not just the congregation. All those who live within the community are members of the parish.

We work with leaders who come from all parts of cities and from many denominational backgrounds. It is abundantly clear that in something as dynamic and diverse as the city, no single expression of the Church is enough to work on healing the city. We are even learning to recognize the contributions of other faith traditions, which often have much deeper roots in a particular location than we do.

Richard Foster, in his book *Streams of Living Water: Celebrating the Great Traditions of Christian Faith*, identifies six streams of the Christian Church: Word, Social Justice, Sacramental, Charismatic, Contemplative, and Holiness.[61] We make it a priority to seek out and affirm all of these streams. A city cannot experience the fullness of transformation until these different "streams" merge into a raging river—the kind of river that mirrors what is described in Revelation 22. These streams flow out of the Catholic, Orthodox, and Protestant traditions alike.

If grace is like water that runs downhill and pools up in the lowest places, then the lowest places will be the confluence of all the streams of God's grace at work in the world. We imagine that these streams are pulled down and gathered together by the gravity of God's love. Perhaps Jesus' prayer for unity in John 17 will find greater expression, not in the lofty heights of the Church's intellectual commitment to ecumenism, but in the depths of urban centers around the world where unity will find practical application in all streams of the church as they work in tandem with brothers and sisters of other faiths to love and heal broken people.

City as Playground

We are learning to see the city as a playground—a place to practice and model the love of God. Dave Hillis, president of the Leadership Foundations (a movement that is committed to the spiritual and social renewal of urban centers throughout the world), has for many years led a movement to embrace the city as God's playground. Hillis builds upon G. K. Chesterton's insight that "the true object of all human life is play" and that "heaven is a playground."[62]

The prophet Zechariah said, "And the streets of the city shall be full of boys and girls playing in its streets" (8:5). It is a vision full of hope and vitality—one that refuses despair. Many of us have been trained to see the city as a battleground between good and evil, God and Satan, where everything becomes a win-or-lose proposition, consisting of zero-sum games and endless rivalries. Nowhere is this more true than among faith-based groups and churches in poor communities who live at the edges of their own existence and are tempted to view their own communities in this way. We have been trained to think of mission in military terms where territory must be conquered or defended. Many proof-texts in Scripture are marshaled to support such a view, but the gospel offers another way forward. The image of playground helps us find our way and invite others.

The book of Proverbs offers a privileged look inside the mystery of God during God's act of creation. "Then I was beside him, like a master worker; and I was daily his delight, rejoicing before him always" (Prov. 8:30). The word for "rejoicing" in this text is the Hebrew word *sachaq*, which means "to laugh" or "to play." So, here we catch a stunning glimpse of God at play in creation. Quite literally, we were created in playful laughter. Creation is the result of God playing around and virtually all great movements of God have that same quality to them.

Playgrounds provide open spaces where participation and freedom to try new things is the bottom line. Winning is not the end goal and failure is built into the game. Of course, playing is not just fun and games—our real-world play can be hard work with ample bumps and bruises. But to forsake the city as a playground is to enter into the vicious cycle of violence that turns our cities into ever more dangerous battlegrounds. The

liberating power of the gospel sets us free to disengage and di-
vest battleground tactics that perpetuate and inflame school-
yard rivalries into all-out wars. It can appear nearly impossible
in the context of poverty and violence to do this, but this is the
promise of Jesus and a geography we are determined to explore.

Mary Oliver writes in her poem "Messenger" that "my work
is loving the world."[63] We are discovering the richness of this
work and find ourselves falling more in love with this world
than we ever thought possible. We are not talking about loving the world in some idealized state—the world as it should
be, free from sin and brokenness. We are talking about learning to the love the world as it is, in its aching woundedness and
forlorn beauty. This sort of loving is new to us and comes as a
surprise—a delightful surprise to be sure. If our first conversion was to the Word who is Christ, our second conversion is to
the world, and we are realizing that the first conversion means
nothing without the second.

4

radical presence

I am with you always.
Matthew 28:20

God, rid me of God.
Meister Eckhart[64]

WE CALL IT The Great Commission—"Go therefore and make disciples of all nations, baptizing them in the name of the Father and of the Son and of the Holy Spirit" (Matt. 28:19). It has become such a key text for many Christians devoted to mission that we can imagine Jesus alerting his disciples to get their pens ready. "Ok, listen up! Now I am about to give to you MY GREAT COMMISSION." Or perhaps the disciples looked at each other in awe after Jesus spoke and said, "We must be receiving in this moment THE GREAT COMMISSION."

However, the term *Great Commission* never actually came

from the lips of Jesus nor his disciples. Although it's not certain who coined the term, according to David Bosch in his groundbreaking book *Transforming Mission*,[65] it was William Carey, the founder of the Baptist Missionary Society and the father of modern protestant missions, who put it on the map in the early 1800's while raising support to serve as a missionary in India.

But is this passage really the "Great Commission?" Is it *the* text that should guide how we understand God's mission? Could it be that the near canonization of the term has damaged our understanding of the Christian mission?

We need to remember that there are four Gospel accounts, not one, and each has its own equally valid and important "Great Commission." It's not that there is anything wrong with Matthew's Great Commission, but rather the problem is what happens when Matthew's commission is considered more important than the commissions in the other Gospel accounts. Consider, for example, what could be considered the Great Commission of John's Gospel, "As the Father has sent me, so I send you" (John 20:21). Pay attention to the difference from Matthew 28—it is not a matter of accepting one and rejecting the other, but notice the nuance that each brings to the other. Matthew exhorts us to go and make disciples and then to baptize them, but he tells us nothing about the methodology of how those disciples are to be made. John emphasizes the "how."

In John 20, after Jesus has risen, he enters the room where his disciples are gathered and says, "Peace be with you. As the Father has sent me, so I send you" (Jn. 20:21). This prompts us to ask: If Jesus sends us as the Father sent him, exactly how did the Father send Jesus? The answer sings out from the beginning of the Gospel, "And the Word became flesh and lived among us" (Jn. 1:14). God sent Jesus in the flesh, and that is how Jesus sends us—in the flesh.

The Apostle Paul uses another metaphor to unpack the incarnation in Ephesians 2:10, "For we are God's workmanship, created in Christ Jesus to do good works, which he prepared in advance for us to do" (NIV). The Greek word used here for workmanship is *poiema*. This is where we get the English word for poetry. Speaking incarnationally, we are God's poetry to the world. God is speaking poetry *to* us and *through* us to the world. It is our distinct privilege to be in community with people in hard places who live as God's enfleshed poetry. Raising up poets to incarnate God's gospel song to lost, disenfranchised, and marginalized people is a vital enterprise. Wallace Stegner beautifully portrays how poets create place:

> No place is a place *until it has had a poet* . . . What Frost did for New Hampshire and Vermont, what Faulkner did for Mississippi and Steinbeck for the Salinas Valley, Wendell Berry is doing for his family corner of Kentucky, and hundreds of other place loving people, gifted or not, are doing for places they were born in, or reared in, or have adopted and made their own."[66]

So, the incarnation is not merely a doctrine disconnected from street reality, rather it has profound implications for day-to-day life and ministry. At the risk of reducing the incarnation to a formula, we might think about it in three ways:

God in Christ
Christ in us
Us in the world

We exist in the world to point to, lift up, and celebrate the incarnate Christ. We need to learn to hit the streets with the poetic license found in Ephesians 2:10. This calls for a radical presence. To help us grasp this idea, consider the doctrine in light of a simple English grammar lesson.

Prepositions for Mission

We learned in high school that prepositions are small words that connect thoughts or ideas—connectors that show relationship. We use them in spatial relationships, as in "My fingers hover *over* the keyboard." When considering the work of mission in the light of the incarnation, we must pay close attention to the prepositions we use.

There are three primary missional prepositions. The first is "*to*." Ministries focusing on this preposition tend to locate power in very specific places such as the pulpit. They often deal with those they want to reach in a paternalistic manner; that is, they place themselves in a position of superiority over those they feel called to reach. Ministries that see "mission" as something done *to* others may even become oppressive, violating the dignity and freedom of those to whom they minister in the name of Jesus. Some Christians are trapped in churches and deeply oppressed by ministry that is done "to" them.

The second preposition is *for*. Rather than becoming paternalistic, these kinds of ministries can fall into the trap of being maternalistic. Many of us have grown up in families with well-meaning mothers who tried to do far more for us than was healthy. Many youth ministries, for example, tend to do far too many things for young people rather than equipping them act on their own. In these ministries people often have to seek approval of the leader or pastor for everything they do, because they lack confidence or the freedom to think and to act on their own.

A third prepositional option for the mission of the church

is *with*. This is the incarnational preposition—*Immanuel* (God with us). When this preposition drives the mission, whether it's the church, organization, or even a short-term mission project, the potential to transform *both* the leaders *and* the people they seek to serve is heightened. Along with potential there is cost—these ministries require a much higher investment of time and relational energy (though much more is released in the long run). This kind of ministry also demands that leaders give up power rather than guard it. Those already invested with leadership sometimes shy away from this kind of ministry because it means giving up power and initiative to others.

In the form of a grid, the prepositional grammar of ministry looks like this:

Preposition	Relational Stance	Outcome
TO	Paternalistic	Oppression
FOR	Maternalistic	Co-dependence
WITH	Incarnational	Transformation

WHAT *WITH* MINISTRY LOOKS LIKE

The first time the two of us (Kris and Joel) taught together in Central America was during a week-long intensive masters-level course at the Central American Theological Seminary (SETECA) in Guatemala City. On the evening before the last day of the course, we took our students on a field trip to one of our favorite churches, Nueva Jerusalén, in Santa Catalina Pinula, a small city just outside of Guatemala City. There, youth pastor

William Quiñonez lives out incarnational mission in his local church and community.

William introduced us to three young men whom he presented as "cell group leaders." He initiated a conversation between the five of us and then left to speak with someone else. We were shocked to learn that the three had long gang histories, so we were very interested hearing about their experience of leaving the gangs in order to live out new lives as Christian leaders. What had it been like to get out? How did they transition to a new life? None of them chose to respond to us initially, which I (Joel) credited to my very poor Spanish at the time. I tried again to communicate our question and they looked back and forth between themselves as if to say, "Who wants to be the one to break down for these two gringos what's really up?"

The tallest of the three took on the mantle of responsibility, saying, "Well, we've never actually left the gangs, man," he said. Again, I thought my poor Spanish was betraying me, so I asked for clarification of what I was sure was a misunderstanding on my part. "Wait a minute, Pastor William just introduced you three to us as Thursday night cell group leaders. How can you still be in the gang and be church leaders at the same time?" Our tall friend took a deep breath as if to gather the patience he needed to explain himself to these two naïve gringos standing in front of him.

"Well," he said, "Pastor William has been teaching us about 'la incarnación de Jesus' and he broke it down to us like this—Jesus chose to leave heaven in order to join a gang—a really messed up gang full of thieves, murderers, liars, and backstabbers. A gang called 'humanity.' He left heaven in order to join 'la pandilla de la humanidad' (gang of humanity) because he knew the only way to transform that mess into something beautiful would be from the inside out.

"Pastor William challenged us to consider what this means for us as gang members. We thought we might need to leave the gang after giving our allegiance to Jesus, but after considering this, we decided to stay in the gang and work on transforming it from the inside out. The homies (fellow gang members) respect us for how we have changed and realize that there are certain things they do that we just can't be part of anymore, but we decided not to leave the gang. Our Thursday night cell group is focused on our homies."

Our mouths dropped open as we heard them lay out an articulate demonstration of the incarnation that points to a far more radical idea of presence than we had ever considered. I forgot all about translating for Kris for a moment until he saw the amazed expression in my face and asked me what they had said. Kris was as taken aback as I was and asked them point-blank, "Does the senior pastor of this church and the rest of the congregation know that you guys are leading cell groups while still active gang members?"

Now it was time for one of the other gang members to chime in and he very matter-of-factly explained, "Sure they do. Just a few weeks ago they brought us up in front of the congregation to pray over us with the laying on of hands, anointing us as their missionaries to the gangs of Santa Catalina Pinula." Radical presence indeed. The city of Santa Catalina Pinula had become a "place" because some poets of the street had been found, named, and commissioned.

5

beautiful questions

How do we sing the Lord's song in a strange land?
Psalm 137:4

So I kneeled down. But words wouldn't come. Why
wouldn't they?[67]
Huckleberry Finn

OUR EXPLORATION OF the geography of grace has taken us
on a twenty year pilgrimage serving grassroots leaders in
hard places. We have stumbled along, trying to figure out what
a sustainable, missional theology might look like among people
who have been crushed by life. We have worked with strategic
cohorts of grassroots leaders in the capital cities of six countries
throughout Central America and the Caribbean, multiple cities
throughout the United States and in places like Kenya, Romania,
and Thailand among others. We gather in these places to listen

and reflect on what is being learned on the circuitous journey through the landscape of grace. These groups ask questions of Scripture and of one another in pursuit of a theology that will sustain their work in slums, prisons, brothels, and the streets. Quite frankly, we are not convinced that we have a clear sense of even the right questions to ask. We are keenly aware of "proper" questions and "proper" answers, but their correctness for other contexts seems to leave them ill-suited for ours.

The psalmist in Psalm 137:4 asks a haunting question that provides a launching pad for discussion, *"How shall we sing the Lord's song in a strange land?"* (KJV). In this passage, the Israelites find themselves in Babylon, ripped out of their homeland by invading armies. God has instructed them to seek the peace and prosperity of their oppressors, but they're wondering how are they, in a dark and strange place, to sing God's songs of grace, mercy, and love?

We explore this very question with leaders serving in the dark and strange world of incarcerated street gangs, homeless youth on the streets, teenage prostitutes, and families caught in relentless poverty. Learning to ask beautiful questions such as this invites the melody needed for effective outreach as we learn to sing God's songs in strange lands—the very same places where the scandalous grace of God pools in deep reservoirs.

Poet e.e. cummings once wrote, "Always the beautiful answer who asks a more beautiful question."[68] We have come to believe that beautiful questions actually do reveal beautiful answers. If we Christians really believed that beautiful questions are far more important than well-crafted answers, our mission with marginalized people groups would be far more effective.

I (Joel) first stumbled upon the crucial importance of this principle long ago while living in North Philadelphia, trying to work with teenage drug dealers in the streets of our neighborhood, nicknamed "The Badlands." Several local churches began "anti-drug marches" trying to "take back the streets" from the dealers. Our church was desperate to see change, but we saw no fruit whatsoever from these marches. One day, a young man who had recently left the drug scene invited me to meet some of the guys on the street and hear their stories.

I naively accepted his invitation, seeing it as an opportunity to build some relationships with the young men that everyone else was content to demonize. I had no idea what to do or say in this "strange land" to even begin to determine what a beautiful question might be. For the first few hours, I had no significant interaction with the drug dealers, who ran incessantly back and forth delivering their product to passing cars. Finally, in desperation and frustration, I tried to begin a conversation with one of them, "If you had my job as a pastor in this community, what in the world would you do to reach yourself?" That question sparked a conversation that lasted several hours, and it was filled with more profound insights about ecclesiology than I had ever experienced in seminary—even after receiving a piece of paper stating that I had "mastered divinity." I learned that many of these young men had attended the Sunday Schools of the very churches that now denounced them in their marches. They articulated the pain of the marginalization they had experienced and explained what the drug gang had done to win their allegiance.

A young man named Miguel stepped into the conversation and declared, between puffs on a blunt, that the way he would reach out to himself and his posse would be to throw a neighborhood handball tournament. "Listen," he told me, "the only walls we can play on are these fuckin' ones right here with sidewalks in front of them and we're fuckin' up our ankles in the process. They got some great walls up at 5th and Allegheny at the rec center, but they won't let us play there 'cause we're drug dealers. You a pastor, man. They got to give you permission. You throw down a tourney over there, and me and all my boys will jump."

Sure enough, when I approached the rec center at 5th and Allegheny Avenue to use their walls for a Saturday team handball tournament for neighborhood youth, they were more than happy to oblige. Of course, I never told them which neighborhood youth I was referring to. Two other neighborhood churches joined ours in sponsoring the tournament and we received a small grant to buy "bangin'" trophies for the first, second, and third place teams in both age categories. We were also able to pay a local graffiti artist to airbrush personalized t-shirts for every participant.

Miguel, the dealer who had given us the idea, took charge of organizing all the teams and promoting the event. He even had me ask for the rec center's permission to allow them to paint the walls in preparation for the tourney. Ironically, given the nature of my first conversation with him, he consistently scolded any player who cursed during the tournament. He yelled at them, saying they needed to respect the church people who made the tournament possible. They also asked us to set up a sound system and play Christian hip-hop and other "church music." They wanted us to set up a table full of Bibles and other Christian literature so the players and fans could read stuff in between matches.

The tournament started at noon, and we were finally asked to leave at 11:00 p.m. with the championships still not completed. Miguel apologized profusely while asking permission to hold the finals the following Sunday morning. "You guys can all come over after your services and give out the trophies," he said. "We'll all wait for ya." Needless to say, there were a few empty pews in those three neighborhood churches that Sunday morning. Miguel became a good friend, and we began working together on several tournaments a year—getting permission from the local Salvation Army to hold winter tournaments inside their gym. The Army even put up special wood on their walls so that the balls would bounce at maximum efficiency. Several years and many tournaments later, Miguel came looking for me at church one day. He had really messed up and cheated on his girl during a night of partying, so he had come to pour out his heart and learn if there was any way to get his life together. In the middle of a flood of tears, God opened his heart. Miguel stepped into a new life from which he has never turned back.

Many months after the tournament, during a time of reflection on what had occurred, I realized that we as a church had been doing exactly the opposite of asking beautiful questions. We had been going to God asking him to show us what to do to reach these drug dealers, while all along Jesus was just waiting for us to go directly to them armed with beautiful questions. Traditionally, our evangelism strategy involves prayer for God's guidance, asking him *what* we should be doing. We end up putting a rubber-stamp of approval on plans we had already designed, thinking God has approved them because we prayed. We write up our plans and ask God to sign off on *our* dotted line. Then, after receiving God's "approval," we go to the world to find out *how* to accomplish what we already feel compelled to do.

When we ask beautiful questions, we reverse this order. The questions drive us into the world asking what to do, and *then* we turn to God to find out *how*. We give God a blank sheet of paper to write out his plan (by means of consulting the communities we are called to serve), and then we sign off on *God's* dotted line. The fulcrum of this shift rests on a transfer of power. God gave the authority and power to Jesus, and he in turn gave it to the Holy Spirit who then gave it to the church. The problem is that the church often disrupts the flow of power by hoarding it and locating it exclusively in places like the pulpit and Sunday morning services led by professionals. The church should perpetually facilitate the process of giving power away *to the most powerless* in the community instead of hoarding it for itself.

A study of the questions Jesus asks in the Gospels reveals the process by which he transfers power so that beautiful answers may emerge. Often before healing someone, Jesus asks what the person wants him to do for him or her. This approach involves a transformative transfer of power to the world. Likewise, we have learned that true empowerment begins when we ask questions, inviting those around us to speak what they need. If we are faithful to ask, God will be faithful to show us the how. Only then do we learn to sing beautifully together the Lord's songs in strange lands.

WHAT DO YOU WANT ME TO DO FOR YOU?

Our first missional community in Central America took root in a town called Chinandega, Nicaragua. After three years of training in what we call the "Street Psalms Series," we became very impressed with a group of three young men who had come to the training together. By their ability to engage in theological riffs with Scripture and by the examples they shared, it became obvious that these young men were living as the poetry of God in their neighborhood of Managua, which was called *Los Braziles*.

After participating in one of the Street Psalms intensives, we frequently stay in country to see the neighborhoods and visit the ministries of our conversation partners. I (Joel) was determined to visit *Los Braziles* to meet the leadership of the church where these young men were being discipled. Thus, together with my Colombian training partner, Jairo Piraneque, we visited *Los Braziles* and met someone who has become for me a model faithful mission.

Pastor Tomas Ruiz has faithfully lived and served in *Los Braziles* for more than twenty years. He started with twenty-five members and the church stayed roughly that size for the first seven years. Tired of so many years of hard work with little tangible fruit, Pastor Tomas, guided by the Holy Spirit, began to listen to neighborhood residents. It soon became clear that on many occasions he and his church had offended the community by wrongly judging and condemning them. Then, in his personal devotional reading, he had stumbled on the story of Jesus and Bartimeaus in Luke 18:35-43. This story deeply convicted Pastor Ruiz for the paternalistic manner in which he had looked down upon his neighborhood.

As we listened, he explained to us how for many years he and his twenty-five member church tried to figure out what they should be doing to "bless" and "reach" their neighbors. With idea after idea they tried unsuccessfully to reach their neighbors by imposing on them the ideas they had conjured up in their sequestered conversations. When reading the story about Jesus and Bartimaeus, Pastor Tomas recounted how he came to realize that he and his congregation had been "doing" a ministry that was dis-incarnated from the real needs and dreams of their own neighborhood. In Jesus' question to Bartimaeus, "What do you want me to do for you?" Pastor Tomas found a life-giving, power-swapping question. So he called the entire community to a meeting over a dinner. After the food was served, he stood up and passionately begged his neighbors for forgiveness on behalf of the church. This paved the way to ask them the same beautiful question Jesus had asked of Bartimeaus.

Shortly after the dinner, the church members circulated through the community to ask their neighbors, "What can we do as a church to serve and bless you?" The number one response was a plea to help clean up the streets from the garbage and mud holes that were causing so many problems for the neighborhood, including severe illnesses among children from mosquitos breeding in the many potholes. The church members reconvened to compare notes from what they'd learned and collectively committed to respond to the needs of the community, especially the mosquito-infested potholes.

The three-week cleanup was carried out with an amazingly important twist: They chose to work on the streets during their regular Sunday morning worship time. They used the act of picking up garbage and filling up holes as a genuine act of worship before God, a form of worship that was visible and in solidarity with the real needs of their neighbors. The church's ministry was rejuvenated by asking the community what the church could do to bless them instead of deciding for themselves under the guise of prayer meetings or strategic planning sessions.

As the result of a beautiful question, Pastor Tomas's church, Faro de Luz (Lighthouse), began serving the community with renewed vision in the year 2000. They now have 250 "disciples" (Pastor Tomas refuses to count "members" because for him every resident of the community is a "member") in the old, but now reinvigorated sense of a parish. They have a multi-use church building, a neighborhood school of some 300 students, a neighborhood computer center, a gymnasium, and a micro-enterprise project making iron products. They recently purchased land for a baseball diamond and soccer field for the community. In addition, they have built 22 homes for neighborhood families. All of these projects and ministries have been born from asking beautiful questions. In this way, the community takes ownership in the work the church is doing together *with* them. Eventually, Pastor Tomas was voted to be the legal representative of the barrio *Los Braziles* before the city government of Managua because of the trust and respect that had been built and the church has successfully planted several other congregations in neighboring communities.

Who Do You Say That I Am?

The most beautiful question Jesus asked his disciples is found at the very center of the Gospel of Mark. In ancient Jewish literature, the key to a story's meaning is often found in the middle of the story rather than the end, as is often the case in Western storytelling. This emphasis on the center is most obvious in Jewish chiastic poetry, often found in the Psalms; the very center of the poem gives the main point. For the Jewish storyteller, each story has a "sacred center" that contains its unique treasure of meaning.

The Gospel of Mark contains sixteen chapters, so if we follow the notion of the "sacred center," something really important might be found around Chapter 8. There we find Jesus in Cesarea Phillipi. What is so special about this place, and why does Jesus choose it to ask this most important question of his disciples: "Who do you say that I am?" If you look at a map of the time, it will show Ceseara Phillipi to be the extreme northern border of Jesus' ministry—as far as we know, he never ventured further. Perhaps there are some questions that can only be asked in certain places. Why didn't Jesus save this riveting question for Jerusalem, the sacred center of an entire culture? Perhaps because a place like Jerusalem would have elicited a different answer. There, an entire history and culture would have weighed in, making it an unfair place for the disciples to consider the full possibilities regarding Jesus' identity. They needed to be removed from that context in order to even consider anything other than the prevailing viewpoints and accepted norms.

The vision trips that we conduct in Latin America for groups from the United States provide the same kind of space that Jesus gave his disciples before posing his all-important question to them. We simply cannot consider certain questions amid the sacred centers of our personal upbringing or denominational "camps," because those places tend to answer the questions for us. Jesus saves his highest and holiest question for a place on the northernmost edge of his ministry, furthest away from all that is most sacred to his disciples. In the same way, God takes us through circumstances far "north" of our sacred centers of understanding and experience to pose what may be the most vital questions. He holds in reserve his highest and holiest questions for remote and sometimes dark places at the edge of our own cultural, physical, theological, emotional, and spiritual maps.

As we've said, and will keep saying, we have come to realize that a central aspect of our calling as Jesus' disciples is to pursue the pools of God's grace in hard places far north of familiar life and experience. We find that our conversations guide us far from the "sacred centers" of our personal Jerusalems where the questions tend to be answered for us. The question of "Who do you say that I am?" sounds very different when asked in the middle of a cemetery overlooking 3,000 people who work in a garbage dump to scratch out a meager existence than it does from the comfort of a Sunday School classroom.

Of North American pilgrims and gang members alike we ask: Where is your Cesarea Philippi? Where is the northernmost place God has taken you, and how do you answer the question in Mark 8 differently because of where you have been? How has your personal journey opened your eyes to who Jesus is? Are you ready for his beautiful questions once you arrive?

6

holy ground

You will see heaven opened, and the angels of God
ascending and descending on the Son of Man.
John 1:51

There is nothing so secular that it cannot be sa-
cred, and that is one of the deepest messages of the
Incarnation.
Madeline L 'Engle[69]

BEFORE THE CENTER for Transforming Mission or the
Street Psalms Community existed, we called our little ragtag group of street theologians MUD Inc. ("Making Urban
Disciples"). It was a head-turning title that fit nicely with t-shirt
designs and other artistic forms of expression. But perhaps we
shouldn't have "grown up" into more sophisticated titles. The
name MUD came from the word picture of Genesis 2:7, *"and the*

Lord formed the man from the dust of the ground." At the dawn of creation, God's hands are in the mud, shattering our typical expectations of deity behavior. God plays in the mud and proclaims what God made from it to be good—God has no fear of the slimy intimacy of touching God's creation. If God can put God's hands in the mud to sanctify what God touches, what about us? God calls the dirt good. Can we?

Read from another angle, we see God kissing humanity into existence. It was the kiss (breath) of God that brought life to the mud. This idea confounded the Greek mind because, since God is Spirit, any thought of a God touching mud, or even worse, wearing flesh, was completely out of the realm of appropriate imagination.

In his book, *A Grief Observed*, C. S. Lewis writes of his struggle to make sense of the death of his wife. In pondering the immense disappointment that his wife had not been healed, he writes about how our pre-conceived images of God need to be continually challenged:

> Images, I must suppose, have their use or they would not have been so popular. To me however, their danger is more obvious. Images of the Holy easily become holy images—sacrosanct. My idea of God is not a divine idea. It has to be shattered time after time. He shatters it Himself. He is the great Iconoclast. Could we not almost say that this shattering is one of the marks of His presence? The incarnation is the supreme example; it leaves all previous ideas of the Messiah in ruins.[70]

In his experience of grief and loss, Lewis found it necessary to shatter his own faulty and inadequate image of God that he had been worshipping prior to the death of his wife. In fact, as

Lewis puts it, God does the shattering (the word "iconoclast" literally means "image smasher"). In this process, often through our own suffering, God demonstrates how God's transformational touch sanctifies our lives and our world.

THE INCARNATION UNITES WHAT THE WORLD DIVIDES

In John 1:43-51, we read the account of Jesus' call to Philip and Nathanael. Philip immediately accepts the call to follow Jesus, and then he explains to Nathanael what has happened to him. Nathanael evidently remains skeptical but still intrigued by Philip's encounter with this Jesus of Nazareth ("Nazareth, can anything good come from there?"), so he accepts Philip's offer to go and meet Jesus. As Nathanael approaches, Jesus calls him "a true Israelite, in whom there is nothing false." Nathanael is taken aback by Jesus' forthright proclamation and wants to know how it is that Jesus knows him. "I saw you while you were still under the fig tree before Philip called you," Jesus declares. Jesus' supernatural insight inspires Nathanael to declare the Rabbi Jesus to be the Son of God, the King of Israel. To this emphatic declaration by Nathanael, Jesus offers what seems at first glance an odd reply:

> "Do you believe because I told you that I saw you under the fig tree? You will see greater things than these." And he said to him, "Very truly, I tell you, you will see heaven opened and the angels of God ascending and descending upon the Son of Man" (John 1:50-51).

Any listener steeped in Jewish lore would immediately recognize Jesus' reference to the story of Jacob's ladder in Genesis 28. In the ancient world, whenever divinity showed up, that place of epiphany was sacred. Usually, such places were marked with stones as a holy memorial. In the Genesis passage, Jacob falls asleep and has a vision of angels ascending and descending upon a ladder. He awakens from the dream and exclaims, "Surely the Lord is in this place and I did not know it." Upon further consideration of his dream, he becomes reverently fearful and proclaims, "How awesome is this place! This is none other than the house of God; this is the gate of heaven." For Jacob, the ladder image of angels ascending and descending makes the place an intersection between heaven and earth. Jacob renames the place Bethel ("house of God"). He takes the rock that had served as his pillow and uses it as the chief building block of an altar he erects so that God can be worshipped in this holy place—this intersection between heaven and earth.

Returning to the Gospel of John, there is one major difference between Jacob's vision, and Jesus' appropriation of it to refer to himself. In Genesis 28, the angels are ascending and descending upon a *place*. In John 1, the ascending and descending occurs upon a *person*—a profound difference. While a place is *stationary*, Jesus is mobile and thus the holy intersection between heaven and earth is in *motion*. Wherever Jesus goes, that place is holy.

Does that mean that since the Holy Spirit dwells in the hearts of his people, then each of us is, by association, also a mobile intersection between heaven and earth? Is it possible that wherever we go, that place becomes holy? Is it possible that the incarnation sanctifies the world in such a way that all places are made holy? The implications of where grace locates itself through incarnation now become staggering. Wherever God walks by the Spirit's powerful work and indwelling presence, that place is holy!

I (Joel) once visited a soup kitchen for the homeless in

Chicago. Before dinner, the nuns gathered all the homeless men who had come for food into one big circle. In a swarm of unbathed bodies, in a building that should have been condemned, they all began to sing, "We are standing on holy ground. Standing on holy ground. . . . " God walks everywhere. All ground is holy. So how does this change our attitude regarding a place when we consider it holy? How does our behavior change toward a person when you consider him or her sacred?

Bishop George McKinney tells a story in his book *Cross the Line: Reclaiming the Inner City for God* about the early days of his church-planting ministry in San Diego.[71] After midnight one Christmas Eve, he found himself with a message to share, but everyone was in their homes asleep, so he had no congregation to share it with. He and his wife discussed where he should go in their neighborhood to deliver his Christmas Eve message so late at night. They decided that the best place to go was a broken-down local strip joint called "The Funky Ghetto." Upon entering, McKinney spoke with the club manager behind the bar. He told the man that he was a local pastor with a little message he hoped to deliver that night, if he could have just a few minutes on stage between dance acts. The manager, probably thinking this was worth a good laugh, turned on the house lights and told the few patrons in the room that a local pastor had something to tell them. Considering it was Christmas Eve and because the pastor promised to be brief, the patrons accepted the idea with grunted approval. When he finished, he asked for a glass of water and told them that if any of them wanted to speak with him, he would be thrilled to talk before heading back to his home to celebrate Christmas Eve with his wife.

One of the men thanked him for coming, but clearly did not want to talk about anything else. Just before McKinney got up to leave for home, one of the dancers who had been on stage approached his table wearing a terry-cloth robe. She told him about how she had been raised in a Christian home, but had fallen away from the faith as she grew older. She explained how she hated her life of drug use and strip dancing. She then proclaimed, "But you came here tonight and it was like God is tracking me down and telling me to get my act together. I guess it can't get any worse than the Funky Ghetto, huh?"

After talking with him for fifteen minutes, she returned backstage. McKinney waited around another fifteen minutes, but no one else came to talk to him, so he simply returned home. He remained hopeful that he would be able to grasp the lessons the Lord had wanted to teach him from his experience at the Funky Ghetto.

Perhaps Bishop McKinney had not been sure what he was supposed to learn, but we find profound lessons for us in his story. He had been led to share a particular message on this Christmas Eve night in a go-go bar because no one in his church had been there to listen. Angels were ascending and descending inside a sleezy strip joint because a pastor had refused to damn a place simply on account of the behavior there—to do so would have been to double-damn it.

When Jesus lived on earth, the fear of making physical contact with lepers was not about fear of catching a disease. It was the fear of making oneself ritually "unclean." In other words, it was an issue of avoiding spiritual contamination from those who were outcasts and rejects. The power of Jesus' sanctifying work in the incarnation is that he reversed the process of contamination. As opposed to being contaminated by lepers, his touch becomes a contaminating agent in the reverse direction— he "contaminated" others with his righteousness. Paul says that "where sin increased, grace abounded all the more" (Rom. 5:20). Can it be that every attempt to defile something only increases its holiness in God's presence?

The incarnation demands the reality of God's presence everywhere. The incarnation takes a world that we have divided and pulls it back together, for God proclaims that all of life is holy. The incarnation makes all of life sacred and every place holy ground. There is no split between sacred and secular.

When we use this story to reflect on incarnational mission with certain young men, we of course need to warn them not to go running back to their pastors, mentors, or parents saying that we have advised them to frequent strip clubs in order to sanctify strippers—we might quickly find ourselves without any grassroots leaders in our conversations! Bishop McKinney answered a very unique calling for a specific time and place. The point is not to replicate the details of his story; rather, the power lies in his understanding of "sanctified presence" that gave him permission to live into this calling to a particular "strange land."

—section two—
hovering

The earth was formless and void and darkness covered the face of the deep, while a wind from God
swept over the face of the waters.
Genesis 1:2

Christ plays in ten thousand places, lovely in limbs,
and lovely eyes not his to the Father through the
features of men's faces.
Gerard Manley Hopkins[72]

7

symbolic universe

The Lord put a mark on Cain.
Genesis 4:15

Symbols are the natural speech of the soul,
a language older and more universal than words.
C.S. Lewis[73]

OUR FRIEND AND mentor, Dave Hillis, tells the story of when he was a camp counselor and was asked to lead a seminar for urban youth. As he was about to start the session, a young lady from Los Angeles walked in and asked Dave what he was going to talk about. He said it would be about how to survive the city. The young lady replied, loud enough for others to hear and with some attitude, "Oh, that's easy! You only need three things—a gun, a condom, and a Bible."

LISTENING AS AN ETHICAL ACT

Have you ever wondered why Jesus waited thirty years before he began his formal ministry? What was the Word doing, if not listening to the world into which he was sent? Bonhoeffer taught us that the first service we owe to both God and humanity is the ministry of listening, and we learn how to do it from God himself. "It is God's love for us that he not only gives us His Word, but also lends us His ear."[74] Isn't it ironic that the Word would take thirty years to listen to the world before revealing himself? What exactly was he listening for?

Father Ben Beltran suggests that Jesus spent thirty years getting inside what he calls the "symbolic universe" of humanity in a concrete and particular way. Fr. Beltran is a Roman Catholic priest who serves the Smokey Mountain community in the Philippines—a community of garbage dump scavengers. These scavengers taught Fr. Beltran, a priest schooled by the brightest and best of Rome, how to listen to their world and ultimately how to teach and preach good news in their midst.

In his book, *Christology of the Inarticulate*, Father Beltran talks about the classic model of communication—the triad of sender, message, and receiver.[75] He notes that when we focus our attention on the sender of the message, the main concern is the *intent* of the sender.[76] When we focus on the message, we become preoccupied with *content*. When we focus on the receiver, communication is understood to have taken place only when the message has been integrated into what he calls the receiver's symbolic universe.[77] As Beltran points out, much of Western theology has been preoccupied with the *content* of the message, where theory, doctrine, and dogma take precedence.[78] This leads to a generalized, disembodied, and disincarnated faith that creates distance between the sender and receiver and ultimately does violence to both.

Beltran describes the symbolic universe as that place where souls are shaped according to the context in which they live.[79] It is situated within community and culture, and is not the property of an individual. In this sense, we are talking about interpreting the culture in which individuals live. Place matters, and culture is a product of place.

Imagine culture as an iceberg. Two-thirds of an iceberg is hidden under the water line. Only the smallest part of the iceberg is visible. Now change the metaphor slightly and imagine that each culture has three parts: a body, mind, and soul. The body of a place is like the tip of the iceberg. The mind and soul of a place are hidden beneath the surface. The body of a place includes the physical environment—features such as land, architecture, and climate. Though they comprise the most obvious and visible aspects of a place, they can affect us deeply in ways that are not always obvious. For example, Kris lives in the Pacific Northwest where it rains a lot. Joel lives in Guatemala City, the land of eternal spring. One is slightly depressed and the other is slightly manic! People in the Northwest live much of their lives indoors. They drink lots of coffee and hang out in pubs. In Guatemala City, people live most of their lives outside in the perpetual springtime air. Place matters!

The mind of a place sits just beneath the surface. By mind, we mean social norms, language, food, music, rites, religion, values, work, and even humor. We are talking about the peculiar way a people go about living in a particular place. These aspects of culture can be observed, but are not easily discerned by those within the culture itself because they are so ingrained. It often takes an outsider to notice the way a culture functions. For example, consider the role of food in how a culture functions.

Several years ago we visited Thailand where elaborate rituals surround food and meals. Every culture takes its food seriously, but Thai culture is in a league of its own. Virtually every important conversation happens within the context of a meal. The more important the conversation, the more elaborate the meal. In Nairobi, where food is not as plentiful but no less valued, all important conversations happen over a simple cup of chai (tea). In the Northwest, important conversations happen over a cup of coffee in a coffee shop or over a beer at a pub. In Guatemala, important conversations happen over a long and casual lunch.

Beneath the body and mind is the soul of a place, or its "symbolic universe." It is the deepest part of the iceberg—that which gives it its mass and weight. Intuition tells us that this part of the iceberg exists, but it is nearly impossible to see from the surface. The soul of a culture is both unseen and unconscious, and this is what gives it its power. Symbols and stories both hide and reveal the soul at the same time. They are like clothing—they help us trace its particular shape, while at the same time covering it up.

We might think of the symbolic universe as the narrative structure of the soul—those stories that shape the way we interpret all of life. These stories are held together with symbols that fill the story with meaning. In fact, the Latin word "symbolum" literally means "to hold together,"[80] and this is what symbols do. Symbols are the glue that hold the characters and plot lines of our stories together, giving them meaning. C. S. Lewis said, "Symbols are the natural speech of the soul, a language older and more universal than words."[81] Symbols are metaphorical poetry that compresses meaning into its most concentrated form, exploding with possibilities when activated by our imaginations. This is their power. They work on us as much as we work on them.

Theologians have called this the "scandal of particularity"[82]—the mystery of God's transcendent Word incarnated with specific, finite form. Contrary to the ways it is often packaged, the gospel is not a "one size fits all" product. Holistic spirituality that connects with a particular people in a particular place is not imposed from without, it is derived from within the concrete realities unique to each context.

As we mentioned, the Pacific Northwest of the United States is Kris' home. Among other things, it is known as the "None Zone."[83] According to the "Religion by Region Series" that studied religion in eight different regions of the United States, the Northwest is the None Zone because when they filled out the census, most Northwesterners (62%) checked "NONE" with regards to our religious affiliation,[84] making it the least churched region of the country.[85]

Northwesterners earned their title through the accident of geography and years of fierce independence. What drew settlers to the Northwest 200 years ago was a thirst for adventure and opportunity, driven in large part by a desire to escape the people and places from which they came. Not much has changed since then. As a result, things like church and conventional forms of community are not high on the list of priorities—Northwesterners are friendly, but they tend to like each other at a distance.

Of course, it's only when we look beneath the surface that we discover the hidden irony in all this. While the None Zone is clearly non-religious in nature, it is deeply spiritual. While Northwesterners turn away from institutions and practices associated with particular religions, they are creating new and alternative forms of community that express keen spiritual hunger.

Understanding how we are shaped by context helps us

understand the way we see and experience God. Consider a study published by Baylor University about religious life in the United States which revealed that ninty percent of Americans believe in God.[86] That is not surprising. What is surprising is that there is such diversity within how the ninty percent see and experience God.[87] The study suggests that the image of God that people internalize is largely dependent on where they live. It summarizes the various images of God in the United States by using four broad categories: 1. Critical God. 2. Authoritarian God. 3. Benevolent God. 4. Distant God. The researcher argues that each of these images can be broadly tied to a specific geographical region:

View of God	Geography
Critical God	East
Authoritarian God	South
Benevolent God	Midwest
Distant God	West[88]

For those who have travelled throughout the United States these results are not surprising. Easterners can be critical; they live in a fast-paced urban world that demands quick judgments. Their God is the same. In the South, authority and respect, especially for elders, endures as a major value. Their God reflects this. In the breadbasket of the United States, shaped by a culture in which many people live off the land and family is primary,

God is seen as the benevolent provider of rain and sun to grow crops, and shelter to sustain the family. In the West—well, it's the West, where people have made their own way. God is preferred at a distance—friendly, but at arms' length.

However we might evaluate the Baylor study, it points to ways context shapes how we construct meaning, and how the symbolic universe of a people develops over generations. The challenge is this: If our image of God is largely determined, and therefore limited, by where we live and with whom, how can we hope to seeing God as anything more than a mere projection of ourselves? Do culture and context override the Spirit's power to reveal God's true self?

Some might find these questions disturbing to their conception of God, but we must learn to appreciate the unique ways that each region, culture, and community sees and experiences God. It only enhances our conviction that if the church really is the body of Christ, then it will take the *whole* church to see God vibrantly. No single scrap or small fragment will do. On the other hand, the unique strength of each context that deserves to be celebrated also creates equally unique blind spots that deserve to be challenged. The gospel cuts both ways. That is why we must not only celebrate, but also challenge the internal workings of the symbolic universe that are tied to a particular geography. What delights the Spirit in Guatemala City, may grieve the Spirit in Tacoma. Authentic spirituality is not a generalized spirituality. It is always specific and concrete—in dialogue with other particular expressions of God's self-revelation.

Beltran suggests that when we deny the concrete reality of a people or place and misinterpret the symbolic universe of those we serve, we enter into the demonic cycle of "systemic misunderstanding."[89] Systemic misunderstanding has come to characterize much of what passes for good news in the church today. It happens when we fail to get inside the symbolic universe of a particular people and place. As a result, every effort to help further alienates the people being served, in ways that the giver nor receiver fully realize. What is intended to be good news is actually bad, but (and here is the demonic mechanism) the disempowered receivers have been conditioned to accept the bad news as though it were good. Both parties are caught in a vicious, self-imprisoning cycle that masquerades as liberty.

Let us return to the young urban camper to see how this works. She said that survival in her world required a gun, a condom, and a Bible. She is something of a prophet—giving us a glimpse inside the symbolic universe of many urban young people with laser-beam precision. Of course, not every urban kid carries a gun, a condom, or a Bible—at least not in a physical sense. But for young people who grow up in the context of poverty and violence in urban communities, these are important symbols that reside deep within their imaginations and shape them over time. Consider what the urban prophet is saying to us. She assigns the same value to guns and condoms as she does the Bible. What is she teaching? The symbols of guns, condoms, and Bibles are insights into a culture wracked with fear and hungry for power. All three symbols reveal a narrative that says this world is an unsafe and dangerous place that demands protection. If the gun doesn't work, perhaps a condom will. And if these two fail, well, we can always give the Bible a try. Or maybe she's saying that the value of each is determined by the situation. In some cases we need a gun. In others, a condom; in still others a Bible. It all depends. Or maybe she's saying we need all three at once and that's just the way things are. To fail to hear her story and interpret it faithfully in ways that honor her story is to enter into a vicious cycle of systemic misunderstanding.

Now, let's consider how Jesus enters into our symbolic universe. He does this at two levels—the micro level and the macro level. Let's consider first the micro level. A quick survey of the Gospels, particularly the Gospel of John, reveals that all the "signs" that Jesus performs are unique and one of a kind. He never reveals himself the same way twice. As C. S. Lewis says, the one prayer that God refuses to answer is the prayer "encore" or "do it again."[90] Jesus always meets people in particular ways, never in some generalized program. In one instance, he turns water into wine. In another, he spits in the mud. In another, he says a word; in yet another, he simply draws in the sand. In the third chapter of John, Jesus speaks to Nicodemus under the cover of night. In John 4, he speaks to the Samaritan woman in broad daylight. It is always new and different. Jesus meets people in their unique circumstance and addresses their unique stories. The Gospel is never general. It is always specific. This is the scandal of particularity.

And yet there is a storyline that we humans all share—a narrative structure that transcends culture, place, and time. There is likewise a symbolic universe that is common to all people everywhere—one that shows what it means to be human while at the same time honors the particular ways we go about expressing our humanity. This is the symbolic universe at a macro level.

In order to make sense of the symbolic universe common to all of humanity we will follow Jesus into the desert and consider the temptation narrative. Here Jesus reimagines the symbolic universe of humanity in ways that set us free. This is the work of the incarnate Word—to be enfleshed into the symbolic universe of this world. Jesus listens intently to our story and there, from within our story, Jesus begins to reinterpret our symbols and reshape the contours of our soul. He tells the story that we can't quite tell for ourselves. He reveals what has been hidden since the foundation of the world—hidden under layers of fear, anxiety, guilt and shame, all of which have been sacralized and then projected onto God as though heaven-sent. We are eager to say more about the "hidden" thing that Jesus reveals, but for now it is enough to say that the hidden thing is not so much a some*thing* as it is a some*one*, and that someone is not at all what we thought. In a word, God is not mad and never was, or at least not in the way we imagined, and this is what Jesus reveals.

Jesus does the hard work of seeing for us so that we can see for ourselves. He offers a vision of God and of life that the prophets could only see in glimpses—a vision that is rooted in our deepest desires, but is chronically and systematically dismissed by the world around us and avoided by our own timid souls. His life tells a story we always wished could be true but could never fully accept. He repositions the mirror of life so that we can see and worship the one true image of God rather than mere projections and exaggerations of ourselves. He does all of this from within the same reality that we live with day to day, without displacing or dishonoring us. This is the key—Jesus subverts and reimagines life and God himself from within the human experience. He not only subverts our way of seeing reality, but he transforms it. The Word and the world meet with a holy kiss, and from this we are born again.

In order to retell the temptation story, we will borrow from an ancient hermeneutical method of scriptural interpretation known as midrash. Midrash is a Hebrew term for "interpretation," and is the Jewish tradition of reading between the lines of Hebrew Scripture to unearth hidden layers of meaning. There is a playful freedom in this method that has at least two distinct advantages to more modern methods of biblical interpretation. First, it values the work of imagination as an important tool of interpretation. Secondly, it is clear to all who read or hear a midrash that it is an *interpretation* of the text—not a declaration of doctrinal truth. A midrash does not make false claims of authority beyond the authority of the interpreter. In other words, there is a built-in humility to the method of midrash, which is certainly a virtue when interpreting Scripture.

A Midrash of the Temptation Story

Each of the synoptic Gospels marks the beginning of Jesus' public ministry with a tour of Israel's symbolic universe set against the backdrop of an unnamed Middle Eastern desert. In biblical parlance, the desert is that place in Scripture where we go to figure out who is who and what is real. It is the place where souls are revealed.

After traveling forty long days and nights without food, Jesus rests. Exhausted and hungry, he meets the devil and so do we, for this is not Jesus' story alone. This is our story too. Jesus carries all of humanity into this meeting or, to be more precise, he carries the fullness of humanity into his divine appointment with the Tempter. We are rehashing a conversation that began in a garden so many ages ago and continues to this day.

The conversation centers around three symbols that have shaped the soul of Israel, and the world, since the beginning— the symbols of bread, temple, and crown. Each symbol is packed with meaning and a narrative history that represents a way of seeing the world and God. The bread is an economic symbol; the temple is a religious symbol; the crown is a political symbol.

Donald Kraybill, in his very helpful book *The Upside Down Kingdom*, sees Jesus' conversation with Satan as a confrontation with the principalities and powers that have colonized the imaginations of the world.[91] We are not dealing here with merely personal temptations of the flesh or the pride of life—a perspective that has often dominated the teaching and preaching of a hyper-personalized Western culture. When considered symbolically, Jesus is naming the "principalities and powers"[92] of the world (to use the language of Paul). He is naming the economic, religious, and political realities that claim godlike powers for themselves and do great harm when allowed to govern by fear. As it turns out, these systems are the substructure of society. In fact, modern sociology teaches us that these are the systems by which every society and (specifically for our context) every city functions. Jesus is doing battle with the same principalities and powers that he ultimately exposes and defeats on the cross. Jesus meets with Satan to talk about things of ultimate significance— bread, temple, and crown are about reality itself.

BREAD—FROM SCARCITY TO ABUNDANCE

Imagine Jesus after a long fast and a lonely walk in the desert. He sees a barren landscape, a wasteland—no gardens, or streams, no milk or honey, only rocks and sand and the occasional desert fox. The scenery matches his interior. The land is as empty as his stomach and his stomach is as empty as his own story. Relative to the world stage, he comes from an insignificant people who have lived under the thumb of foreign oppression for most of its existence. Israel had been a slave state tossed between Egypt, Assyria, Babylon, Greece, and now the Roman Empire. The glory days under David and Solomon are a distant and sometimes cruel memory. And so Jesus' story mirrors the story of his people. He was conceived in scandal and born on the run in a place of no account. His birth inflamed the paranoia of those in power, so his family fled to Egypt to survive persecution. He re-entered the "promised land" quietly, with little fanfare. The promised land looked anything but promising, much like the deserted place where Jesus is now—here he is, the "anointed one," sitting on a pile of rocks in the middle of nowhere. He is filled with all the same longings and frustrations of his people whose spirits were being crushed under the weight of their failed dreams.

Wandering the desert for forty days must have brought to mind the many wanderings of Israel. Certainly Jesus would have recalled Israel's forty years in the desert. Perhaps he would have also recalled Moses' encounter with God at Mt. Horeb, an encounter that set all this wandering in motion so many years ago (Ex. 3:1). Mt. Horeb was the place of God's self-revelation as the great I AM. Ironically, the Horeb means "desolate wasteland." That God would reveal himself in a desolate wasteland could not have escaped the mind of Jesus. Perhaps Jesus was expecting God to show up and reveal himself in the wasteland that he now occupied. Not this time. Instead, the tempter appears. If the primary power of evil is derived from its ability to masquerade as good, we must assume that Satan's appearance to Jesus was veiled in some kind of righteous exterior, for evil unveiled is powerless to persuade.

The devil speaks first. "If you are the Son of God, command these stones to become loaves of bread" (Matt. 4:3). On the surface this seems less like a temptation and more like a reasonable invitation, perhaps even inspired by God. What is the harm in turning stones into loaves of bread, especially after a long fast? How much more so, in light of the fact that so many of his brothers and sisters also suffer from empty stomachs? Not long after this temptation, doesn't Jesus do this very miracle

of providing bread? Why not now? One can hear the wheels in
Jesus' head turning much like the sound of his stomach grumbling: *Why not?* Along with Jesus we can envision the stones
turning to bread. No longer would the bellies of starving children distend and bloat. No longer would the world starve for
food or wonder if there was a God who loved them.

We often like to emphasize the Son's love for the Father, but
we must not forget his love for the world. He had walked for
thirty years among his own people and seen their misery, and
he had a growing sense of his own power to alleviate suffering. Self-respecting adults cannot watch children suffer without
wanting to alleviate their pain, especially if they have the power to do something about it. The consuming presence of suffering drowns out our most noble theories and theologies. Like a
grumbling stomach, the only way to quiet its deafening noise is
to satisfy its desire, and to do so *now*! It is not hard to imagine
Jesus being overwhelmed by the vision of scarcity before him.
What kind of God allows his people to starve? When seduced by
a worldview of scarcity, the mystery of God's abundance is not
easy to see.

In this anguish, the Spirit that led Jesus into the wasteland of
temptation compels him to look deeper. Jesus takes another look
at the barrenness that surrounds him and listens more carefully to his own stomach. Here, deep in the soil of relentless scarcity, Jesus discerns the seeds of his Father's abundant and fruitful love. It takes some time, but eventually he begins to smile
when he sees the peculiar farming techniques of his Father who
wildly, extravagantly, and perhaps even irresponsibly throws
the precious seed of his love on all kinds of soil—the good, bad,
and ugly. The indiscriminate and unconventional nature of the
Father's farming technique is almost laughable. What kind of

farmer scatters precious seed with such liberty and recklessness? Jesus also sees 120 gallons of the finest wine flowing from six stone jars of stagnant dishwater. He remembers the table God sets for humanity—a table with room for all, especially those who least deserve a seat. He smiles because God's abundant love allows him (and us) to re-imagine the whole of God's economy as one of reckless abundance. When one sees all of humanity (even one's enemy) as a friend, the possibilities for generosity multiply thirty, sixty, even one hundredfold. In such light, generosity begets generosity and five loaves become 5,000. Radical generosity lays down life itself, against which nothing, not even death, can prevail. As Dostoevsky imagined in *The Brothers Karamazov,* in his famous chapter called The Grand Inquisitor, had Jesus thought less of God and less of humanity's capacity to act on what he saw, perhaps Jesus would have caved into the temptation and enslaved us with miracles. Instead, Jesus replies to the Tempter, "One does not live by bread alone, but by every word that comes from the mouth of God" (Matt 4:4).[93] Jesus resists the myth of scarcity and declares God's Word reliable in the face of deprivation. God is friend, not foe. God can be trusted. There is enough!

There are many authors who have debunked the myth of scarcity that Jesus confronts in the desert, but none so succinctly as Mary Jo Leddy who writes,

> The economics of God's love is not based on a law of scarcity but rather rooted in the mystery of superabundance. The personal or political decision to declare that there is not enough is the beginning of social cruelty, war, and violence on a petty or vast scale. On the other hand, the choice to affirm that there is enough for all is the beginning of social

community, peace, and justice. The option to assume that there is enough frees the imagination to
think of new political and economic possibilities.[94]

Jesus' fidelity to the "mystery of superabundance" moves humanity from the bondage of scarcity born of fear to the freedom
of God's abundance, born of love. There is enough bread for all,
if we can only see and embrace it.

TEMPLE: FROM SACRIFICE TO MERCY

No symbol made greater claims on the imagination of Israel
than the temple. What bread was to the body of Israel, the temple was to its soul. The temple was the center of religious life,
and it embodied Israel's hopes and dreams. It was a reminder
of their status as the "chosen ones." At the sacred center of the
temple was the Holy of Holies—the very dwelling place of God,
located in the city of God. It was the center of Israel's universe,
and this center continually transformed and re-invented Israel's
faith from deep within, far deeper than any could imagine.

The temple's beauty was a testimony to God's glory, but the
economics of scarcity had infiltrated Israel's religious life over
the years. Ironically, it produced a lucrative temple industry. The
temple was the largest single economic engine of Jerusalem, one
that Jesus ultimately rendered useless. The economics of scarcity had produced a religion of scarcity and it followed the same
deadly logic. As is always the case with scarcity, violence was its
governing principle, hidden under layers of rules and regulations that masked the fear that sustained it. This was the sacrificial system of the temple—it was a highly regulated and sophisticated system of violence that had been given sacred meaning
and justified by virtually every religious authority, except a
handful of prophets.

In the second temptation, the devil takes Jesus to the top of the temple overlooking Jerusalem where he says to Jesus, "If you are the Son of God, throw yourself down."[95] The tempter reminds Jesus that the angels will protect him if he does, and no harm will come to him. Jesus is promised immunity. In our reading of the text, the devil sees the temple system for what it is—a system governed by the principle of violence that we have just described. It makes sense that he would see it for what it is, because it is a system he takes great pride in and has a vested interest in sustaining. He sees a den of thieves profiting off the fears of the people. He sees a sacrificial system steeped in violence, maintained and justified by a complicated system of rules and regulations. He sees and enjoys all of this.

Together, the devil and Jesus witness the controlled chaos below. They see the same thing. One is pleased, the other is angry. Jesus' anger creates an opening for the devil, who tries to seduce Jesus with the logic of violence itself. And so he tempts Jesus to "throw" himself into the middle of the violent mess below and do something about it. He tempts Jesus to clean up a violent system with violence.

The word for "throw" (*ballo*) actually means to "throw" or "cast" in a violent way.[96] It is imbedded in the name "devil" (*diabolos*). The word *diabolos* means to cast alongside or to cast apart. It means to divide or separate and to do so forcefully or violently. This is what the devil does, he divides and separates through violence. It is the essence of the diabolical mind. So, the essence of this temptation is an invitation to violence. It is the oldest trick in the book, dating all the way back to Cain and Abel. Put more softly, Jesus is being asked to condone a temple system that is governed by violence. The problem of course, as Einstein pointed out, is that "a problem cannot be solved by the same consciousness that created it."⁹⁷ In other words, though it remains one of the most seductive of all temptations and carries within it a convincing logic, violence cannot cast out violence any more than Satan can cast out Satan. Humanity has tried, and failed.

Jesus looks down at the temple courts teeming with activity. He sees people buying and selling God's favor as well as each other's. He smells burnt flesh and raw blood floating up on the prayers of the people. He sees those who can afford the price of admission and those who cannot. Anger burns, and the logical wheels of violence begin to turn. Why not throw myself into this violent mess with an act of merciful vengeance and put an end to a system gone mad? Weren't the prophets of old permitted as much? Jesus is tempted to strengthen himself with the thought he will be protected in such a battle. After all, he is God's anointed, and he has been promised victory. If God protected Cain in his violence, how much more will God protect Jesus in his? *Why not put God's forgiveness to the test with an act of violence? Why not throw myself into the sacred center of my own house and deal with it on its own terms. I will not only turn over the tables of injustice, I will tear the whole damn thing down to its foundations with my bare hands. Vengeance is mine!*

Moved by the Spirit, Jesus takes another look. He discerns the faint outlines of the lie. Violence cannot cast out violence, and Satan cannot cast out Satan (Mark 3:23). The whole sacrificial system testifies to the lie. Yes, it contains violence for a while but it can never bring peace. Jesus remembers the prophets of old who declared God's heart to a people trapped in cycle upon cycle of violence:

To this one I will look,
To him who is humble and contrite of spirit, and who

trembles at My word.

"But he who kills an ox is like one who slays a man;
He who sacrifices a lamb is like the one who breaks a
dog's neck;
He who offers a grain offering is like one who offers
swine's blood;
He who burns incense is like the one who blesses an
idol.
As they have chosen their own ways,
And their soul delights in their abominations.
(Is. 66:2-3, NASB)

Mercy rises within Jesus' heart there at the top of the temple and he is struck by a new reality—that what lies beneath him is a people who do not know what they are doing. They are like sheep without a shepherd. They delight in their abominations because they have lost touch with their deepest and truest delight, and God's. They don't know what else to do. They have confused their own need for blood with God's. Once again, Jesus hears a still small voice rising from within, "I desire mercy, not sacrifice" (Hosea 6:6, NIV).

Jesus looks again at the meticulously designed religious system with all its rules and regulations and discerns another law at work. It is the law that rules his own heart. It is the inviolable law of love. Jesus discerns within himself the desire for mercy. It is mercy, not vengeance that will dismantle the temple. It is mercy that sits behind the veil, and it is mercy that will lovingly subvert the system from within. It is in and through this mercy that Jesus sees a new temple. He imagines a day when he will finally declare, "It is finished." Having been exposed for what it is, the entire temple cult will collapse under its own weight.

Jesus pulls back from the temple ledge. Could it be that he is reminded that God's patience with a violent humanity and his slowness to anger is no excuse to test that patience with his own act of violence. He quotes the ancient text, "Do not put the Lord your God to the test" (Matt. 4:7). Jesus refuses to throw himself into the temple trap and test God's love with his own act of violence. He opts for another way—the way of mercy—a way that would one day turn the temple inside-out and become the hope of all those who have ever cried out, "Lord have mercy."

CROWN: FROM DOMINATION TO DOXOLOGY

The crown is the symbol of the political system, which is concerned with the stewardship of power. While this symbol is not named directly in the temptation narrative, it is clear from the context that we are dealing with the temptation to power. In a monarchial system, the crown is the ultimate symbol of power. As such, it is something of a summary of the previous temptations. The economic, religious, and political systems are of one piece—each needs the other to survive. There is no bread and temple without the crown, and there is no crown without the bread and temple. They are interconnected. As Eugene Peterson says, each temptation deals with the "exercise of power,"[98] but none of them so boldly as the final temptation.

Throughout the temptation narrative, we witness Satan's systematic efforts to get Jesus to use his power, not for harm but for "good." This is the way temptation works. The good that the devil seeks is twisted to be sure, but as we have said before, this is the only way forward for the tempter. We are dealing here with Lucifer, the "light bearer." His entire existence is derived from God's goodness. There is no inherent badness in him. At best, he is a parasite of goodness—twisting and perverting it. At worst, as Augustine said, he is the absence of goodness. Satan exists the way darkness exists, which modern science tells us is not the opposite of light but the absence of light. It is therefore the tempter's ability to twist and manipulate that which *is* in order to call forth that which *is not*. This is what makes the temptations so tempting.

"Again, the devil took him to a very high mountain and showed him all the kingdoms of the world and their splendor . . . All these I will give you, if you will fall down and worship me" (Matt. 4:8). Jesus stands atop the world, looking down on all the kingdoms. From this great distance, the devil shows Jesus their "splendor." The word "splendor" or "glory" is a key word in this text. The word is *doxa*, literally meaning "praise."[99] At such lofty heights, their glory evokes a deep primal praise—a kind of holy doxology. It all looks quite good and praiseworthy. The kingdoms are good gifts that deserve a good king. It is hard to see the underbelly of those kingdoms and the moral principle of death by which they operate at such a distance. It is even harder to see the devil as anything other than the light-bearer of God at this point—perhaps the better angel of his own nature has finally come to set him straight.

Jesus ponders the potential of wearing the crown—the potential for good, not evil; the potential for life, not death. *Who better to wear the crown and steward power than a benevolent king who genuinely cares for creation?* Could it be that in the thin air of these great heights Jesus is disoriented and begins to reconsider his position on the bread and the temple? *What if I am wrong? What if there really is not enough to go around? What if a certain kind of violence really can bring peace? What if there is some truth to all this? Why not seize the crown? If they want a king, why not at least give them a good one? If anyone can handle power, wouldn't it be the one who is all powerful? And given the cruelty of this world, why not dominate it with goodness and bring it to its knees for its own sake? After all, will not one day every knee bow and every tongue confess that I am Lord? And if I am Lord, the angel of light that stands before me is here to remind me that it is my duty to bow to the truth of all I am seeing now.*

What we are witnessing here is not only a call to kingship, but a call to "worship." In fact, the word for worship in this text is the same word for "splendor" or "glory" that was used earlier, *doxa*. The devil is offering a kind of twisted doxology, a distorted form of praise—Jesus is being tempted to praise a kind of power that violates his own nature. From the outside looking in, it all looks quite innocent. Jesus is tempted to take his rightful place as king, but to do so in a way that gives praise to a false kind of power. He is being tempted to abstract power from relationship, imposing his will from the outside, taking control and using force to get what he wants, and because what he wants is good it seems quite reasonable. It is the temptation to define power in terms of might. This is what it means to take the throne in a way that gives praise to Satan. As Walter Wink reminds us, "Whatever the power of the Spirit means, bullying force isn't part of it . . . the power of God is often exercised in personal ways, creating, saving and blessing. It is never an impersonal application of force from without."[100]

The rules of Satan's politics are simple—take by force and get by grabbing. The end justifies the means. When seen from the perspective of motives, it looks benevolent, but in the end it is self-serving. Only when it is exposed do we see what Wink calls "the Domination System," with Satan as its "world-encompassing spirit."[101] We see a system that requires absolute allegiance, requiring subjects and laws and force. In religious parlance, it requires a twisted form of forced "worship," not freely-given praise, as Galadriel knew in *The Lord of the Rings* when, in response to Frodo offering her the one ring, she says, "All will love me and despair!"[102] Such a system sees itself as sovereign before which there can be no other, and it maintains its godlike status through fear and force. This is why William Stringfellow can say that the *only* moral authority of such power is "that which is disclosed as its last authority, which is death."[103] The power of domination has mastered the ability to hide its real purposes, but when fully disclosed, it is not a call to open and freely-offered praise, it is rather a call to enslavement and death. Such forms of worship are fallen forms that require the sacrifice of all for their own survival.

Empowered by another Spirit, Jesus takes a second look at the "splendor" below. Another praise comes forth, a new doxology. It is not the doxology of coercion, but of freely-given praise. He remembers it as a nursery song his mother used to sing to him as a child. A reminder that another power is at work in the world, a deeper and more potent power, a new kind of kingdom—one that brings down the powerful from their thrones and lifts up the lowly—one that fills the hungry with good things and sends the rich away empty (Lk. 1:51-53). It is a song for the Servant-King.

This nursery song brings him back to reality. He envisions a power made perfect in weakness, not strength. He envisions a power that pours itself out and divests itself of any and all coercion. He envisions a power that divests itself of the principalities of this world and in doing so makes "a public example of them, triumphing over them" (Col. 2:15) by exposing them for what they are. He envisions a power that not only transforms life, but also death itself. Such power is foolishness to those who only know the power of force and might. It is a stumbling block to those who are perishing, but to those who are being saved, it is the very power of God, a power that makes salvation possible.

The glittering gems on the crown being offered are seen for what they are—a crown of thorns. Satan's twisted view of power is exposed. The whole world is turned upside-down. The cross ascends and Jesus is "lifted up." Jesus, along with the rest of us, can now see Satan's plea for what it is—a call to bow down to death itself. Jesus declares, "Away with you, Satan! For it is written, 'Worship the Lord your God and serve only him'" (Matt. 4:10).

Interestingly it is only in this last temptation that Jesus addresses the devil as "Satan," whose name means "accuser." Jesus sees the accusation for what it is—that God is not God, nor is God worthy of praise. Lies, lies, lies, it is all a lie. "Woe to those who call evil good and good evil" (Is. 5:20, NASB). This is the work of Satan. But God is good. There is enough. He is the God of peace who is worthy of our praise.

Having emptied himself of the voice of the accuser, Jesus allowed himself to receive attentive care from the angels (literally "messengers," in contrast with the one who accused and manipulated). The very next sentence in Luke 4:14 reads, "Then Jesus, filled with the power of the Spirit, returned to Galilee." It is a beautiful image. Having re-imagined the symbolic universe in the wasteland of Israel, Jesus is free to preach and teach Good News to his people. For the next three years, Jesus demonstrates to the world what, up to then, had only been known by "hints and guesses."[104] Jesus reveals God's economy by offering new bread in new ways—he declares there is enough! Jesus reveals God's religion and builds a new temple—he puts an end to the sacrificial system, steeped in violence and declares mercy for all. Jesus reveals God's politics—he demonstrates the presence of a new kingdom, a new power in the land. He is the Anointed One, empowered to preach good news to the poor, proclaim release to the captives, recovery of sight to the blind, bring freedom for the oppressed, and proclaim the year of the Lord's favor for all. All of life is re-imagined in Christ.

As Brueggemann reminds us, because of this we too can re-imagine the world. We are called to an artful dance of gospel subversion:

> [To] get up and utter a *sub-version* of reality, an alternative version of reality that says another way of life in the world is not only possible but is peculiarly mandated and peculiarly valid. It is a *sub-version* because we must fly low, stay under the radar, and hope not to be detected too soon, a *sub-version* because it does indeed intend to *sub-vert* the dominant version of and to empower a community of *sub-versives* who are determined to practice their lives according to a different way of imagining."[105]

All of this is fueled by what Mary Jo Leddy calls "radical gratitude"[106] that fills the heart of Jesus and beckons him to the cross where all of life is re-imagined once and for all.

8

insiders and outsiders

Be wise in the way you act towards outsiders; make
the most of every opportunity.
Colossians 4:5 (NIV)

The Church is the only society in the world
which exists for the sake of those
who are not members of it.
Archbishop William Temple[107]

THE ENGLISH WORD for "church" is derived from the Greek
word *ekklesia*, meaning "the called-out ones."[108] In John 17,
Jesus prays that his disciples would remain in the world without
being defined by the world. More often than not, this prayer is
interpreted through the lens of morality: "Don't drink, smoke
or chew, or run around with those who do." This interpretation
suggests that superior moral behavior allows us to be "in but not

of the world," and our job is to call the "world" to the same kind of moral superiority.

Unfortunately, the moralistic approach is not working. Consider the difference between the moral behavior of the "church" and the moral behavior of the "world." Studies routinely reveal that church members cheat, lie, steal, have affairs, divorce, watch pornography, abuse drugs and alcohol, and even kill at roughly the same rates as the general population—there is no appreciable difference between "us" and "them." We are not simply talking about poor or permissive behavior of nominal Christians or members of "liberal" traditions. Ironically, the more conservative and literal our expressions of faith, the worse some aspects of our moral behaviors are, statistically speaking. Here are three examples:

Divorce. Non-denominational Christians divorce at higher rates than other Christians—Catholics and Lutherans being the least.[109]

Domestic violence. Research suggests that some religious men and women tend to stay longer in unhealthy, violent relationships because religion is sometimes used to justify domestic violence.[110]

State-sanctioned violence. 62% of white Evangelical Protestants support torture, compared to 40% of religiously unaffiliated.[111]

One could argue that the more intensely we fix our eyes on achieving moral superiority, the worse our morality becomes. The one thing we can say for certain is that the way out of moral degradation is not moral fixation. In an attempt to understand God's unusual grammar regarding what it means to be *in* but not *of* the world, we explore a way that has less to do with developing a superior morality, and more to do with learning to relax into relationship—a way that transforms all of life. Moving from a fixation on morality into relationships is a counter-intuitive path to the promise of the gospel. Christians are not primarily called to some kind of superior moral code, instead we are invited into a radically fresh way of relating with each other and God—a way of relating that became Jesus' fervent prayer in John 17. It is a way of relating that is grounded in the abundance of God's love.

Such an approach frees us to see God at work in the world and to celebrate what we see God doing. Gospel sight and gospel celebration are the gifts of the Spirit that we desire. As our friends from the Eastern Orthodox Church remind us, if we want the "wisdom" of these gifts we must learn to "pay attention"—pay attention to the fact that they are already given to us all in abundance. Here is our hunch: the line between insiders and outsiders, us and them, is largely an invention of our own making. It is primarily a tool of control, grounded in a worldview of scarcity, and it has little to do with Jesus' prayer in John 17.

I (Kris) will never forget when Joel invited me to join him on a visit to a prison in Guatemala. I don't like confined spaces, and I am not a fan of extemporaneous speaking, especially when it has to do with speaking to gangs in prison. When the guards released us inside, we were greeted by warm hugs and a thick haze of marijuana. It had been some time since I had last been high. Given the quickened pace of my nervous breathing and the thick haze I was inhaling, I soon discovered myself relaxing a bit. I'd like to think it was just the Spirit calming my nerves, but in this case I think what I was experiencing was slightly more "natural." After an hour or so of casual conversation with the inmates, Joel gathered the young men in a group for a more formal conversation.

I vaguely remember mentioning the story of the gun, condom, and Bible to see what their thoughts might be. To be honest, I was just spit-balling, trying to draw out a conversation. They were amused, but I don't think it was connecting. Somehow the conversation turned toward the church and whether or not there is good news for young men who find themselves in their position. Honestly, I was wondering the same thing. Dozens of eager and sometimes angry faces stared at me—faces filled with intricate tattoos that marked so much of the shame and pain in their lives. I felt like I was staring at Cain himself, and so I asked if they knew that God was the first tattoo artist in the world. There were a few smiles of recognition and pride as they recounted the story of Cain who had killed his brother only to have God mark him with a tattoo for his own protection. Scripture calls it the "mark of Cain." It is the mark of grace.

Up to this point in the conversation, the distinction in my mind between "us" and "them" was clear. I was on *Team Us,* and they were on *Team Them.* I was there to assist the Spirit in recruiting Team Them to join Team Us. Maybe it was the other hazy spirit at work in me, but something began to happen to my vision. Their faces seemed to soften. What stood before us was not a bunch of thieves, murderers, and thugs. What stood before us was a cluster of little boys. Yes, many if not all of them had done unspeakable things. And yet their faces continued to soften. They looked more and more like little boys to me. Not innocent little boys, but boys who had done horrible things for reasons that they still didn't understand. *Father forgive them, for they do not know what they are doing.*

I began to tell them the story of how God got his name. When God revealed himself to Moses, Moses asked God's name.

God said, I AM. The Hebrews formed a word for this name, called YHWH (pronounced yah-weh), a word that mirrors the way we breathe and mimics the sound of our breathing.[112] When we inhale we gasp "yah." When we exhale we say, "weh." Joel and I began to demonstrate the sound of God's name in our breathing. We invited the inmates to join us in saying God's name this way—Yah-weh, Yah-weh, Yah-weh.

The Hebrews were looking for a word that would honor God's nature. They wanted a word around which the lips would not close, nor the tongue clasp, as a way of signifying that God is free and unbound by humanity. We stood together in the prison breathing the name of God. Some did it openly. Others tried to hide their participation, but we all breathed. As we breathed, I reminded them that the first thing they did when they came into this world was say the name of God (YHWH). I also reminded them that the last thing they will do when they leave this world is say the name of God. I reminded them that this is the gospel. God is with us—completely! God loves us—completely. God lives with us and God dies with us. God is with us! If anybody ever tries to make the gospel more complicated, it's not the gospel.

As we breathed the name of God together that day, the line between us and them began to blur. They were no longer the bad guys and we were no longer the good guys. We were just the guys—all of us children of God.

We first heard the story of God's name from Fr. Richard Rohr, who reminds us that the beauty of this whole thing is that the name of God unites us all. There is no Christian way to breathe, no Jewish way to breathe. There is no Buddhist or Muslim way to breathe. There is no male or female way to breathe. There is no slave or free way to breathe. There is no black, white, or brown way to breathe. There is no conservative or liberal way to breathe. There is no Protestant or Catholic way to breathe. We simply breathe, and with every breath we take we declare God's name. We are all God's children, even and most especially "the least of these."[113]

THE LINES BETWEEN US

When we recall experiences such as breathing the name of God with gang members, we find ourselves fascinated by the question of whether there are boundary lines in the geography of grace. Archbishop William Temple wrote, "The church is the only cooperative society in the world that exists for the benefit of its non-members."[114] Could it actually be true that the church exists for those who do not show up? What would such a church look like? The idea of being part of a body of people that exists for others is a radical and largely untested notion. We confess that we do not know exactly what this looks like, though we have seen it in glimpses.

How do you exist for those who may never show up? It would be interesting if we put an empty chair on the altar each Sunday to remind ourselves for whom the Church exists. Similarly, some Jews still observe the tradition of the cup of Elijah where an extra cup of wine is left on the table in case a stranger happens by. Who knows, but that stranger might be the Messiah? A church in Guatemala City has taken William Temple's notion seriously, and it radically altered the way they worship.

When I (Joel) entered Nueva Jerusalén church in Santa Catalina Pinula, I immediately noticed the graffiti-splattered wall behind the pulpit. It was loaded with the street nicknames of three or four-dozen youth. The names were artistically scattered around the periphery of the wall. In the middle of the names was a big, beautiful question. The question read, "Do you know who is *not* in church today?" The entire service occurred without any reference to the graffiti, so afterward I asked youth pastor William Quiñonez, a core member of our Guatemala City network, about the names and the question. He responded simply, "Oh, those are the nicknames of the gang members of our pueblo. We decided to put all of their names behind the pulpit so that during the service the people can think about who is *not* here instead of only who is."

Pastor Quiñonez and his church would have put a huge smile on the face of the Apostle Paul who wrote to the Colossians, "Be wise in the way you act towards outsiders, make the most of every opportunity." (Col. 4:5, NIV). Paul was writing to a group of people very concerned about who was "in" and who was "out." They had all kinds of dietary restrictions and other ways of measuring the insiders versus the outsiders. Instead of teasing out the intricacies of what is clean and what is not, Paul implores the Colossian Christans to be wise in the way they act toward those who are on the outside and he connects the fruitful use of time to the way we treat outsiders. Picking up on the same theme, the writer of Hebrews maps the geography of outside versus inside in a fascinating way, employing layers of Jewish imagery:

> The high priest carries the blood of animals into the Most Holy Place as a sin offering, but the bodies are burned outside the camp. And so Jesus also suffered outside the city gate to make the people holy through his own blood. Let us, then, go to him outside the camp, bearing the disgrace he bore (Heb. 13:11-13, NIV).

The writer references Jewish religious regulations that

required sacrifices to be burned outside the camp. We are invited to consider this peripheral location in connection to the central event in the story of Jesus—where did he suffer? Outside the city gate, and in doing so he sanctified the people who were inside. *"Let us, then, go to him outside the camp bearing the disgrace he bore."*

Speaking symbolically of our own world, we recognize "the camp" to be those things we use to define ourselves—church, family, upbringing, culture, ideology, money, doctrine, sexuality, etc. The redemption of these things lies outside of them. As Karl Barth taught, grace is always an outside gift.

Typically, when we go looking for Jesus, we go inside—once a week on Sunday to church. But Jesus is inviting us to join him outside the camp. Anyone who has ever been an outsider knows that to be outside is to bear the shame of the ones inside the camp. The identity of the camp is always formed over and against anything and anyone who is different. It is always risky business to go outside.

Remember Paul's admonition to the Colossians regarding how they were to treat outsiders? Paul is urging us to be wise toward outsiders, because sanctification (the process of being "set apart" for a sacred purpose) for those of us on the "inside" is integral to shameful realities on the outside. Consider the implications for mission. Traditionally, the Church approaches mission with the idea that there are many unconverted people out there who need the good news of Jesus Christ; therefore, it is our responsibility to go to them for *their* benefit. This might be true, but what else might be happening as we go *out there*? We discover Jesus. This gives us invigorating freedom to greet Jesus in the name of Jesus and say, "Hi, it's been so long since we talked. I had no idea you would look this way. Are you hungry? Are you naked?" Going outside allows us to see mission as the process of falling on our knees saying, "Lord, where are you? We went outside the church so that those of us within the church could live and breathe." There is no air in the church without this counterintuitive geography of mission.

There is no greater "outside place" than between two thieves on a little hill just outside of Jerusalem. Perhaps a lesson from hip-hop culture can shed some light here for us.

8 MILE

The film *8 Mile* is loosely based on the life of Eminem, one of hip-hop's most controversial and respected artists. Eminem plays the character B-Rabbit in the film. B-Rabbit is an aspiring rapper from Detroit who grew up on the "wrong" side of 8 Mile Road in Detroit, Michigan. The road literally separates the haves from the have-nots, the "insiders" from the "outsiders." It divides the city from the suburbs, the rich from the poor, and black from white. 8 Mile is a graphic metaphor for that which divides the world. B-Rabbit lives on the Detroit side of 8 Mile, which puts him with the have-nots. What complicates things is that B-Rabbit is poor and white. He lives in a trailer park with his mother who is hardly a model citizen, and he is deeply ashamed of her. He's a white kid trying to make it inside the black world of urban hip-hop.

Some of us have been "insiders" for so long it is hard to imagine what it is like to be on the outside. Others of us have been outsiders for so long that we have no idea how to function as an insider. Crossing 8 Mile seems impossible. If you ever sit with a group of grassroots leaders talk about their own city or neighborhood, you will most likely here them discuss the geographical, cultural, racial, religious, and social boundaries that exist there—physical or geographical boundaries such as certain streets, parks, bridges, or schools. Similar boundaries show up in the language of economics (rich vs. poor), race (black vs. white), and culture (indigenous vs. mestizo or mixed populations). Inside the church, the boundaries often surround generational issues, musical preferences, educational style, dress codes, gender, or sexual orientation. We even have huge boundaries within our own psyche—places in our personal lives we are afraid to visit, such as family expectations, family secrets, or places of personal shame.

In the Gospels, we see Jesus breaking boundaries at every turn. He was perhaps the greatest boundary-breaker in the history of the world. He shattered boundaries related to culture (the woman at the well), gender (Mary and Martha), religion (sabbath laws), and generations ("Let the little children come to me"—Matt. 19:14). He also broke through boundaries around tradition and social strata. The ultimate 8 Mile boundary that Jesus crossed was the chasm between heaven and earth, life and death, and all of this has radical implications for the church on a mission.

Unfortunately, the institutional church in cities where we serve grassroots leaders is stymied by 8 Mile boundaries, and thus often separates herself from the very people and places that could bring about the vision she so desperately needs. This was reinforced for us when we were asked to consult on gang outreach in the capital of a Central American country. Beforehand, we asked incarcerated gang members from a neighboring country to share some thoughts that we could carry to leaders who would be attending the event. Here is a small sample of their response—read the following with the image of tattoo-plastered Central American gang members in a maximum-security prison:

Frequently we have seen growth in the physical
structure of many churches. We see leaders with a
competitive attitude choosing, it seems, to compete
with other churches while abandoning the needs
that exist in prisons, neighborhoods, slums, and re-
habilitation centers. The priority of these churches
always seems to be focused on the comfort of their
respective members so they can feel like VIPs. They
have lost, or perhaps just forgotten, the vision of
Jesus Christ, who said, "Therefore go and make disciples of all nations." We don't want to criticize just
for the sake of being critical. [We do want] to stand
for the *truth* that while churches are constructing
huge sanctuaries, there are children dying of hunger, gang members killing one another, and pris-
oners suffering greatly—while Christians comfort
themselves in their big churches."[115]

This is a prophetic wake-up call from some of the most extreme "outsiders" one could ever meet. What do their words as
outsiders say to us as insiders? In a sermon focused on Luke
23, Tim Keller notes the "outsiders" gathered around the cross.
There is Simon of Cyrene—an ethnic, cultural outsider. Simon,
an African, carries the cross of Jesus. A convicted criminal—a
moral outsider—seeks a place in God's kingdom as he hangs by
Jesus' side. The Roman centurion, a racial outsider and part of
the hated Roman guard, comes to an authentic understanding
of what is really happening on the cross. Finally, there are the
women, social outsiders, lingering when other followers have
fled. Luke locates only one religious insider at the cross, Joseph
of Arimathea, who seems to recognize the significance of Jesus'
death. Joseph asks for the opportunity to bury Jesus. Luke is

trying to teach us something about the inverted roles of out-siders in the Gospel through the choice of characters he locates around the cross:

Simon of Cyrene	Cultural Outsider
Thief	Moral Outsider
Centurion	Racial Outsider
Women	Social Outsider
Joseph of Arimathea	Religious Insider

In reflecting on this inversion of roles, Keller notes that be-cause of the way salvation is accomplished, those on the outside tend to understand and embrace the cross before those on the inside. In other words, because of the unsavory way salvation is accomplished, outsiders tend to "get it" before insiders. Women tend to get it before men. Children tend to get it before adults. The poor tend to get it before the rich. It is all in the way salva-tion was accomplished. Outsiders are familiar with the rejec-tion, shame, and scandal at the core of the gospel story. Not only do they tend to connect more quickly, they have the stomach for it. For example, the women at the cross were able to stand and watch what Jesus went through because they knew the ex-perience of pain, suffering, and rejection—they had lived the story of shame and marginalization their entire lives. There is a deep intelligence in all victims about such things. And just when we think the cross only speaks to outsiders, Luke reminds us of Joseph, the religious insider. Not all outsiders embrace the cross, any more than all insiders reject it. But outsiders often appropriate it more quickly than insiders because they recognize themselves in the cross. On the other hand, many of us religious insiders often stumble at the cross because we have so much to lose.

It is our experience as religious insiders that we often come late to the party. If we do come, it is often with great reluctance and offense, much like the elder son in Jesus' parable in Luke 15. Jesus leaves the story open and unfinished. We are left wondering if the elder son (insider) ever decides to join the party in honor of the younger son (outsider). We see the unfinished story as Jesus' open invitation to religious insiders everywhere.

PRAYING WITH PROSTITUTES[116]

Pastor Francis Montas and his wife, Loly, shepherd a church of young people—Casa Joven—that meets on Saturday nights in a converted Santo Domingo nightclub. They have been core members since the beginning of our Dominican Republic missional community, led by CTM Caribbean Director Mario Matos. Their work with street kids, incarcerated juvenile delinquents, and *las chicas de Sarasota* (prostitutes) serves as a prophetic wake-up call to many others in the Dominican church.

One Thursday night, Francis and Loly called a special prayer service because so many young people in their flock were having serious problems. They did not know what else to do in the face of such difficult circumstances. They met in a little house near one of Santo Domingo's most infamous streets for prostitution—La Avenida Sarasota. Their prayers for one another seemed strained and "blocked" somehow in a way that they had not experienced before. Their prayerful attention shifted to the

young women working on the street who they had passed by to
enter their prayer meeting. They began talking about the wom-
en and praying for them. Eventually they left the building, as if
a magnet were pulling them toward the women, and they spent
the next several hours asking beautiful questions of the "Chicas
de Sarasota."

I (Joel) had the chance to go out to the streets with Francis
and Loly and their team seven weeks later, during which time
they had not missed a Thursday night encounter with the girls.
We experienced a numbness-shattering picture of God's scandalous grace in the strange world of evening call girls. Each sex
worker we talked to lit up as the young women from the church
called them by name and embraced them with bear hugs. The
women on the street updated us on their week, sharing stories
about their children, and receiving prayer with eager anticipation—all the while completely ignoring potential clients who
passed by.

We had just finished sharing and praying with a group of
three sex workers when one of them, whom I will call Gloria,
asked if she could pray *for us*. Needless to say, that was an inversion of roles I had not anticipated. We all joined hands on the
sidewalk of Avenida Sarasota at 2:30 a.m., and I heard one of
the most beautiful prayers of my life. When Gloria uttered her
"amen," a smile exploded onto her face. She sheepishly confessed
that it was the first time she had ever prayed out loud. I pretend-
ed to cough while trying to wipe away tears, embarrassed that I
was not upholding a strong male exterior. Gloria received more
bear hugs from the ladies and an awkward handshake from me.
She said that she planned to come to church that Saturday night
when I was scheduled to preach.

I thought about her promise several times over the next

several days, and on Saturday night, Gloria indeed came. When the service concluded, she received hug after hug from the young worshipers, including the guest preacher, whose awkward handshake on the street a few nights earlier would no longer suffice for Gloria. She approached me with arms opened wide and a smile erupting with joy.

How blessed the church in Casa Joven has become, and how their vision and mission for their city has been recalibrated through their interaction with these young women! Casa Joven is living out the missional implications that Keller describes in Luke 23 where the outsiders "get it." As a result they are encouraging many other "insiders" throughout Central America and the Caribbean to exchange hugs with the "outsiders" of their respective cities and neighborhoods. In so doing, they are learning to sing God's song in their own "strange lands."

9

drama of embrace

His father saw him and felt compassion for him
and embraced him.
Luke 15:20 (NASB)

Embrace is grace, and grace is gamble, always.
Lewis Smedes[117]

OUR DISCUSSION OF insiders and outsiders becomes especially explosive in the context of violence and oppression, when outsiders are perpetrators of injustice against insiders. This, unfortunately, is where many of the grassroots leaders we serve live, move, and have their being. In the preface to his book *Exclusion and Embrace: A Theological Exploration of Identity, Otherness and Reconciliation*, theologian Miroslav Volf shares an encounter after a lecture he gave on the need to embrace one's enemies.[118] Theologian Jurgen Moltman had asked whether or not Volf felt he could embrace a Chetnik. The Chetniks were Serbian fighters who, in the early 1990s, devastated Volf's homeland of Croatia, destroying cities, throwing people into concentration camps, raping women, and burning down churches. So, how serious was Volf willing to take this "embrace your enemy" reasoning when it got really personal? Moltmann figured it all sounded good in theory, but could Volf bring himself to embrace a Chetnik — the ultimate *other?* After a pregnant pause, Volf replied, "No, I cannot—but as a follower of Christ I think I should be able to."

Over the years, in the networks of leaders we serve in difficult places around the world, there have been many occasions where ministries and individuals have found themselves up against their own outsider "Chetnik" groups. Often, these groups of violent outsiders have sown destruction and preyed on the neighborhoods our friends love, in the very places where they are laying down their lives. What does it mean to follow Jesus when he tells us to "love our enemies"—those groups of "ultimate others?" It is one thing to consider this as an objective concept or principle, but quite another when our lives and our children's lives are threatened by "Chetniks" in Croatia, Nairobi, Guatemala City, or San Salvador. This is the daily reality that many of our leaders face. Volf shares his personal internal battle on the subject with gut-wrenching honesty when he writes, "I felt that my very faith was at odds with itself, divided between the God who delivers the needy and the God who abandons the Crucified, between the demand to bring about justice for the victims and the call to embrace the perpetrator." *The call to embrace the perpetrator?* Can that really be from God? How in the world are these servant-leaders supposed to embrace someone who is threatening to take their lives, destroy their ministries, and hurt and kill the people they love most?

To get a handle on this, one image we have explored is what Volf describes as "The Drama of Embrace."[119] Consider the theological implications of "embracing the perpetrator," of loving hostile outsiders through the simple physical act of a *hug*. Hugs are made up of four distinct movements: (1) opening the arms, (2) waiting, (3) closing the arms, and (4) opening them up again.

Act 1: Opening our arms. Volf describes the open arms of a hug as the "code of desire" for the other. Open arms toward another person indicate that space has been created for the other to come in. It is an invitation into the space of another—the "soft knock" on the door of the other's heart.

Act 2: The period of waiting. Here is a "desire held in check," as the initiator with open arms awaits the response of the person to whom he or she has extended an invitation. Will the "other" move toward the extended open arms? Herein lies a big difference between embracing and grasping—waiting for a response requires patience and discipline.

Act 3: The closing of the arms around the other. Here one finds the goal of embrace, the time of mutual indwelling. Two individual spaces are mutually encountered. The key is reciprocity—each holds and is held by the other. In an embrace, "a host is a guest and a guest is a host." It takes, after all, two pairs of arms for one embrace, and this act is laced with tenderness. It must not be perverted into an obtrusive, forced "bear-hug," or a passive unwillingness to reciprocate.

Act 4: The reopening of the arms again. For an embrace to come to fulfillment, there must be a release. The end of an embrace is, in a sense, already a beginning of another embrace, for the ultimate goal of an embrace is not the fusion of two "others" into one dissolved "whole," but the celebration of two "others" in momentary unity and intimacy that leaves its indelible mark on each.

If these are the physical mechanics of what we call a hug, then what does it look like with our enemies—the hostile "others" in our lives? It is easy to celebrate the joy and warmth of a reciprocal embrace with a friend or a beloved family member, but can we embrace the "Chetniks" in our lives, the "ultimate others" who seek to destroy and ruin us? This is a beautiful but also intensely difficult question. A *cruciform* spirituality (shaped by Jesus' death on the cross, which we will explore in detail in section three) includes not only the other who is a friend, but the other who is an enemy as well. Such a spirituality, Volf writes, "will seek to open its arms toward the other even when the other holds a sword."[120]

That is exactly what our friends around the world have taught us. They do take precautions to protect themselves, their loved ones, and their property, but in the process they have not let down their extended arms, hoping against all odds for the joy of reciprocal embrace.

Our network in Kenya, coordinated by Gideon Ochieng, is made up of at least twelve tribes and twenty-five members of the network will soon graduate with a master's degree in Global Urban Leadership. Not long after we began the master's program, the country erupted in violence following the 2007 presidential election and came to the brink of civil war. Many Kenyans died, hundreds of thousands were displaced, and every member of our network was personally affected by emotional, physical, and relational violence. Some guarded their churches and homes from looters, while others consoled families ravaged by physical violence, death, and deceit from those they had previously considered friends and neighbors.

Following the elections, skepticism grew across lines of "otherness," especially across tribal and political affiliations. Morning and afternoon chai breaks, city taxi rides, and even churches became exclusive of the "other," and Nairobi shifted from an inclusive urban epicenter to 42 separate tribes, 2 distinct political affiliations, 199 informal settlements, and rich vs. poor.

Amid the tension, members of our network graciously agreed to come together for a retreat of reconciliation in a town outside of Nairobi. We originally thought that this would be a retreat from daily demands on them as doctors, teachers, preachers, counselors, parents, and many other roles. In many ways, it was—yet the real retreat was marked by the opportunity to leave the pressure of living out the political and tribal roles that their communities had attached to them. Leaders in the network found room for laughter, for stories, and for watching soccer (which in some ways might be the global metaphor of embrace). Although it only lasted two days, the retreat represented a gracious space where arms could open and "soft knocks on the door of the other's heart" could be heard.

We do not pretend to suggest that these leaders flawlessly modeled full inclusion. Who has? They argued about contentious issues and occasionally excluded others by using tribal language, but they also opened their arms wide enough to make room for "the other" at a time when their entire country was fraught with skepticism, anger, and violence. Their little retreat loosened the chains of otherness and modeled a way for them to open their arms to the "Chetniks" who represented immense pain and violence in their homes, churches, and communities.

Examples of embrace like these abound in our network. They are not perfect models of embrace, but they are real. Consider a ministry leader in Guatemala City who appealed to her supporters to fund a special initiative that focused on an entrenched group that preyed on her community by charging extortion money ("protection taxes") and then responding violently through assaults and murder against those who refused to pay. She received very few responses to her plea, but one was very notable. A poor elderly widow wrote back, saying that she and her adult children felt God prodding them to give a monthly offering to the project. This was very remarkable because we learned later that she and her family had been personally terrorized by this particular group and had even lost a family member to their violence. In supporting the project, they chose to extend their open arms toward the others, even though those others stood with sword in hand.

Consider the lesson taught by the example of a ten-year-old boy—the son of a woman in one of our missional communities. Upon learning that his and his mother's lives had been threatened by a violent group from his neighborhood, he wrote a beautiful prayer in his journal that his mother shared with us. He asked that the Lord would forgive the young man making the threats (he mentioned him by name), and that he would realize how much he was hurting other people. The young boy asked that God would show the man making the threats the error of his ways, and that he would find the truth of God's love even for him. I (Joel) was astounded to read the words of a child asking God to forgive an oppressor who was threatening to take his and his mother's lives.

On another occasion, we learned of a leadership team in one of our Central American cohorts that had endured a period of extremely serious threats of extortion. The leader of this ministry team called to tell us that she and her team had spent two hours in prayer focused on the very group threatening to kill them. With deep sincerity in her voice she told me, "Joel, it was so beautiful. God gave us such a love for these young men tonight. We love them, all of them. We are full of God's love for them." The threats had not ceased, the situation was nowhere near a favorable resolution, but this leader and her ministry team had chosen to extend their arms to people threatening to kill them.

But it is one thing to open your arms to the enemy—it is quite another to be on the receiving end of such an embrace. It is deeply humbling. Several years ago, I (Kris) attended a camp for kids with disabilities. I am not exactly sure why I went, but I remember thinking it would be good for me to go—perhaps as an act of charity or penance, I am not sure. I arrived at the camp in good spirits, but by the end of the week I was emotionally and spiritually drained. I felt increasingly alone and isolated among the kids as the week dragged on. Ironically, it was just the opposite for the kids. They arrived suspicious and withdrawn, but by the end of the week they were open and present, eager to celebrate.

On the last night, the camp gathered for a concert. It was festive and full of celebration. I sat near the back, wishing I was home. I grew impatient and anxious, and I felt horribly alone. I counted the minutes before it was over. The carnival of disordered and disabled humanity made me more and more irritated—kids slobbering, arms flaying, awkward gestures, social miscues, strange grunts, awful smells. It was becoming more and more grotesque.

In the back stood Stephanie. Her body was eight-years-old, but she was stuck inside a mind that would never advance beyond the age of two or three. She couldn't speak, and her parents kept her leashed to a long bungie cord so that she could walk but not run away and hurt herself. She had two beautiful older twin sisters who were able-bodied and full of life. Stephanie and I had made a small connection earlier in the week, but it wasn't much since she couldn't speak and I had little patience to know how to take the relationship further.

So, as I sat on the aisle seat near the back of the room with my hood over my head, I heard some commotion near the back and turned to see Stephanie lumbering awkwardly up the center aisle. It wasn't clear where she was headed or what she was doing. She continued up the aisle, stretching her leash just about as far as it would go. As she approached, she suddenly turned toward me and lunged her body forward, arms flaying in the air. I was completely unprepared and she hit me in the face. I wasn't sure what she was doing. Had she fallen? Was she angry? It took me a second to realize that she was giving me a hug. I responded as best I could, but I was mostly embarrassed by the scene she was causing. Stephanie left as awkwardly as she came and returned down the center aisle.

Happy that the ordeal was over, I watched Stephanie lumber away. As she reached the end of the aisle she took a sharp left turn and headed for the back left corner of the room. There in the corner sat an older gentleman that none of us had seen all week. He sat hunched over on a bench. He was rocking back and forth with his head buried in his arms. This was a camp for special-needs kids, but apparently nobody told him that. He lived near the camp and had shown up for the final celebration. I watched as Stephanie found her way to the back corner and threw herself at the man who was completely oblivious to what was happening. It looked more like a collision than a hug, but he soon gathered himself and with great ease and affection he returned her hug in kind. I figured that was the end of that.

It wasn't.

Stephanie again began the long awkward journey back up the center aisle. I was watching to see where she would go next. I grew anxious. The music was playing, the kids were shouting, and damn, she was coming back my way. Again she threw herself at me. I knew what was coming, but for some reason I was still unprepared for another hug. I did what I could to be a little more affectionate this time, but it was still awkward, and to be honest I was hoping she would go away. She left and headed down the aisle. I again thought it was over.

It wasn't.

She headed for the man in the back who by this time was eagerly awaiting her return. She threw herself at him. He was beaming! He could hardly wait for her to get there. She turned and headed back up the aisle. Something was happening in me. Like the man in the back this time, I found myself waiting for Stephanie to arrive, half-hoping she would choose me again. All of a sudden it didn't matter that we had become the center of attention and celebration. The music and mayhem continued around us but that didn't matter much to me now. My desire to be hugged by Stephanie grew. I was really hoping she would choose me again. She did! Of all the people present that night, she chose me! She threw herself at me once again and we hugged. It was a real hug—a mutual hug—a non-self-conscious hug—a hug that has stuck with me all these years.

Perhaps it has stuck because the drama that night continued. Back and forth, back and forth, back and forth, Stephanie just kept going back and forth between me and the old man. She gave us hug after hug in what became a beautiful dance between one little spirit-filled girl and two alienated men, desperate for a hug. We were the happiest guys in the place. The music rang out, the kids slobbered and grunted their joy all over the place, and for a moment I was transformed. I doubt very much that Stephanie is still alive, but I will never forget her embrace and I suspect neither will that man in the back of the room, whoever he was.

We are constantly humbled and challenged by the people we have the privilege of walking with in some of the world's dark places. Our friends, following Christ's example, wait with open arms patiently extended in eager anticipation of someday entering into the joy of reciprocal embrace. Someone once wrote that forgiveness is the scent that a flower leaves on the heel that has crushed it. Over the years, we have had the chance to smell the scent of some beautiful flowers. Forgiveness carries with it a huge risk and a very high price. But, as Lewis Smedes writes, "Embrace is grace, and grace is gamble, always."[121]

10

unbounded spirit

I will pour out my spirit on all flesh.
Joel 2:28

Out beyond ideas of right thinking and wrong
thinking, there is a field. I'll meet you there.
Rumi[122]

WE HAVE REFLECTED extensively on the "Word made flesh" (Jn. 1:14) and tried to unpack the street-level implications of the incarnation from a variety of vantage points. In jazz-like fashion, we loop back now and consider the first picture of God in Scripture. It is a preview of the incarnation: "In the beginning God created the heavens and the earth. Now the earth was formless and empty, darkness was over the surface of the deep, and the Spirit of God was hovering over the waters" (Gen. 1:2, NIV).

Here we see God intimately involved in creation and the first image of God is the image of the Spirit tenderly and passionately "hovering" over chaos. The word "hovering" is associated with the word "brood." It is the image of a mother hen on her eggs, drawing them into life, a mother in the midst of chaos, nurturing life. This imagery animates our conversations with grassroots leaders who serve in the daily chaos of incredible pain, suffering, violence, and injustice—the image of God as mother is more than comforting to them. The feminine face of God is an essential part of healing not only our image of God but the communities we serve. It is an image that has largely been denied by the mainstream church. For this reason we often refer to the Spirit as She. In fact, the word for Spirit in Hebrew is feminine *(ruach)*. The word for Spirit in Greek is neuter *(pnuema)*.[123] We are socialized to use the masculine pronoun, but we are convinced that for those who have experienced the abandonment and abuse of their father, the image of God as mother drawing life into existence holds great promise. It is both Biblical and practical. Perhaps this is why we are seeing women leaders being welcomed and received in some very hard communities in ways that male leaders are not.

For those who want to make sense of serving marginalized populations in hard places, the image of God "hovering" in chaos also frees us from the need to *bring* God to those we serve in order to *fix* them or their circumstances. Rather, it gives us license to awaken people to the God who hovers there in the midst of their mess. This means we can greet the Holy Spirit in the hardest places with a holy kiss as opposed to having to bring Her there as a special delivery package. We have challenged hundreds of grassroots leaders in hard places to work with this image in their ministries to see what happens. It has had a revolutionary impact, as we shall see.

THE WORK OF THE SPIRIT

Before we take a tour of Acts to explore how the Spirit worked in those early days of the Church, consider first how our view of the Holy Spirit might help or hinder our ability to recognize and join the Spirit's work. In the West, we gravitate toward a belief that, given enough of the right information, we can explain anything. Buried in that notion is a powerful compulsion to control. As a result, we are not so comfortable with the idea of a Holy Spirit. If God is present in some kind of Spirit—how can I be sure this Spirit behaves itself? How can I define it, tap into it, control it? How can I be sure the Spirit isn't acting without my prior approval and full consent? How can I be sure this Spirit will do things my way?

The Eastern Orthodox Church, for theological and perhaps cultural reasons, is far more comfortable accepting the inexplicable mystery and unbounded nature of the Holy Spirit. In this sense, they follow Mary's example: When she was told that the Spirit of God would come over her and she would conceive a child, she simply replied, "Let it be." Likewise, the Orthodox mind is perhaps more willing to embrace Jesus' depiction of the Spirit's work, "The wind blows where it chooses, and you hear the sound of it, but you do know where it comes from or where it goes. So it is with everyone who is born of the Spirit" (Jn. 3:8). Just *how* the Spirit recreates and gives new birth is a mystery and beyond our control.

One of the words used in the Eastern Church to describe the Holy Trinity is the Greek word *perichorisis,* which comes from the world of dance.[124] Embraced by God, we are invited to join in, but the Holy Spirit initiates and choreographs this dance of life. At first, we are simply the marveling spectators, but the wonder of it all is that the Spirit comes to the edge of the dance floor, extends a hand of invitation, and graciously leads us to join the dance.

Consider how our understanding of the Spirit affects the way we think about mission. When we believe *we* are leading the dance, we also think it is our job to usher in the Spirit, to bring Her with us to the places where She is not presently located or to people groups who don't know Her. By contrast, if we understand that the *Spirit* is in control, then She proceeds as She sees fit. Instead of bringing the Spirit wherever we go, we find Her already present (hovering in chaos) there. Our job is to greet the Spirit already at work.

This may seem an abstract and benign idea, until we think of the Spirit's presence in some of the worst and most shocking people and places in the world. It makes the hair on the back of our necks stand on end. We protest, "There is no way you can tell me that the Spirit is already there in such dark places, at least not a *Holy* Spirit."

If we believe our job is to bring the Holy Spirit with us, does this not have a profound effect on the way we see the people we are called to serve? It very often leads to the first step of judgment, not blessing. In its worst iteration, we end up as conquerors with a perceived spiritual mandate, and there are plenty of historical examples of such faulty and destructive thinking. Historically, we have sometimes ripped Matthew 28 out of context, canonized it as The Great Commission, and then gone about making disciples of all nations in whatever form or style and by whatever method we considered most efficient and effective.

Many of us still live out of this tradition. Our first step

toward the neighborhood is seldom blessing. We see only deficits in hard places as opposed to seeing and celebrating community and neighborhood assets, which are likely the result of the Spirit already at work. The Spirit has been way ahead of us, working without our help. When we believe we need to *bring* the Holy Spirit to the lost, we become heroes in our story—forgetting that this is entirely God's story, in which we are invited participants.

If we understand that the Spirit precedes us everywhere we go, we will realize we do not need to bring the Spirit with us, for the Spirit is already there and active. She has been working, and invites us to dance with Her as She hovers in chaos, lovingly extending her hand of grace to us. The Holy Spirit is free to roam, and roam She does as a mother gathering her chicks, or as a lover wooing her partner to the dance floor.

Consider a story from Alaska and the Aleutian tribal cultures that dominated that landscape for thousands of years. Eastern Orthodox Christians were the first to bring the good news of Jesus to this part of the world and, upon encountering the Aleutian people, they began to listen—because they had the expectation that the Spirit was already active and at work. They saw it as their job to locate the Spirit and bear witness to Her presence and work. When the Orthodox missionaries listened carefully to the people's stories, they could recognize the Spirit at work in the culture. For example, Michael Oleska in his book *Orthodox Alaska—A Theology of Mission* narrates the traditional understanding of an Eskimo whale hunt in which the victim whale possesses a kind of intelligence that is foreign to Western Culture:

> The bowhead whale . . . is a huge and powerful creature, perfectly capable of escaping a small skin boat

paddled by a dozen men. To catch a whale, the
hunters need the cooperation of their prey. It must
not swim away. It must not dive to the ocean depths.
It must not attack. It must float on the surface and
wait for the hunter to arrive, allow them to maneu-
ver their tiny boat directly in front of its head and
permit them to throw their hand-made harpoons
directly into its face . . . the whales allow themselves
to be killed, trusting that the People will treat them
respectfully and allow them to be reborn. Very little in traditional Eskimo culture can be understood
without grasping this fundamental intuition.[125]

When the Orthodox missionaries witnessed this intuition
at work they could see the faint outlines of the Spirit hovering.
They recognized that the Holy Spirit was at work in this culture
long before they had even heard the name of the Aleutians. Their
theological reference point allowed them to see God at work
among these people, preparing the way for them as Christians
to come and point that story back to its origin in their own faith.

How does this thinking shape the way one enters a society
made up of gangs, drug addicts, families in extreme poverty, or
street youth? We come asking beautiful questions, listening and
looking for the dance of the Holy Spirit. As John Howard Yoder
wrote, "God is working in the world, and it is the task of the
Church to know how he is working; that is to say, 'Behold, here
is Christ. This is where God is at work!'"[126]

The historical backdrop to these two perspectives regarding
the Spirit is important. Five hundred years before Luther initiated the Reformation, resulting in the split between Protestants
and Catholics, there was arguably an even greater division between the Western Church and the Eastern Orthodox Church

that occurred near the end of the first 1,000 years of church history. In our trainings with grassroots leaders, we have found it helpful to take time to review this history before pushing back further into the book of Acts where we see the unbounded Spirit in full bloom.

The split between the Eastern Church and the Western Church was complex, but at the center of the controversy was the question of how to understand the Spirit. To put it simply, there was a tug-of-war over the person and work of the Holy Spirit. The whole controversy hinged on three words known as the "filioque clause," which changed the course of church history. The Western church declared unequivocally, "I believe in the Holy Spirit who proceeds from the Father *and the Son.*" The Eastern Church took issue with the phrase "and the Son." They felt it diminished the third person of the Trinity and turned the Spirit into a kind of property of the Father and the Son, thus reducing the Spirit to a second-tier god. They insisted that the Spirit simply proceeds from the Father in the same way the Son does. There was no need to submit the Spirit to the Son, as if somehow the two might be rivals.

Whatever we think of this debate, there have been huge implications in the history and practice of Christian mission. The Western Church has traditionally (though not always) seen mission as a way of bringing the Spirit to a people or place. In this view, the Spirit can only be active where the Son is recognized and worshipped, because the Spirit proceeds from the Son. The Eastern Church (though not always) has tended to search for the Spirit at work in the world, even in places where Christ is not recognized. There is much more to the debate and subsequent history than this generalization, but when it hit the street, this was often the net effect. In our work, we are learning how to recover a view of the Spirit that might be considered more Eastern than Western—and find it energizes our missional presence in hard places. With this in mind, let us take a look at the book of Acts to see examples of the unbounded Spirit at work.

A Study in Acts

The book of Acts is filled with beautiful examples of the Spirit already at work, long before the apostles appear on the scene. Ray Bakke has written and lectured extensively on this and we will draw heavily on what we have learned from him as we embark on this rapid tour.

Martin Kahler said, "Mission is the mother of theology," suggesting that theology is the Church's attempt to make sense of God at work in the world.[127] Theology is always trying to catch up to God and God's work in the world. We are always a step or two behind. In other words, our truest theological insights are a reflection of God's activity, and God's activity is always out front, just ahead of and beyond our reach. This is one reason why we think theology from below is such a critical gift to the academy. Academies take a long time to catch up to what is happening on the ground, and that is not all bad. Grassroots conversations, however, are helpful in that we more vividly see and reflect on God's movement in the real world.

When we look at the whole narrative of Acts, we find the Spirit out in front, crossing boundaries and dancing in strange places in every chapter—all the way to the heart of power in Rome. Each step of the way, the church is thrown on her heels and forced to consider the movement of God for whom she had no categories. The activity of the Spirit in mission creates shock waves among the people of God, forcing them time and time again to re-imagine God in light of the new realities that are created. It is an amazing thing to watch.

The Spirit moves at Pentecost in Acts chapter 2, where we are told that the crowd spoke spontaneously in foreign languages. The emphasis in the text is not the new languages, or "tongues." The text emphasizes the fact that people actually *heard* each other. The verb "to hear" occurs four times in a tight span of only seven verses. Whenever people truly hear one another, we can be assured that the Spirit is at work. It is the reverse of the Tower of Babel that brought so much confusion.

In Acts 2:17-18, Peter recalls Old Testament prophecy from the book of Joel to make sense of the Spirit's mission. He directly quotes the prophet Joel speaking of how the Spirit would cross four of the most challenging 8 Miles of the ancient world—and ours too:

> In the last days it will be, God
>   declares,
> that I will pour out my Spirit
>   upon all flesh,
> and your sons and your
>   daughters shall prophesy,
> and your young men shall
>   see visions,
> and your old men shall
>   dream dreams.
> Even upon my slaves, both men
>   and women,
> in those days I will pour out
>   my Spirit;
> and they shall prophesy (Acts 2:17-18).

First, "I will pour out my Spirit on all flesh." All people, everywhere, are bathed in the Spirit. There are no longer ethnic or cultural boundaries in Christ. We can be proud of our ethnic and cultural heritage while also understanding that they don't define the sum of who we are. Celebration and appreciation for cultural and ethnic diversity is vital, but walls of division between groups are brought low in the Spirit.

Second, "sons and daughters will prophesy." The boundary of gender is erased. Many cultures have come a long way with this boundary, but it is still a great divide, even in relatively egalitarian Western societies. Jesus was a great prophet of gender equality at a time when good Jewish men would daily thank God that they were not created a woman, gentile, or dog.[128]

Third, "young men will see visions and old men will dream dreams." This marks the crossing of the generational divide. Young people are forever frustrated with the older generation, complaining that their resistance to change slows everything down. The contemporary concept of "youth churches" and professionalized models of youth ministry exacerbate the great 8 Mile generational divide, and youth are cut off from any interaction with the wisdom of the elderly. Social media further spreads the distance between the generations as both communicate socially in entirely different worlds. In North America, the elderly are readily deposited into nursing homes under someone else's watch, so the younger generation can continue their lives uninterrupted, not having to deal with infirmity and death. We are in desperate need for ministry models that bridge the ever-increasing gap between young and old, and the boundary-breaking Holy Spirit is leading the way.

Finally, Peter (quoting Joel) says, "Even on my servants, both men and women, I will pour out my Spirit." This is the great economic divide. Slavery is historically and foundationally about economics, even as it has been frequently overlaid thickly with racial oppression. The history of wars in Central and South America, and the abuse and enslavement of indigenous populations, is rooted primarily in economics. Slavery has been dressed up and legitimized in all sorts of ways, but a central thread in a wide variety of contexts has been money. W. E. B. Du Bois said of the 20th century that the most significant boundary was the color line.[129] In the 21st century, we wonder if the most significant boundary might be economic class distinctions.

Joel's prophecy functions like a table of contents of the book of Acts. At breathtaking pace, the Spirit moves ahead of the Church crossing boundary after boundary and inviting us to do the same. Then and now, the Church is taken aback by the movement of God and must struggle to make sense of it and keep up. Several times in Acts, the faithful gathered to debate and reflect on what the Spirit was doing. This seems to be a normative pattern for the Church in keeping with the invitation of Judges 19 to "Consider it. Take council. Speak out."

In Acts 6, Grecian Jews complain to Hebraic Jews that their women were being overlooked in the daily distribution of food. It is important to understand that these were Greek women because in the eyes of traditional Judaism, that fact alone meant they had to wait at the back of the line. However, the twelve apostles decided to appoint seven men to *wait on the tables of the women*. Is it not just like the unbounded Holy Spirit to crash the gender power boundary by putting men in the service of women, rather than in charge of them? The men became butlers for the women—a work of the boundary-breaking Spirit.

In Acts 7, we read Stephen's speech to the Sanhedrin. In his address, Stephen locates the Spirit of God outside the map of Israel, and this angers his listeners. Their blood was boiling by the time he finished, because he kept showing how God was acting outside of Israel's borders. The Jewish leaders "gnashed their teeth at him" because they mistakenly understood that God acted exclusively on their map, on Israeli soil. They were so angry that Stephen transgressed this boundary that they decided to execute him by stoning. Stephen, full of the Holy Spirit who led him across this lethal 8 Mile boundary, looked heavenward and saw Jesus standing by his throne in anticipation to receive in glory this faithful saint. Bakke and others have pointed out that it is the only place in Scripture where Jesus is *standing* near the throne—standing to pay honor to this Spirit-filled boundary breaker.[130]

After the murder of Stephen in Chapter 7, the Church scatters because of the suffocating persecution inflicted by Saul. The Holy Spirit is doing her unbounded dance in the chaos of that trial, and those who were scattered "preached the word wherever they went." Philip crosses a borderline into the cursed region of Samaria, and miracles begin to happen—filling the city with great joy. Peter hears about what is happening and travels through Samaria to see it with his own eyes. He is convinced of the authenticity of all that is taking place, before he returns to Jerusalem, "preaching the Gospel in many Samaritan villages."

Here, one of the most shocking 8 Mile boundary lines gets crossed. The Holy Spirit directs Philip to a "wilderness road" to meet a eunuch, a court official for the Queen of Ethiopia. Bakke describes the eunuch as "a sexually-altered Ethiopian finance minister." In the ancient world, it was not unusual for royalty to castrate court officials who were close to the monarchy. As Bakke points out, there was nothing more offensive to the Hebrew circumcision culture than the castration culture. Eunuchs were considered permanently defiled by mainstream Jews. But here in the 8th chapter of Acts, we see a eunuch

receiving the Spirit. The language in this story is carefully craft-
ed to make the point—because of its contemporary implications
we want to slow things down here and carefully consider how
the story is worded. For example, the eunuch was reading from
the prophet Isaiah when Philip approaches him:

> He was oppressed, and he was
>   afflicted,
> yet he did not open his mouth;
> like a lamb that is led to the
>   slaughter,
> and like a sheep that before its
>   shearers is silent,
> so he did not open his mouth.
> By a perversion of justice he was
>   taken away.
> Who could have imagined his
>   future?
> For he was cut off from the land
>   of the living,
> stricken for the transgression of
>   my people (Is. 53:7-8).

Notice the graphic and poetic irony here. The eunuch is an
African, quite possibly part of the Jewish diaspora of the Old
Testament. He has been "cut off" from the center of Jewish
culture. Philip is directed by the Spirit to join him (Acts 8:29).
Notice also that he was reading from Isaiah about a messianic figure who, like a lamb, was "slaughtered" by its "shearers."
There was a "perversion of justice," and the messianic figure in
the text was "cut off" from the land of the living. This graphic
language is something a eunuch could relate to. If this eunuch
was familiar with Isaiah 53, it is quite possible that he was also

aware that three chapters later, in Isaiah 56, God offers hope to eunuchs when he says, "To the eunuchs . . . I will give, in my house and within my walls, a monument and a name better than sons and daughters; I will give them an everlasting name that shall not be cut off" (Is. 56:4-5).

Eunuchs are rare today, though female sexual mutilation is still being practiced in many parts of the world. More prevalent are entire communities who have been "cut off" from mainstream society, and particularly from the Church, because of their sexual orientation and gender identity. Many young people feel completely foreign to their own bodies. Many more completely heterosexual men and women feel equally "cut off" sexually from their partners. Engagement on these issues within communities of faith is growing, and in many of the missional communities we serve around the world there are hopeful strides among lesbian, gay, bisexual, and transgendered people who are finding authentic ways to follow Jesus. What cannot be overstated is the radical inclusion we see in Acts 8 and the way the suffering servant who was "cut off" and "stricken" identifies with the eunuch, or how the eunuch is "joined" to the community of the faithful.

We understand that this is a particularly painful and divisive topic for many of us within the church. Between the two of us authors and the respective networks that we serve, there are widely divergent viewpoints. We serve within conservative Protestant Evangelical/Reformed churches and mission agencies and mainline liberal church communities, in addition to nurturing partnerships with Roman Catholics. We have dear friends and family who have suffered horribly under the weight of this issue on both sides of the aisle. We do not intend to debate here the morality of various sexual lifestyles or suggest that gays or lesbians are the only ones "cut off" from community or in need of sexual healing. Our basic assumption is that we are all in need of healing. Where the two of us are in full agreement is that our call is to create room for leaders to see and celebrate God at work in the world even when God's movement does not fit prescribed theological categories. As long as there are young people who identify themselves as lesbian, gay, bi-sexual, or transgendered and who feel cut off from Jesus and the faith community, the gospel of Jesus compels us to stand with and for them. Whatever else the gospel means, it means that we stand with and for those who find themselves on the outside looking in. Our call is to remind people that there is always a seat at the table. The good news of Jesus invites us to bear the shame not just of those with whom we agree, but also those marginalized people with whom we might radically disagree.

Several years ago, I (Kris) was teaching a class in which the question of homosexuality came up. The rhetoric quickly turned hateful, and one of the more outspoken students said, "God hates faggots!" I was deeply disturbed, but unsure of what to say. I found myself pushing back and offering alternative points of view that might create room for dialogue. In doing so, I had painted myself into a corner. Some of the students began to question why I was defending the gay community. Soon it was clear that they wanted to know if I was gay or straight. I was not married at the time, so it was an open question in their minds.

I realized at that moment that I had a choice to make. If I claimed my identity as a heterosexual male in front the class, it would ease the tension and quite possibly let us all off the hook. But given the law of averages, at least one person in that room might well be gay or lesbian, and I felt compelled to honor them. I was not trying to be heroic—I'm not that courageous. I just felt compelled. I refused to answer the question, which could only mean one thing in their mind. I must be gay! In a sense, *I was gay,* at least for that class. I learned what it felt like to be on the outside and shamed. The incarnation invites us to stand with those who cannot stand for themselves, whether we agree with them or not. As we stand with those who are shamed, our own identities will be called into question. We are reminded that because of Jesus' associations with people at the edges of society, he was himself assumed to be a drunkard, glutton, "sinner," and "Beelzebub" (the devil) himself. He endured epithets of the same sort intended to demean the gay, lesbian, bi-sexual, transgendered, and queer community. His radical identification with outsiders is most instructive for the church amid controversy over sexual identity.

Perhaps we have hit an 8 Mile here that the Church cannot yet cross. In our experience the Spirit never forces us anywhere that we are not ready to go. She simply moves and invites. There is never a hint of coercion in the work the Spirit. However, we think it is important to remember that doing theology from below has a way of surfacing our personal 8 Miles with alarming regularity. For many of us, our ultimate 8 Mile is quite simply our need to be right. It is a borderline addiction that easily hides under the cover of righteousness. The addiction works just as easily for those on the Left as it does for those on the Right, but our beliefs do not save us. Therefore, we offer in response the beautiful words of the poet and mystic Rumi who said, "Out beyond ideas of rightdoing and wrongdoing, there is a field. I'll meet you there."[131] We want to cultivate this field. It is what we do. It is where we have come to see and experience the Spirit at work. Perhaps the most scandalous aspect of grace is the room it creates for us all to be wrong—joyfully and happily wrong.

Between the two of us, we have had a great deal of experience in being wrong. It has become something of a spiritual gift and we intend to exercise it regularly. And so for other weary travelers also looking for the courage to be wrong, we turn again to Saint Huckleberry Finn, whose love for "Nigger Jim" allowed him to forsake all that he believed, and all that he had been taught was right, for the sake of living in the grace of being wrong. What a gift!

As if to anticipate the tension of "right versus wrong," "us versus them," Luke (the writer of Acts) pushes on to chapter 10 where he tells the story of Peter confronted with his own cultural and religious chauvinism. It takes ten chapters for the Spirit to dance Her way into Peter's perceived racial superiority. She works on Peter through a dream concerning clean and unclean food. Peter resists by hiding behind his own sense of righteousness. He refuses God, thinking he is doing God a favor—"By no means," Peter says. The Spirit persists three times and finally leaves Peter "perplexed." Meanwhile, unbeknown to Peter, the Spirit was also speaking to the "unclean" Cornelius. Cornelius found himself favored by God and sent some messengers to Peter. The irony here is delicious. Messengers of the "unclean" one are sent looking for Peter, the one who is lost this time!

The story continues in Chapter 11, where the word "Christian" appears, initially as a term of derision given to followers of Jesus or "The Way" in Antioch. Critics of "The Way" mocked the followers of Jesus for trying to be "little Christs." It was a label of shame used intended to demean the first recorded church in Scripture. It just so happens to be a multi-cultural, urban church. They have a strange leadership team as described at the beginning of chapter 13—also the first pastoral team that we know anything about—made up of five men (Joel's prophecy of gender inclusion apparently had not yet taken hold).

Consider these five: Barnabas is a Greek from Cypress; Simeon is from Africa; Lucius is an African from Cyrene; Manaen is an ex-court official of Herod Antipas; and Saul, a Roman citizen from Tarsus, completes the group. Here we have a Greek thinker, two Africans, a man who worked for the Jewish King Herod, and a Roman citizen. Now if you were going to pick the leadership team for the first church, would you have picked these guys? They should have been killing each other, not working together. Church growth specialists tell us that this kind of leadership team is a recipe for disaster. The unbounded Spirit, however, dances to the beat of a different drummer and says, "I do as I please, I gather these."

Here we see the Church in her finest dress, when she becomes a place where natural enemies gather. How does that speak to us? What does that look like? If the church is only a gathering of friends, it's just a club, not a church. When the church functions as an exclusive club—where like-minded people who normally and naturally like each other gather—it becomes toxic to mission. Homogeneity is a natural arrangement, easy to fall into. But what happens when the Holy Spirit shows up? Boundaries and dividing lines between natural enemies are transgressed. The Spirit says, "I dance in order to gather natural enemies who, in any other circumstance, would hate one another. In their midst, I declare my glory by allowing them to work together."

In Antioch, this is exactly what happened. Skeptics who looked at the peculiar way the followers of Jesus related to each other invented an epithet that stuck—a group of people trying to be little Christs by loving their enemies. When natural enemies gather and begin to really love one another, we have something unique and special. It takes a miracle of the Spirit to launch that kind of fellowship, and an even bigger miracle to keep it together, because nothing short of a miracle can keep a group of enemies together in loving relationship.

We complete our tour with Acts 15, which is chiastically the climax of Acts. After Acts 15, the Spirit moves the early church all the way to Rome and beyond—continuing to break boundary after boundary. It is in Acts 15 that the early church pauses to "consider and take council." They needed a break in the action to reflect. It is what Bakke calls the first "faith and culture" council of the Church. They gathered to address the question of their own cultural and religious chauvinism and to ask whether or not God was free to move beyond their religious boundaries. It was about insiders (Jews) and outsiders (Gentiles). Which camp was God's favorite? Peter of all people, who had undergone his own conversion on this question in Acts 10, stood up and spoke on behalf of the Gentiles. Paul and Barnabas also told story after story of how God had been moving among the Gentiles. Finally it was Jesus' brother James who spoke the word of wisdom that settled the dispute. Altogether, it is a wonderful example of Kahler's notion that "mission is the mother of theology."

In his letter to the Galatians, the Apostle Paul writes that in Christ, "There is no longer Jew or Greek, there is no longer slave or free, there is no longer male and female; for all of you are one in Christ Jesus." (Gal. 3:28). He may have even shared these words at the faith and culture council (the Galatian epistle is Paul's earliest, and probably predates the council). Years later, while sitting in a prison in Rome awaiting his trial and execution, he reflects again on the Spirit's work. It is the reflection of a seasoned veteran to a young and impetuous community—a community still held captive to a binary, dualistic worldview in which all of life is seen as a battle of black verses white, clean verses unclean, us versus them, insiders versus outsiders, right versus wrong. He writes as a grandfather to his grandchildren, urging them to another way. He writes as a mystic who has seen and experienced another reality. He reminds them that they have been reconciled in Christ, and in that renewal "there is no longer Greek and Jew, circumcised and uncircumcised, barbarian, Scythian, slave and free; but Christ is all and in all!" (Col. 3:11). Now that is inclusive!

All of this is the work of the unfettered Spirit in Her playful, joyful, inviting dance across every 8 Mile borderline in the book of Acts. We end our journey through Acts here, but the dance of the Spirit continues. All of this is the work of the unfettered Spirit in her playful, joyful, inviting dance across every borderline in the book of Acts. We end our journey through Acts but the dance of the Spirit continues. We leave you with the words of Mary Oliver whose little poem titled "Instructions for Living a Life" is a fitting summary of the ever-expanding call of the Spirit. After urging us to "pay attention," she advises, "Be astonished./Tell about it."[132]

11
riddles of grace

I will open my mouth to speak in parables;
I will proclaim what has been hidden from the
foundation of the world.

Matthew 13:35

The shortest distance between a human and
Truth is a story.

Father Anthony de Mello[133]

IN MATTHEW 13, Jesus tells a variety of parables to describe the kingdom of heaven. In one of the most striking of all, we are told that the kingdom of heaven is like a net (v. 47-48). The fishing net of that day was a dragnet, which interests both of us, Joel and Kris, because we are wannabe fishermen. When we go sport fishing, we use specific lures of just the right color and size, and just the right test-line for certain conditions—all to land a specific fish during a specific season. (At least this is what we think real sport fisherman do.) The fishing culture in Jesus' day was markedly different. The dragnet was tied to a weight that would go down to the bottom and scrape up everything from bottom feeders to the fish on the surface and all that comes between. It's a crazy way to fish from our perspective.

Of course, Jesus' real subject here is the spreading of the good news (*euangelion*) of the kingdom of God—what Christians call evangelism. But even in evangelism, the dragnet seems a wasteful way to do mission. For effective and economical evangelism today, we try to be very specific and targeted about the kind of "prize fish" we want to reach for Christ, perfectly placing very specific evangelistic lures. A dragnet is a messy way to fish, and when applied to fishing for souls, it sure makes for complicated evangelism.

Why do we engage in what we think is a better way to "fish" than what Jesus first taught? Aspiring evangelists try to get really good at "winning souls for Jesus" using a host of freshly painted, pristine, specifically designed lures (programs, events, strategies, media). After all, in our modern world we certainly have better tools and techniques than Jesus' disciples ever had.

But, perhaps it is time to look again at this messy and indiscriminate dragnet ministry that Jesus recommends. It is difficult to argue for such a ministry today, and even more difficult to fund, but if we are going to cross 8 Mile dividing lines, we must pursue it. The dragnet approach may sound like the opposite of the "scandal of particularity" that we spoke of earlier. It is rather the other side of the same coin. Jesus was at once particular in his approach to individuals and scandalously indiscriminate about whom he loved. The dragnet of God's love reminds us that we must be careful about being too caught up in our evangelistic tricks and techniques that tempt us to land a "trophy fish." With the dragnet approach, we'll catch something we do not expect or even want. We'll be tempted to throw it back, but we must learn to live with the tension of a net that scoops up everything.

In another parable of Jesus, often called the parable of the wheat and the tares (Matt. 13:24-30), he says the kingdom of God is like "a man who sowed good seed in his field." The big question is who is the sower in this parable? The answer will determine how we apply the implications of the parable to evangelism. If you are like us, you have always interpreted the sower as the church, or perhaps followers of Christ. A closer look at the text reveals the difficulties in that interpretation. What if the sower is God rather than the church? How differently does the text read then?

As the parable goes, while everyone sleeps the enemy sneaks in at night to plant tares (a kind of weed), and then goes away. Tares and wheat look so similar to one another that even the experienced farmer finds it very hard to tell the difference between the two. Maybe the distinction between good and bad, or wheat and tares ("insiders" and "outsiders"), is not as clear-cut as we think it is. Maybe a lesson here is that we do not know as much as we think do. In verses 27-30, the servants ask the owner if they should "right the wrong" by ripping out the tares that were planted during the night, but the sower warns that if they do, they could very well root up the wheat as well. So he tells them to let it go, to let the wheat and the tares both grow together until the harvest time. Is it possible that part of the reason God refuses us the right to separate wheat from tares is that we can't always recognize the difference between good and evil, insiders and outsiders, as much as we think we do?

To have a dragnet ministry, we need to cultivate a wheat and tare discipline—one that humbly recognizes our limitations in discerning the difference between good and evil. This is crucial because when we cast a dragnet among the least, last, and lost, we scoop up some strange specimens indeed, and the temptation is to protect our ministry from the "bottom feeders" by separation—"I can't have that gang member in my group. He will mess up everything." Or "That girl with tight jeans from a non-Christian family is going to be a bad influence on the impressionable church kids." Looking at what our big net scooped up, we are tempted to take the job of separating wheat and tares into our own hands. However, boundary-breaking ministry demands that we humbly admit we should leave the separating for the harvest time. What might it mean to run a ministry like this? To name only one challenge, can we run a dragnet ministry with wheat and tare inclusiveness and still find the funding we need?

Practically speaking, huge obstacles stand in the way of building a ministry of this kind. For example, it is nearly impossible to (and often counterproductive) to attempt to develop large programs. Many of the leaders we serve describe how some youth or families they work with take up so much oxygen in the church or program that others are left suffocating. These leaders have to learn how to handle people that demand all of their attention, leaving them nothing to give to others. They have a very hard choice to make—the simple solution is to prioritize the maintenance of neatly run programs over the "tares" who mess everything up. Some leaders tell us, "I can't run a decent program with those kinds of kids in my room. They will prevent the other kids from hearing the gospel." They feel as if they face a choice between exclusively serving the kids who are ready to hear or letting chaos reign.

That's why so many ministries are designed for only a particular kind of fish. If we cannot accommodate the "bottom feeders," we end up prioritizing programs over people and adjusting our message to fit our program. Dragnet ministry in hard places is chaotic and messy. It sometimes only works as it did with Jesus, a dozen people at a time.

In 2 Corinthians 12, Paul writes about the "thorn in the flesh" he so desperately wanted removed. He called it a "messenger from Satan," designed to keep him from conceit in the face of the "surpassing great revelations" that he had been given. Three times Paul prayed for the removal of the thorn, and each time God said, "No." In this way, Paul confronts the crazy notion that God sometimes refuses to get rid of something Paul considers truly evil. Instead God tells Paul, "My grace is sufficient for you, for my power is made perfect in weakness" (2 Cor. 12:9).

What kind of a God uses evil to bring about good? Why doesn't Jesus kick Judas out of his circle of disciples, the tare of all tares? It seems that God is doing the unthinkable—choosing here to literally encircle evil and use it for a divine purpose beyond our comprehension.

How far do we go with this? We have no neat theological categories for this type of thinking. Have you ever thought that Satan's activity in your life might be the very thing that opens your eyes to God's dancing grace? Large segments of the church today consistently tell people that if they come to Jesus everything will be made right and that God, held captive by God's own word, will surely set them free of all thorns stuck in their sides. But is that always true? Perhaps we need a gospel that gives us grace to recognize and live with the demons that we just can't get rid of. Do we have a gospel big enough to handle that?

All the great spiritual guides teach that maturity in Christ is not so much about the demons we get rid of, but the demons that we are able to live with. If we are honest, some of us have "demons" that we can never seem to get rid of. Don't we at times give people a false hope when we say that accepting Jesus automatically makes everything all right for them if they can only muster up enough faith to make it happen?

Are preachers or church leaders willing to say, "I want you to learn to live with that demon in your life because God's power in you is made perfect in weakness?" Put that way, it sounds absolutely crazy, but is that not what God is saying to Paul in the 2 Corinthians passage? There are certain things that we pray and beg God to release us from, but in effect God is telling us, "No, leave that thorn right where it is. Don't remove it. For it is there that you will see my strength." Beat poet and songwriter Leonard Cohen put it this way in his song "Anthem," "There is a crack in everything, that's how the light gets in."

The temptation to separate the wheat from the tares is more than a ministry issue, it is also an intensely personal dance between power and weakness. What is it that we have been trying to rip from our own lives? What have we spent our entire lives ashamed of or wished never existed? What part of our stories have we suppressed and denied a hearing—trying to pull it out and call it a tare? Are we proclaiming a false gospel when we declare that God will always rid us of our weaknesses and problems?

Jesus said, "And I, when I am lifted up from the earth, will draw all people to myself" (Jn. 12:32, NIV). In this startling declaration, Jesus foreshadows that the powerlessness and defeat of his crucifixion will break down all boundaries between people. Matthew's passion narrative describes this in the powerful symbol of the curtain in the temple. The architecture of the temple created boundaries called "courts." The Gentiles had their court; the women had theirs; and the Holy of Holies, cordoned off by the great curtain, was reserved for God and an annual visit from a priest. In the moment of Jesus' greatest humiliation, in the moment of evil's greatest triumph, the curtain separating the Holy of Holies from everyone else is ripped from top to bottom. The meaning was stunning: In the most wrenching moment of apparent weakness and defeat, our most tightly guarded, sacred boundaries are shattered.

Sometimes the Church re-creates the "temple courts" that block the throne of Jesus. How many boundaries and barriers do people have to cross before finding their way to Jesus? Do they have to conform to our rules? Do they have to learn our "language" and figure out how to effectively navigate our church culture before they can gain access to the throne of Christ? Are we sport-fishing for the fish we desire, or laying the dragnet that brings in all kinds? Are we trying to sort our crops before the harvest or trusting the sower to do the harvesting? If we dare, a dragnet ministry with a wheat and tares discipline radically broadens access to the one whose cross welcomes all.

—section three—
hanging

Cursed is anyone who hangs on the tree.
Galatians 3:13

I have been all the way to the bottom.
It is solid down there.
Madeleine L'Engle[134]

12

cruciform mission

Then God said, "Let Us make man in Our image, according to Our likeness" . . . And there was evening and there was morning, the sixth day.
Genesis 1:26,31

God seems to be gifting me with a heart, a terrifying thing, since hearts only grow as they break.
James Alison[135]

G OD CREATED HUMANITY on the sixth day, which according to the Hebrew week, is a Friday. God called his work "very good." At the center of our faith is another Friday. It too was good. Two Fridays linked together in the most unusual way—creation and the cross. Both are good, very good! The cross is hidden in creation and creation is hidden within the cross. Creation calls forth the cross, and the cross calls forth creation. This is a mystery, and mysteries by definition can't be explained—at least not fully.

Karl Rahner taught that what the mind wants most is not explanation but communion. In fact, explanation very often diminishes the experience of communion. Perhaps this is why Jesus so consistently speaks in riddles and parables, performing a kind of street theater that disorients the mind and opens the heart. The gospel calls us to encounter Jesus—such is the way of the cross.

It took several centuries for the cross to become the dominant image of the Church. The early Church may have heeded Paul's exhortation to preach Christ crucified, but it took a while to adopt the cross as its primary symbol. Perhaps it was too scandalous, too embarrassing, too shameful, especially for an already shamed and marginalized community like the early church. It was not until the third century that the cross became the dominant symbol of Christianity, which ironically coincides with the Church's rise to power. We dare not lose sight of the irony. When the dominant religious culture co-opts the meaning of the cross, the cross tends to become a transactional tool of control that keeps power in the hands of the powerful, and God on the side of the status quo. We must be willing to admit that some of the most cherished theological ways of seeing the cross were formed in the context of power. This does not make them wrong, but we think it is wise to be cautious and even a little suspicious of such approaches.

Despite the fact that roughly half of the content in the Gospels is dedicated to discussing the last week of Jesus' life, and despite the fact that the Apostle Paul resolved to "know nothing among you except Jesus Christ, and him crucified"(1 Cor. 2:2), the most frequently used image of the early church was not the cross, but the image of a fish—the sign of Jonah. The crowds asked Jesus for a sign and Jesus said none would be given except the sign of Jonah. What does this mean?

The cross reveals the sign of Jonah—it *is*, in fact, the sign of Jonah, and much more. Jonah is the story of a reluctant prophet running from the reality of God's love for his enemies, only to be swallowed up by a whale and three days later delivered to the shore of those very same enemies with good news. We are runaways from the God who, when we follow God's way of love and reconciliation, brings us through death of the self to new life. This is the gospel in a nutshell, in both personal and social terms.

The sign of Jonah is the paschal mystery—life, death, and resurrection—and his journey is baptismal. In baptism, we are buried with Christ so that we might live with Christ. We go down into the water, runaways from God, passing through the chaotic waters of death, and then we are resurrected into the reality of God's love. There in the depths we die to all that is false, so that we might live to all that is true. Down there, in the belly of the beast is where we truly meet God, the ultimate being. It is where the real I meets the real Thou. That is why the Church has always insisted that our faith begins in baptism, the watery grave.

Jonah. Baptism. Cross. They all speak to the same journey. The cross tells us that for life to be the blessing that God intends, it must pass through death. Paul teaches us that death is not the enemy we imagined, "O death, where is your sting?" (1 Cor. 15:55). Death, in its natural state, is part of life—just as a seed *must* die, in dying we live. On the cross, Jesus not only shows us how to expose and disempower death as a demonic principality that holds humanity hostage, he also shows us how to die that we might truly live. And so we arrive at the lowest point of our

journey, where words falter and fray under the weight of such glory.

What follows is a series of meditations and stories that we hope will illustrate the way of the cross. We have chosen not to wade into explanations of various historical and contemporary theories of atonement here. We will resist the temptation to dissect the mechanisms of how salvation at the cross works, or be so foolish as to try to explain the mystery of suffering. Rather, our hope is to encounter and seek communion with the crucified one.

A trusted companion for such an encounter is the centurion at the cross. The text tells us that when the centurion "stood facing" Jesus on the cross and "saw that in this way he breathed his last, he said, 'Truly this man was God's Son'" (Mk. 15:39). We ask for the grace to see what the centurion saw, which was more than simply a man being crucified. After all, there were three who were crucified that day and many more who had been crucified throughout history. The text clearly indicates that the centurion saw something different in Jesus, something very peculiar about the way in which Jesus experienced his own death. If we can see this, we can join the centurion and all the faithful throughout history to proclaim with great confidence, "This is God's Son."

BEARING THE SHAME OF THE CROSS

One of the earliest known depictions of Jesus is the Alexamenos Graffito, dating from c.200 AD or earlier.[136] It is an early parody of Christianity. It was discovered in 1857 in Rome and is now in the Palatine Antiquarian Museum. This wall carving is much like the graffiti we might find in a public restroom today. It shows a man with an ass's head being crucified and a youth raising his hand, as if in prayer. The Greek text in the graffito is: *ALEXAMENOS SEBETE THEON* or "Alexamenos worships his god."

Before the development of Christianity, the Jews had been charged by some within Roman empire with worshiping an ass—a shameful accusation. It is likely that the same accusation was being directed at Christians through this ancient cartoon. If we are too easily offended, we will miss the unintended genius of insight here. The irony within the irony of this cartoon is that it makes a profoundly Christian statement.

As it turns out, the image of a youth worshiping a crucified ass, sums up the gospel beautifully. God's willingness to play the ass is what makes Christianity, well, Christian. The artist's attempt to discredit the faith only serves to highlight its power. God bears the shame of humanity and does so in a way that is unthinkable. He bears our shame—literally occupying the space of shame with us—so that we might be shameless.

God does the "full monty," so to speak. God does what Adam and Eve could not do when they tried to cover their shame in the garden. When Jesus was nailed to the cross, naked and exposed to the world, he showed us that it is possible to occupy the space of shame in a way that ends it and brings forth life. The cost is terrible, though. A careful reading of the passion narratives shows a relentless process of shaming the crucified one, and there is every reason to believe his torturers were as successful at inflicting psychic pain as they were physical pain. In solidarity with all of humanity, God was exposed, degraded, and humiliated.

The world has always cursed that which it is ashamed of. Even the ancient Hebrews believed that "Cursed is everyone who hangs on a tree" (Gal. 3:13, Deut. 21:23). Jesus changes all that, or at least rearranges it and gives it new meaning. As James Alison says,

> Ever since God occupied that space himself in Jesus, and showed that it could be occupied and dwelt in, painfully but forgivingly, God pulled the plug on our way of constructing goodness over against people like himself. And that means, God introduces suspicion into our midst, suspicion that our goodness may be fake, and our "evil ones" after all innocent, or at least, no more guilty than everybody else.[137]

If we follow this insight, perhaps we can begin to see what the centurion saw at the foot of the cross. He saw Jesus in a new light—that Jesus was not the one who was cursed by God, as many who witnessed the crucifixion might have expected. Rather, he saw Jesus as cursed by humanity, bearing the brunt of humanity's shame and doing so with a forgiveness in his heart so profound and so deep that it had to come from God. Jesus reflects back to the centurion the centurion's own shame but with one exception, the curse was gone. It is a mystery why or how the centurion saw this and others did not, but the centurion sees his shame through the lens of love and forgiveness. Jesus does not return curse with curse. He absorbs it and puts an end to it. This transforms the centurion, and he declares Jesus to be God's son.

Stunningly, the pattern of Jesus occupying our shame "forgivingly" does not end at the cross. Jesus continues to occupy our shame in the resurrection. He bares the wounds of our shame in his resurrected body as if to say, "I am not ashamed to carry your shame—there is nothing to be ashamed of." Here is the theological key to the redemption of our shame: The shame of Jesus has passed through death into utter shamelessness. If this view is correct then God stands freely with the shamed refusing to give power to that which scandalizes the world. Standing freely with the shamed, God refuses to give power to that which scandalizes the world. God takes the sting out of our shame by occupying it without shame. God takes the curse out of the curse by showing there is no curse at all, at least not from God's side. In doing so, Jesus exposes the truth that has been hidden for ages—a truth that lies far beyond the imaginations of all but the most inspired prophets, buried under layers and layers of failed hopes and dreams. It is nearly impossible for a shame-filled humanity to see it. It took the cross to awaken us to the truth and the truth is quite simple:

God is not mad at us. All is already forgiven.

Paul writes that this message is utter foolishness to those who are perishing, but it is the very power of God to those who are being saved (1 Cor. 1:18).

We stand in awe of a God who is secure enough not only to ride an ass, but in the end, to be one. As we pointed out earlier,

Jesus never allowed fear for his reputation (in any conventional sense) to guide his steps. He occupies all of insulting epithets
hurled at him with surprisingly little concern. He barely acknowledges his accusers, let alone defends himself against them.
His interests lie elsewhere. He allows himself to be so thoroughly associated with the shameful ones as to be one of them. In
fact, the only titles that seem to bother Jesus are the ones that
we might consider good. It is one thing to stand *for* the shamed
or *with* the shamed, it is quite another to be *one of the shamed*
and to do so in a shameless way. As it turns out, the cartoon is
true. God is an *ass*. And we are desperate for a Gospel that frees
us up to become the same. To miss the joke here is to miss the
Gospel. "Let us then go to him outside the camp and bear the
abuse he endured" (Heb. 13:12-13).

In South Africa, Stephan Debeer helps to organize an annual "Feast of the Clowns" where 4,000 clowns march to create
dialogue about some of the deepest hurts and pains of their city.
Each year more than 20,000 people from all walks of life gather to celebrate life in the midst of chaos. The clowns give voice
to the voiceless, playfully defending the rights of the underclass
who continue to endure oppression even after the fall of apart-
heid. They speak truth to power, but they do so as clowns. They
perform a radical form of street theater that accepts the role of
the fool as if to say to those in power, "Look at us! See in us what
you have denied in yourself. We are playing the fool and are
happy to do so. Let your shame fall on us. Let us bear the curse
that you yourself cannot (will not) bear." The organizers of the
festival write,

> A city without festivals is a city without a soul. A city
> without laughter is a city without hope. A city with-
> out clowns will forget its frailty and bask in pride.

The Feast of the Clowns will continue to bring laughter and a smile, to hear and broadcast the many cries of our people, and to create space for dialogue and encounter that will not leave us unchanged.[138]

In Guatemala City, a clown named "Payaso Chitin" (whose real name was Italo Castro) loved the unlovable of his city with reckless abandon and unbridled passion. My wife Marilyn and I (Joel) first met Italo Castro after some friends told us about a professional clown who had a ministry with street kids. Late one evening, we left our children with a babysitter in the comfort of our home and went out with Italo to meet some youth who called the streets their home. It was an experience that profoundly marked our lives.

We zigzagged throughout the city that night, stopping at different *puntos* or points where the street youth of our city gathered to lick the wounds of the day. They would replenish their little bottles of "wipe" used as inhalants to mask their pain and cover their hunger before eventually falling asleep together in "bundles" for shared body heat. When we finally returned to our home at about 2:30 a.m., we lay in bed staring at the ceiling, haunted by the smell of paint thinner and the faces of the youth we had left on the street when it started to rain. Neither of us slept that night.

As I recall that experience now, I'll never forget the way Italo lovingly moved in his clown garb between the youth, gently slipping their hands, filled with rags drenched with mind-numbing inhalants, off of their faces. "Let me see the beautiful face that God has created," he would say. "*Dejame verte* (let me see you)." He would also burst out in a chant over and over again yelling, "*Me siento bien, me siento bien,*" to which the kids would respond,

"Me siento bien, me siento bien" ("I feel good"). For all who had
the privilege of spending time with Italo, as he met with the
kids he so dearly loved, that chant became the unforgettable
stamp in the passport of their journey to the streets.

He embodied the truth captured in the words of poet Galway
Kinnell in his poem "Saint Francis and the Sow"—"Sometimes
it is necessary to re-teach a thing its loveliness."[139] Italo lived to
re-teach loveliness and purpose to children and teens that everyone else saw as ugly and useless. Through him many of those
kids—for the first time in their lives— experienced the love of
a father, big brother, and a friend, and through Italo, God embraced them.

One day Italo was out swimming after spending a weekend
with other clowns at a special event. He was caught in a strong
current that dragged him further and further from the shore
while friends looked on helplessly after realizing too late what
was happening. Italo died that day.

At the memorial service, when the street kids came into
the church, they immediately surrounded the coffin and cried.
The people in the front rows reverently made space for them so
they could have the best seats in the house. Several local pastors spoke of their deep respect for Italo and how they had been
touched by his infectious joy—in and out of face paint.

At the funeral the next day, there was a parade of colorful
clowns shouting, *"Me siento bien,"* and *"Viva Chitin!"* At the
gravesite, even as the bricklayers boarded up the crypt, clown
after clown spoke of the incredible inspiration Italo had been
in their lives. After almost everyone else had left, the street kids
huddled close and held each other while showering one another
in tears. They each took turns speaking of the love of God they
knew in the man who taught them how to feel good in their

souls, and who saw them for who they really were.

Italo's life and ministry represents the best of the grass-roots leaders we have had the privilege of serving and learning from throughout the world. With hundreds of street kids in Guatemala City, he lived fully into a sense of "kinship," which Father Gregory Boyle describes in his book *Tattoos on the Heart* (quoting Pema Chodron, an ordained Buddhist nun): "Kinship's truest measure lies not in our service of those on the margins, but in our willingness to see ourselves in kinship with them."[140]

Italio's story provides more than simply a model for be-friending street youth. In his very life and death, Italio embodied the heart of the gospel we are trying to communicate in these pages—our attempts at explanation fall woefully short. In revealing to us the geography of grace, Jesus occupies the shame of humanity, and he does so without the slightest a hint of judg-ment. On the contrary, he prayed for the forgiveness of the very ones who exposed him to ridicule on the cross. On a garbage-strewn hillside outside the city, Jesus absorbs our shame and our violence and then he steadfastly refuses to return it in kind. Instead, Jesus disempowers death. Jesus exposes the principal-ity of death that has fallen under the power of sin and holds hu-manity hostage. He takes the sting out of such death by expos-ing it and absorbing it and ultimately transforming it. This is God's "victory over death." Death is no longer the curse that it was. It is no longer the power that rules. It is no longer the en-emy to be feared. But here's the twist. In doing so, Jesus also re-claims death and befriends it—not death in its perverted form, but death in its state of grace. Jesus reclaims death as a natural blessing to the rhythm of life and shows us that it is possible to befriend it.

This sounds crazy.

A culture that has not befriended death, is ironically, a dangerous, death-dealing culture. It is true that in Christ we have "victory over death," but the great paradox of our faith is that Jesus shows us that our victory over death is achieved not by entering into rivalry against it, not by fighting it or trying to cast it out with violence, but by finally and fully accepting its place in the rhythm of life. By submitting to it, we are freed from it. This is the great mystery.

After an extensive tour of the United States, German pastor/ theologian Helmut Thielicke was asked what he had observed as the greatest deficiency among American Christians. His reply was an incisive laser, "They have an inadequate view of suffering."[141] It is estimated that Americans spend over four billion dollars annually on painkiller medications alone.[142] Pain has been turned into a problem to be solved by a commodity to be produced. It is something we desire to eliminate and fix.

Of course, there is no more basic and natural human instinct than avoiding pain. But what happens when an entire society becomes obsessed with denying pain and makes it an organizing principle? What happens when pain is denied, dismissed, demonized, and systematically hidden? Unfortunately, it creates a society that cannot tolerate honest dialogue with God about our pain. Such a society suffers from unacknowledged despair that lurks just beneath the surface. It creates churches that seldom take up the exhortation of Judges 19:30 ("Consider it! Take council. Speak out."). With this in view, author Douglas Hall can say, "Covert despair and repressed hopelessness characterizes the spiritual condition of North American culture." In contrast, "Unlike the despair of the poor and afflicted around the globe who know too well their true condition, the despair of the dominant culture of North America is a denied despair, not merely hidden by wealth and power, but forcibly refused."[143]

Our wholesale commitment to deny the reality of suffering and our refusal to engage it leads not only to despair but to violence. Hall argues that a society that cannot tolerate suffering ironically suffers three consequences: First, we lose the ability to enter our own pain. Second, we lose the ability to imaginatively enter the pain of others. Finally, we seek out a scapegoat to bear the pain that we feel but can't articulate or engage ourselves.[144] In other words, our inability to suffer breeds a kind of despair that eventually erupts in violence. A culture that denies death becomes death-dealing. Consider the 105 million people killed in wars of the 20th century.[145] More people were killed in the 20th century than in the previous ten thousand years combined.[146] It is no accident that most of these deaths occurred at the hands of "civilized" and "prosperous" societies who have tried to hermetically seal themselves away from suffering and death.

If that sounds like a heady leap, consider the miniature forms of violence that erupt in our daily lives as a result of our inability to suffer and hold the pain. For example, on our way home from a hard day's work in congested traffic, we can easily summon a few choice words for the screwballs who can't drive. Arriving home, now more agitated than when we left work, we find ourselves arguing with our spouse, yelling at the kids, and kicking the dog. In this case our denial is externalized and we project our frustrations on others. At other times, we turn inward in our denial, thus also internalizing violence and self-inflicting wounds. One way we commit violence on ourselves is depression—we victimize ourselves, especially that part of ourselves that we feel most ashamed of. Denial is always dangerous, especially for the vulnerable, who become the scapegoats of our denial, whether it's other people or the weak part of ourselves.

But, the cross stands at the bottom of the arc of incarnation, sanctifying the wounds of the world and declaring them holy too. If the incarnation expresses what William Stringfellow calls God's "preemptive concern for life,"[147] the cross expresses God's preemptive concern for death, sanctifying both with the mark of his presence. If the gospel declares anything, it declares that through the wounds of Christ, our wounds become the wombs of transformation.

We are not saying that the cross explains or justifies suffering—Jesus gets no answer to his question "Why?" as he hangs on the cross. Neither do we. The cross does not glorify or worship suffering. As Jürgen Moltmann says in the opening line of his book *The Crucified God*, "The cross is not and cannot be loved."[148] It would be morbid to love the cross. While the cross does not explain or justify suffering, it does enter into suffering and, in so doing, redeems it. Moltmann goes on to say:

> Only the crucified Christ can bring the freedom which changes the world because it is no longer afraid of death. In his time the crucified Christ was regarded as a scandal and as foolishness. Today, too, it is considered old-fashioned to put him in the centre of Christian faith and of theology. Yet only when men are reminded of him, however untimely this may be, can they be set free from the power of the facts of the present time, and from the laws and compulsions of history, and be offered a future which will never grow dark again. Today the church and theology must turn to the crucified Christ in order to show the world the freedom he offers.[149]

The cross draws out the meaning of the incarnation to its depths. In his great incarnation hymn, Paul declares that Christ

emptied himself,
>   taking the form of a slave,
>   being born in human likeness.
> And being found in human form,
>   he humbled himself
>   and became obedient to the
>   point of death—
> even death on a cross (Phil. 2:7-8)

The incarnation declares that God lives with us, the cross declares that God dies with us—God is present in both life and death. And herein lies our hope: that God's resurrection power is forever at work not only in life but also in death. For this reason we can declare that the cross is God's ultimate YES to humanity.[150] This raises dissonance within us, because God's ultimate YES is often our greatest NO.

Ernest Bekker, in his book *Denial of Death,* illustrates this denial in its most absurd form. He compares North American culture to the men of the Chagga tribe in Tanzania who wear anal plugs all their lives, "pretending to seal up the anus and not to need to defecate."[151] This act of denial is, of course, completely absurd, but perhaps it is no more absurd than some of the metaphorical anal plugs that divert North American culture from reality on a daily basis. At least the men of Chagga are forced to admit their humanity each morning when they pull the plug in obedience to their flesh. Our "plugs" are probably much more difficult to remove. They have been lodged in deeper, hidden places, such as our hearts, minds, and souls, blocking anything that exposes the illusion of a painless world.

In such a cultural context, God's great *Yes* becomes our great *No!* That is why Hendrikus Berkof wrote, "Whatever else the cross may tell us, it certainly proves that we cannot stand God and that he must be eliminated if he comes too close to us."[152] God reveals too much reality for our timid souls. Nothing is closer to the sacred center of our being or a greater threat to our illusions than the scandal of the cross itself. Bruggeman suggests that when God must be praised at all times prayer becomes a lie, a cover up, and a warrant for the status quo.[153] In other words, a gospel that does not allow for heartbreak, lament, or crying to God from a place of pain is in reality no gospel at all.

THE CONFESSION OF THE CROSS— CALLING THINGS AS THEY ARE

Martin Luther said that a theology of the cross *(theologia cruces)* "calls a thing what it is."[154] It is rooted in reality and derives its power in weakness. On the other hand, a "theology of glory," as Luther taught, tends to avoid reality and seeks power in strength. It lives in illusion and denial and ultimately erupts in violence. Luther argued that a theology of glory "calls good evil and evil good."[155] In a world of great fear and denial, never has the Church been in greater need of a theology of the cross.

A theology of the cross calls us to be a confessing church— to confess the truth of what is, while embracing the hope of what ought to be. Likewise we are called to confess truthfully who we are, even while we participate in what we are becoming. Without the grace of confession we are cut off from real life, and in our illusion we try to build utopias that only hurt the hurting. Utopia literally means "no place,"[156] which is precisely where we arrive when we build our lives on ideals rather than reality. One of the best contemporary examples of what it means to be a confessing church and live in reality is found in the remarkable character named B-Rabbit in the movie *8 Mile* that we first introduced in chapter 7.

B-Rabbit seeks refuge in the streets, where he learns to battle with words to protect his dignity. "Battling," or free-style rapping, is an urban art form of hip-hop which is very much like boxing only with words instead of gloves. It is verbal jujitsu.

B-Rabbit grew up as a poor white kid on the "wrong" side of 8 Mile. He is a skilled artist but has failed miserably throughout the story. He's choked several times at the hip-hop club in front of his peers and has suffered humiliation at the hands of his archrival Papa Doc. His home life is a wreck and his love life is even worse. Papa Doc and his boys have not only jumped B-Rabbit and his friends and beat him up, but have "had" B-Rabbit's girlfriend and everybody knows it. The ironic twist, intended to shatter stereotypes, is that Papa Doc, though African-American, grew up on the "right" side of 8 Mile in a good home with a mom and dad who gave him his real name, Clarence—a source of shame that B-Rabbit eventually exposes.

The climax of the movie finds B-Rabbit at his lowest point, with nothing left to lose. It is here that he finds his voice at the club. B-Rabbit makes his way to the finals where he meets Papa Doc in the battle for the championship. The tension is thick. What will B-Rabbit say to the man who has beat him up, had his girlfriend, and humiliated him before all his peers?

B-Rabbit loses the coin-toss and is handed the microphone first. What will he say? What can he say, given that Papa Doc has all the ammunition? Having lived the cross, B-Rabbit raises the cross. He calls things what they are. He makes a confession in front of his world. He simply says what is true. He spends the next minute of his life telling everybody what they already know about him; without shame, he proclaims the most degrading details of his own white-trash existence and embarrassments at the hands of Papa Doc's friends. It's at once scathing and humiliating—yet brilliant, even inspired. In stripping himself bare, B-Rabbit leaves nothing for Papa Doc to say against him and thus exposes him for who he really is. Clarence is speechless and B-Rabbit wins.

A theology of the cross calls for the courage of B-Rabbit. It gives us the grace to call things what they are, especially ourselves. We acknowledge that not many of us have the courage to confess with the naked honesty of B-Rabbit, nor should we. There is hope in the gracious consolation of Frederick Buechner who says, "I don't think that it is always necessary to talk about the deepest and most private dimension of who we are, but I think we are called to talk to each other out of it, and just as importantly to listen to each other out of it, to live out of our depths as well as our shadows."[157]

What lurks in our depths is the reality that we are wounded people who are scared to death of death, and we do great harm to each other in our attempts to protect ourselves from it. The cross exposes this painful—though ultimately liberating—truth. The cross reveals to us that, given the chance, we will kill even God in the name of righteousness. The illusions we have come to accept as real are so real that we will shout with the rest of the crowd, "crucify him, crucify him," all the while feeling justified that we are doing the world a favor. Even those too enlightened to join the crowd will quietly step aside and let it happen.

Jesus looks upon all this and says, "Father, forgive them; for they do not know what they are doing."(Luke 23:34). The cross exposes not only our willful sin, but also our passive ignorance. We don't often know what we are doing when we do it, so we are compelled to cry out, "Lord have mercy."

COVERING OF THE CROSS—FORGIVING WHAT IS EXPOSED

The cross of Jesus offers forgiveness with outrageous freedom. In fact, whatever else the cross is, it is the gift of God's love before we even recognize that love as God's gift. While Jesus is naked and exposed to the world, he calls things what they are, while simultaneously clothing with forgiveness that which he exposes. B-Rabbit gives us a powerful demonstration of confession and the liberty that comes from it, but he only demonstrates half the gospel message. B-Rabbit fails to clothe the enemy that he exposes. We do the same, whenever we withhold forgiveness for that which is exposed in ourselves as well as others.

We have found great hope in remembering God's act of mercy with Adam and Eve after they had eaten from the tree. God "clothed them." God did not send them forth from the Garden of Eden until they were clothed. We see this as a metaphor for forgiveness. The cross makes forgiveness possible, but it is not as if that possibility did not exist before, for that would turn the cross into a tool of transaction between humanity and God. Rather, the cross fundamentally reveals God's forgiving heart. We are clothed in and through God's grace from the beginning.

THE DESIRE OF THE CROSS

We hope it is clear by now that a theology of the cross is not masochism, or doom-and-gloom. It is the power and wisdom of God. It is completely gratuitous and free, but what a strange sort of grace and freedom it holds:

> The faith that emanates from the cross is a faith
> that enables its disciples to follow the crucified God
> into the heart of darkness, into the very kingdom of

death, and to look for light that shines in the darkness—the life that is given beyond the baptismal
brush with death.[158]

No one should enter into a theology of the cross without having tasted the grace of the incarnation, for it is the grace of the
incarnation leads us to the cross. God's passion for life necessarily leads God into death. This is a paradox because it is here, in
death, that the incarnation reveals its deepest desire, which is to
enter death itself and establish life even there, so that nothing
may separate God from us—nothing, not even death.

The night before Jesus was crucified, Jesus introduced the
Passover meal with a peculiar comment. He said, "I have eagerly desired to eat this Passover with you" (Luke 22:15). The
phrase "eagerly desired" is a double intensive, which is inflat-
ed language, extreme and even a bit risqué. The Greek word is
epithumia, which can mean "lust."[159] A more literal translation
would be, "It is with desire that I desire." It's strong language, to
say the least. The point here is that the deepest desire of the incarnation is revealed not just in the meal before the cross, but
in the cross to which the meal points. Jesus' entire being is so
thoroughly constituted in and through a desire for life that he is
willing to enter death. And there, in the midst of death, he declares life.

THE SECRET OF THE CROSS

Jürgen Moltman said, "God weeps with us, so that one day we
might laugh with Him."[160] What stands behind the cross, and in
its very heart, is the laughter of God. It is a silent laughter to be
sure, but it is there. Tears of joy and sorrow are not easily discerned within the realm of God's desire. They mix with ease and
will not be separated, but they are both there. God is laughing

in death for those who can hear it—it is the same laughter with which we were created. Proverbs tells us that in the beginning when God created humanity, the Word played at the Father's side like a little child, "rejoicing before him always, rejoicing (*sachak* or "laughing") in his inhabited world and delighting in the human race" (Prov. 8.30-31).[161] Perhaps it is a stretch, but could we imagine that God created humanity in laughter and, with that same laughter, re-created humanity and the rest of the world in the bowels of death itself? Herein, it could be argued, lies the secret of the universe.

The cross makes no sense apart from this secret and neither do we. Were it not for the writer of the book of Hebrews, we might never have had the courage to name it. The secret of the universe is the very same secret that stands behind the cross and gave Jesus—and us—the courage to endure it. "For the sake of the joy that was set before him endured the cross" (Heb. 12:2). The secret of the cross is joy. It is what G. K. Chesterton called the "gigantic secret" of the faith.[162] Joy is what keeps the theology of the cross from being a morbid preoccupation with death. Chesterton writes:

> The Stoics, ancient and modern, were proud of concealing their tears. [Jesus] never concealed His tears; He showed them plainly on His open face at any daily sight, such as the far sight of His native city. Yet He concealed something. Solemn supermen and imperial diplomatists are proud of restraining their anger. He never restrained His anger. He flung furniture down the front steps of the Temple, and asked men how they expected to escape the damnation of Hell. Yet He restrained something. I say it with reverence; there was in

that shattering personality a thread that must be
called shyness. There was something that He hid
from all men when He went up a mountain to pray.
There was something that He covered constantly by abrupt silence or impetuous isolation. There
was some one thing that was too great for God to
show us when He walked upon or earth; and I have
sometimes fancied that it was His mirth.[163]

It is with this joy in mind that Jesus submits to death, believing that even in death, God will breathe life into existence.
Three days later, we hear the laughter of God that was hidden
in Jesus.

How else do we explain the unimaginable grace in which
Jesus breathes his last breath? In Luke's account of the cross, he
says that "darkness came over the whole land," and the "sun's
light failed." We suggest that Luke is taking us back to a place
we have been before, back to Genesis when "darkness covered the face of the deep." In the midst of that darkness, Jesus
says, "Father into your hands, I commend my spirit" (Lk. 23:46).
The word spirit here is the Greek word *pnuema*, which means
"breath."[164] In other words, "Into your hands I breathe." And
then Luke says, "Having said this, he breathed his last." Quite
literally, Jesus exhaled.

Can we see it? Jesus releases into the darkness the breath
of life. He releases the same Spirit that hovered in Genesis. He
releases the same Spirit that brooded over the chaotic waters
and drew life into existence in the beginning, the Spirit that
breathed the breath of life into the dust of humanity. He released the same Spirit that sustains all of Creation and that filled
his lungs for 33 years. He released that Spirit to hover in darkness—to brood like a mother hen and re-create the world. Three

days later, we see new creation.

When Jesus breathes his last breath, he confesses the name of his Father. It is his last act of blessing on the world—*Yah-weh*. He does not cave into the temptation of scarcity, but declares God's abundant love to the end. Christ is resurrected in that love, and so are we. Jesus' last breath is our first.

Some stories only make sense in the end, and this is one of those. Only through the resurrection can we begin to discern the faint outlines of "joy" that were set before Jesus, calling him—and us—to the cross. It is only in and through abundant joy that we can make sense of Jesus' life and death, his passion and pathos. Without joy the whole thing falls apart and so do we. Without joy, Jesus' journey to the cross becomes a mad march to death to appease the wrath of an angry God, but our story is different. In the end, laughter trumps the bitterness of wrath. Joy trumps sorrow in a surprising subversive twist—and that is our subject in Section Four.

13

the poetry of truth telling

Look at me.
Lamentations 1:12

To speak a true word is to transform the world.
Paolo Freire[165]

I N OUR INTRODUCTION we described the "blue note" as that
bittersweet note in jazz and blues that gives voice to pain. We
said there are actually three blue notes: the flatted 3rd, the flatted 5th, and the flatted 7th. The bluest of the blue notes is the flatted 5th because it creates the most tension and dissonance. It resists resolve and awakens us to our shattered hopes and dreams.
Ironically, this is part of its allure. When blended with the larger
score, it gives voice to the longing for healing that comes from
pain.

In a sense, a large part of our work is to function like the blue note—to give voice to pain—but to do so runs the risk of becoming stuck there. We can easily define ourselves by our wounds, or even actually *become* our wounds, in which case we end up passing the wounds on to others—and back to ourselves. In the same way, denying pain is as dangerous as wallowing in it. Both lead to violence. The gospel provides a way forward, but it is always by way of the wound. Whatever else Scripture is, it is a relentlessly truthful journey through the blue notes of humanity and God. All of the great stories play out like an extended Miles Davis jazz riff on a hot summer night, finally yielding to resolution, though not easily or predictably. Over one-third of the Psalms are laments. The book of Job itself is a long psalm of lament. An entire book in the Bible bears the name Lamentations. Jesus said, "Blessed are those who mourn." And, of course, the cross is the ultimate blue note.

It often goes unnoticed that the blue note continues even after the resurrection. Jesus continues to bear the wounds of his suffering, and ours, in his resurrected body. The resurrection does not mark the end of woundedness, but its transformation. There is a difference. Just ask Thomas, whom Jesus invited to literally put his finger on the gospel. The gospel declares that the resurrection not only heals our wounds but also dares to honor and give voice to them—for eternity. There is something profoundly gentle and intimate about a God whose redemption includes our suffering. Apparently in God's economy, there is a place in heaven for our highest praise and our deepest pain. Nothing is wasted in Christ. The crazy claim of the cross is that somehow we are healed in and through the wound, eternally.

This is a particularly important topic in our work in the Street Psalms network since we find ourselves walking with dear brothers and sisters who have suffered much. In seeking how to effectively give voice to their pain and ours, we explore with them the ministry of lament and the scandal of the cross. Not that we always walk confidently and speak assuredly in the midst of suffering—because we often feel paralyzed by our fears and insecurities at profoundly distressing levels. We do not write from a place of personal triumph, but from a growing acceptance of the gospel that assures us of God's goodness in a sea of chaos, even our own. If pain is the water in which the Gospel swims, then we are invited to dive in. There is goodness in the darkness. That's why we can go there.

Every year since 2000, one of our Street Psalms Community colleagues, Scott Dewey, has helped lead a team of two-dozen people to Eastern Europe to provide a summer camp for abandoned children living in a government-run institution. This orphanage is filled with bruised, broken, abused, and marginalized children. The suffering and pain they have experienced is beyond comprehension, and the leaders who work with them each year are shattered each time the camp concludes. The "goodbyes" are always thick with gratefulness and grief—with plenty of crying from team members and children alike.

The throw-away young people of this society (most are Roma, or "Gypsies") have become like dearest family members to the "missional discipleship community" that Dewey is a part of. The relationships they have developed with the orphans have profoundly enriched their lives and nurtured their faith. Nothing else could explain, after all, why team members have oriented so much of their lives around nurturing relationships with these children and advocating for their long-term welfare. Their experiences with these orphans have at times taken them to the far edges of their faith in God as they cope with the horror of what the children experience, but their story also profoundly illustrates the power of the blue note—giving voice to pain. In 2005, Scott was immersed in a study on lament just prior to heading off on his yearly trek to the orphanage. That year, the team moved deeper into the darkness of the children's experiences than ever before.

During the course of summer camps, one team member invited campers to create a video project from their stories. The project was conducted in a secret location in the forest because some of the orphanage staff had threatened to beat the children if they disclosed details about orphanage life. The idea of sharing their stories resonated with the orphans far beyond all expectation, and doing so led them into their own grief further than they had ever gone before.

On the third night of the camp, during an evening worship time, something occurred that took everyone by surprise. While crying and tears would always begin the evening before camp was over (crying is not tolerated in the orphanage), this time the tears began early. It started with a catch in the throat during a time of singing to the gentle music of guitars, but it quickly swept through the room until all the children were weeping. Singing gave way to sobs and cries of anguish. Before long, some of the campers had collapsed on the floor, wailing. When words were possible within their shrieks, phrases emerged such as *"De ce? (why?)," "De ce, Tata, de ce, Mama? (Why Daddy, why Mama?),"* and *"Nu Plecat! (Don't leave!)."* The screaming went on for hours into the night, echoing from the walls and drifting into the valley. In the early hours of the morning, the children could only lie gasping in the arms of the camp leaders, where they eventually fell asleep. The same thing happened the following evening during worship, and again the night after that.

The team was confused, and there was considerable debate

how to respond. They realized they were swimming in deep waters far from the shores of their ministerial and personal comfort zones. They decided to let the process run its course, wherever it might go, because they believed that profound spiritual things were happening for the children, far beyond their ability as leaders to comprehend.

They returned home to the United States and remained haunted for weeks on end by memories of the children's screams. They wondered if it had been perhaps the first time the pain in these children's souls had been given a chance to find a collective voice. They saw parallels between the children's cries and that of Jesus on the cross, "Why have you forsaken me?" which in turn echo (and thus affirm) the lament of the psalmist, "My God, My God, why?" They came to believe that the cries of the children constituted the highest and most holy worship possible and that they could do no better than to join them in it.

After months of reflection by the team, the theme of "Immanuel—God with Us" emerged for their next camp experience. Scott encouraged the team to think about how they might explore this message with the children. At one point he poured out his thoughts with the team in an email, warning that he wasn't interested in "a low-voltage version of this theme, to the effect of 'cheer up, everything's ok because God's in the orphanage, take our word for it.'" He wanted, instead, for the team to have the courage to journey with the orphans on a journey "straight through the agony of the crucifixion before arriving at Easter—refusing shortcuts or detours."

He knew the task would not be easy, though he suspected the orphans might grasp the journey more readily than they would. He wrote, "They already live much of their lives in Good Friday and Holy Saturday. It may be more important for us to learn to see through their eyes, than for them to see through ours." In this spirit, he outlined the following four main areas of focus for the next camp:

1. The Bible "denies denial." Drawing from Kathleen O'Connor's book *Lamentations and the Tears of the World,* Scott observed that "crushed spirits cannot worship unless that worship speaks from the pain." He argued that God places a high priority on those who are crushed because "a good deal of the Bible is devoted to hearing cries of people in pain—and even giving voice to it for those who have lost their voice." His experience with the orphans and subsequent re-examination of Scripture led him to conclude that mourning is a form of truth telling and a process that God uses for healing. He pointed as evidence to Jesus' words, "Blessed are those who mourn." He hoped to give the children (and themselves) permission to do just that.

2. Jesus, Immanuel, shared our suffering. In his reflections, Scott also expressed how we easily miss the fact that Jesus suffered not just *for* or *instead* of us, but also *with* us. In other words, he enters our suffering, clothes himself with it, and in so doing identifies with us in the most profound manner. He challenged his team to see that Jesus shared the orphans' (and their own) "experience of abandonment, powerlessness, and shame."

3. We are called to compassion. Focusing on the literal meaning of compassion (to "suffer with"), Scott challenged his team to understand compassion as far more than "simply feeling sorry for the kids . . . or even helping them." He focused on Philippians 2 which portrays Christ emptying and offering himself from a position of weakness. He encouraged his team to be real with the children, to share their own fears, shame, and doubts, versus coming in as "super-Christians" who have everything together: "Jesus is the only super one, and he himself became weak and shamed for us. Can we have this attitude with each other?"

4. We need to tell the truth to each other. Here, he challenged his team to honesty and vulnerability with one another and with the kids. If they could do that, he believed God's sufficient grace would rise to the fore: "This will be our witness—and theirs as they return to the orphanage. We know they go back each year, fail to live up to ideals from our camp, and cycle back into guilt and shame all over again. I hope the kids can hear a grace-full, truth-full message of God-with-us *especially* in the mess, rather than when we've gotten our act together."

The team returned the next year with their curriculum centered on the theme "Immanuel: God with Us—Weak, Abandoned, and Shamed." There were challenges at every turn that might have derailed a less determined bunch. Local officials cut electricity to their building. The orphanage decided half the kids could not attend due to "disciplinary reasons" (a decision later overturned). The hired cooks stole a large quantity of food. The water pump failed. Neighbors threw trash in the pool. Emotions flared, team members hit emotional walls, or became exasperated with one another. Most of the team got sick. All of these difficulties, though, faded in contrast to the extraordinary work of God among the children and adults during the camp.

In one object lesson with the kids, they peeled onions to explore how each layer represented layers of pain and shame. Just as tears come from peeling an onion, the deeper one goes into the layers, the more painful it is. One by one, campers and team members offered their own stories, while peeling an onion.

"Is shame from God?" they asked by way of reflection afterward. The children had often been shamed with religious talk about them at the orphanage, so responses varied. The team encouraged them, "Shame never comes from God. God is never the accusing voice. Shame is something that comes from others, or from ourselves. God chooses to accept, embrace, and lift up." Together, they read from Psalm 22:1, 2, 6, and 7, where the psalmist honestly tells God of his anger, suffering and confusion. They explored what it meant to give God their shame and their pain, allowing the layers to be peeled away.

In one art project, they encouraged the children to draw two things—one picture to show what was good in the past year and one to show what was painful. They explored with the children the question of whether God was present in both. One team member broke the ice, telling of her husband's arrest and imprisonment and of her own shame over an eating disorder. Her risk bore much fruit in the openness of the group through the week. The children also began to take risks in personal disclosure. One girl broke down crying, explaining her drawing of a betrayal by her best friend. Another was so moved she could not speak, but, instead, folded the drawing and asked for a private conversation later.

On another occasion, after reading a passage from Psalm 6 ("My soul is in anguish/How long, O Lord, how long?"), the group participated in a "liturgy of lament." The group of 70 team members and orphans were encouraged to speak aloud, one by one, any anguish in their hearts. To each cry, the group responded unison, "*Până când, Doamne, până când?* (How long, Lord, how long?)."

The first orphan spoke, "We want the beatings at the orphanage to stop."

Până când, Doamne, până când was the cry from all.

"We want to know the love of a mother and father."

Până când, Doamne, până când.

"We want to feel safe."

Până când, Doamne, până când.

"We want to have enough food in the orphanage, so we will not be hungry."

Până când, Doamne, până când.

On and on it went. There were many tears, (though not the hysterical wailing of the previous year). They finished with a hymn and many hugs. Afterward, they went outside for hours of talks, games, and walks under the stars.

During another worship time, the team presented a multimedia piece that juxtaposed images of the crucified Christ from art and film with wrenching photographs of modern human suffering. The photos elicited stunned silence and tears from many in the group, both team members and campers. Afterward, in small groups they asked two questions: Which pictures stood out to you and why? Are there images from your own memory that you might have added to the images of suffering we saw?

One boy started by recounting the memory of seeing his father beat his mother, finally hanging her in view of the other children. "I think of her hanging there in the kitchen, and I think of Jesus hanging there on the cross."

The next boy spoke of the beatings he had endured and a stabbing. "Yes, I think also of Jesus and what he endured."

Another girl could not speak, but slow tears dripped off her nose as she bowed her head. Finally she said only, "I am ashamed."

They read Matthew 27:27-44, where Jesus is mocked, and they asked the children how his experience might be like their own. Together they discussed the possibility that in times of our greatest weakness, vulnerability, and shame, we may in fact be sharing in God's own experience.

Especially poignant was a foot-washing ceremony. Campers (and even the interpreters) expressed anxiety about what they were being asked to do, but the session lasted well over an hour with every single person volunteering to participate—both in washing and being washed. It was messy. It was tender. It was an intensely intimate time.

After concluding the camp and returning to the US, Scott reflected in writing on all that had occurred during their time with the children:

> Our orphan friends' lives are lived in Lent and Good Friday. Together for a week, we tasted a bit of Holy Saturday and Easter. What a taste! The last two evenings at camp, the orphans and our team danced long into the night under the light of the stars and a string of Christmas lights somebody found in the attic. The look on the children's faces was one of almost incredulity that they could be permitted such happiness. It is now their long Lenten season again—fifty-one weeks of the year. Our prayers are with them.

14

voices from below

Mortal, can these bones live?
Ezekiel 37:3

We are prophets of a future not our own.
Archbishop Oscar Romero[166]

THE DEAD STILL speak—at least they do in Guatemala. One of the unspoken lessons of the incarnation that we explored in Section Two was that before Jesus preached his first sermon, he spent thirty years listening to the world he loved so much. That God would lend an ear to humanity and listen for thirty years before God speaks is in itself a parable of what God values—honoring the people's response to the petition of the Levite in Judges 19:30. For every year of public preaching, Jesus spends ten years quietly listening. That's ten parts listening to one part speaking. If the Word honors the world by listening intently to its pain, hopes, and fears, perhaps we would do well to spend the majority of our time listening to those we serve.

Another word for listening is discernment. Discernment is learning to see the Spirit at work in the world. It is the discipline and art of mapping the movement of God. As we unpacked in chapter two, the mapping process we use in our network includes three exercises: *mapping the hurt, hope,* and *heart.* Through greater awareness of our hurts and hopes we come to understand our heart and the hearts of those we serve. One of the most powerful experiences of mapping the hurt, hope, and heart of a place for us has been with the Forensic Anthropology Foundation of Guatemala (FAFG). The FAFG uses forensic science to investigate human rights violations that occurred during Guatemala's 30-year internal armed conflict. Forensic anthropologists exhume mass graves, identify the bodies through interviews from witnesses and DNA samplings, and then determine the cause of death to create the possibility for criminal prosecutions. FAFG has exhumed more than 5,000 of the more than 200,000 skeletal remains of victims of the war, 20% of which are children.

The decades-long conflict left in its wake a profound level of desolation and pain among the Guatemalan people, marking a wound in Guatemalan history that is still bleeding profusely. In its wake are anguish, resentment, misery, poverty, underdevelopment, and seeds of violence, which have in turn led to further injustice.

The work of the FAFG teaches us that while the victors usually write history, in modern-day Guatemala there are chapters that can only be written in the blood of these innocent victims. Through their silent tears, truth is slowly being uncovered and hope regained for a devastated people. The peace accord signed in 1996 was a step toward reconciliation, and soon after, the FAFG was established by Guatemalan anthropologists dedicated to the scientific quest for the truth across (and under) the landscape of Guatemala.

There is unbelievable tedium involved in meticulously re-assembling body parts and identifying cause of death for each victim. In visits to the FAFG labs, we see the skeletal remains of men, women, and children exhumed from mass graves in the highlands. We see skulls and reassembled skeletons respectfully laid out on tables so the scientists can determine age, identity, and cause of death. We see bullet holes in many of the skulls, including those of teens and children. We enter storage rooms full of cardboard boxes with the already-inspected remains of hundreds of yet-unclaimed people labeled with a special coding system. This system points to files where one can locate victim information such as village, region, and specific gravesite where the remains were located and exhumed.

Despite this gruesomeness, there is also a beautifully redemptive aspect that shines through. As bones are meticulously exhumed, inventoried, x-rayed, washed, and assembled by the forensic scientists, the social anthropologists set to work on biological profiles of each individual. Interviews are conducted with living witnesses and family members. The purpose is to gather all pertinent information to help uniquely identify the victim. Biological profiles and forensic data are matched to provide an even fuller picture of the individual.

As the bones of each "case" are carefully laid out on tables and the skeletons reassembled, they slowly take the shape of a person. The bones begin to speak and tell the story of what happened until they eventually are reconnected to their names, faces, and histories. Their stories are honored, and they are then ultimately returned to their families for burial.

The day we first arrived together at the FAFG, they showed us a particularly complicated case that involved the remains of a family of four. We were shown the skeleton of a mother carefully laid out on a table. Next to her was her son. Beginning with the mother, one of the forensic scientists pointed out the trauma to the skull (meticulously reassembled with glue). She pointed out the entrance wound to the front of the head and the exit wound to the back. She slowly scanned down the body where even our untrained eyes could make out massive fractures to the ribs, arms, and legs. She showed us metal fragments. Based on what we saw, she asked us what we thought might have happened. We rightly guessed that there was a grenade involved as well as a gun to the head. We saw the same in her son who lay next to her. It was still too early to tell, but the rough outlines of a theory had begun to emerge. Either each member of the family was shot in the head and then a grenade was exploded, or the grenade was exploded and then each member shot in the head to finish them off. Given the way the bones were traumatized there was evidence that the mother was trying to cover the grenade to protect her children, all of whom were eventually shot in the head. A forgotten story is now being retold. A blue note is reverberating as it gives voice to indescribable pain.

Once the bones have said all that they can say, Rob, the FAFG photographer, comes to document the findings with photographs, which are archived for evidence in case of a future trial. When we walked into Rob's simple office, we saw photos of skeletons revolving continuously on his desktop monitor. He had a small photo table off to the side where he documented the evidence. The office was strangely peaceful with beautiful classical arias playing in the background. Rob is meticulous about his work. He needs to be. He shared that one of his greatest joys of his work is when the Foundation finishes all its forensic work and finally returns the bones to the family members—most of whom are Maya campesinos (peasants) who live in the hill country. When they return the skeletal remains to the families, the FAFG staff engages in a process called "dressing the bones." The image is as intense as it is intimate. The family insists on re-dressing the skeleton with clothing—a painstaking process as you might imagine. What used to be just a pile of unidentified bones in a mass grave, denied the dignity of name and story, let alone their very lives, are now not only reassembled and named, but they are carefully clothed. It is a process exploding with theological significance.

For us, it is difficult to miss the profound connection between a visit to the FAFG and the story of the nameless concubine (sex slave) of Judges 19, a story that has become the baseline for our journey into the geography of grace. Her story ends with the shocked reaction to the dismembered body, "'Has such a thing ever happened since the day that the Israelites came up from the land of Egypt until this day?" (Judges 19:30a). In the Judges 19 narrative, we are invited to "consider it, take counsel, and speak out" (Judges 19:30b). Here, while mapping the pain of the 36-year Guatemalan internal armed conflict, a beam of hope begins to shine in the darkness of this nation's deepest wound.

Through the work of the FAFG, we can witness a literal reversal of Judges 19—not by dismissing or avoiding reality, but by embracing it—a literal "submersion" into the midst of the wound. We can see the caring, painstaking task of renaming, reclaiming, restoring and the literally "reassembling" of present day Judges 19 dismembered and discarded victims.

The significance of this work takes on further importance when considered in light of elements of Mayan culture so poignantly described to us by the FAFG staff. The Mayan peoples, we were told, believe that the elderly, children, and female victims are still crying because they weren't buried with dignity. Mayans believe that as long as their dead relatives are not at peace, the living cannot be at peace either. In Mayan culture, the dead are brought to the church to be before God, not to be prayed for as in other cultures, but to face God in person, to tell God of their angers, tears, and indignation, and to make their cry for justice in hope that God will adopt their cause. While lying dismembered in mass graves like forgotten animal carcasses, this healing process was not possible for the victims or their families.

Furthermore when a body is taken out of the church after such a "God encounter," the open casket is taken out into the daylight to publicly honor the deceased. To the Mayan families, the re-burial of the remains is more important than the exhumation. The re-burial is a public proclamation by the deceased of their ordeal, pointing to the need to make amends.

The FAFG believes it is important for the world to know that innocent people were killed in Guatemala and that the relatives have now been able to recapture their stories. It is impossible to fully recover from the deplorable loss of so many innocent lives, but they say one thing that can be retrieved is the memory and dignity of a wounded people. The FAFG has its work cut out for them as they continue to find Guatemala's missing sons and daughters so they can be named, their stories told, proper burials given, and justice served—all necessary steps to forgiveness and healing of a wounded nation.

For many of the leaders, seminary students, and "vision trip"

participants who have journeyed to the FAFG with us, it is usually the first time they have entered into a deep wound by way
of a "mapping process." According to many of their written reflections, their theology had not allowed for such an experience.
They had been taught that the gospel allows them to escape pain
and suffering as opposed to giving them a license to enter it and
embrace it. In the "secular" work of the FAFG, we are confronted by the reality of the Holy Spirit hovering in the midst of a
deep, bleeding national wound, inviting us to come and dance
with her in the midst of unimaginable pain and suffering.

At the conclusion of one of our trips to the FAFG, we were
ushered into a little space set aside for religious ceremonies related to the victims. We stood there as a class, with table after
table of individual skeletal remains of men, women, and children in plain view. We held a Moment of Blessing—a public liturgy for victims of violent homicide, on behalf of the 250,000
victims of the Guatemalan armed conflict. Several of the FAFG
staff joined us, and at the time of the parting blessing, I (Joel)
asked one of our staff to read the closing prayer. But when I said
her name (Liz), one of the FAFG scientists named Luis thought
I had called upon him. Thus, he began reading the closing blessing, stating these words: "Beloved of God, leave this place in
love. Leave this place in peace. Do not seek to return evil for
evil. Give strength to the broken hearted and support the weak.
Love one another as God has loved you. As this is home to many
of us, it is also the home of God. May God bless both this place
and each of us as well. Let us go in peace. Amen."

Here a forensic lab scientist offered a prayer that the church
of this nation had seemed reluctant to pray. By entering the pain
and the hope that a "listening post" such as the FAFG provides,
it is our prayer that the church in hard places will follow the

example of our dear and brave friends at the FAFG—to go deeply into the bleeding wounds of their nations to pray, reflect, and embrace the stories so the tears will no longer remain silent.

Richard Rohr affirms that evil is not overcome by attack, or even avoidance, but by fusion.[167] We are learning from the graceful dance of our friends at the FAFG that their work is indeed "fusion" with pain and suffering—union at a higher level. It is a slow and tedious task, requiring incredible perseverance. We have come to value this deliberate pace by remembering that those who vigorously seek peace often pay a great price.

If we read the gospel rightly, genuine peacemaking uncovers the mechanisms of violence that are at work in our hearts, and as Gil Bailie points out in his book *Violence Unveiled*, doing so may even hasten and intensify the violence it exposes.[168] When violence is exposed and unmasked, it very often breeds more violence before it subsides. In the end, the gospel of peace offers us another way by absorbing violence and transforming it. Peacemaking is not for the faint of heart. Jesus referred to the slow but sure path of peace when he said, "Until now, the kingdom of heaven has suffered violence, and the violent take it by force" (Matt. 11:12). Some Christians have used this passage to justify violence, but if we place the emphasis on the phrase "until now," Jesus' words take on new meaning. In other words, until now humanity has been trying to bring about the kingdom of God (i.e. peace) and has done so by means of violence and force. Until now the kingdom of God has suffered because of this approach. In fact, all of creation has suffered—*until now,* that is. The implication is quite clear. In Jesus, there is a *new now* and another way.

The leaders we serve live and work in places that are rampant with violence. These hard places typically operate with the world's formula for transformation, which is peace through force. Jesus reveals this as the way of the Evil One (see Mark 3:23). But unlike the Evil One, Jesus refuses to cast out violence by means of violence. Jesus says, "My peace I give to you. I do not give to you as the world gives" (Jn. 14:27). God's peace is not like our peace in that it is not achieved through violence. Peace is not only the end of the gospel, but also its means. In a word, the gospel is Peace!

In our visits to the FAFG, we have been deeply moved to witness the process of "the new now" created through digging up the remains of forgotten people and "re-membering" the bones before returning them to their families for a proper burial. On one trip after visiting the lab, we were led to a small house church in the hills outside Guatemala City, where we were asked to bless a woman and her daughter. The woman's husband had recently been murdered, but not before he had killed more than 200 others—he was a lead assassin for a local gang. What kind of blessing do you give a little girl whose father was murdered after killing 200 people? What does peace look like for her?

What about the rest of us whose violence may be less obvious, but no less destructive?

We are still exploring. And while we explore, we continue to consider the words of our resurrected Lord. He speaks words of comfort and promise. He speaks words that are radically subversive. He speaks to the reality of God's kingdom at work in the world now. Three times he repeats these words, as if they are the sum total of his life and message. They are the words of the "new now" in Christ: "Peace be with you. . . . Peace be with you. . . . Peace be with you" (Jn. 20:19-26). May it be so.

15
ministry of memory

Do this in remembrance of me.
Luke 22:19

Remember in the dark what you knew in the light.
Richard Rohr[169]

WE ARE LEARNING through our interactions with leaders in the hardest places of their respective cities that if we are to move transformatively into the future, we need a long memory. In the last chapter we excavated this truth in the work of the Forensic Anthropology Foundation of Guatemala. Another method for developing a long memory is to invite the elders of a particular city to help the younger generation reclaim the memory of a particular place. In doing so, new possibilities for the future open up. In other words, we dream new dreams for the future via the process of remembering.

It is inspiring to watch a group of young leaders catch renewed vision when elders are enabled to reclaim the best dreams of a city, community, or even a particular church or organization with their voices. This is a vitally important process for emerging leaders. It is our joy to stand on the shoulders of those who have gone before us, to see all that they have seen, and then go beyond. That is what we seek to do through the process of "seeing through memory."

We conduct this process with bands of grassroots leaders of missional communities in all the countries where we serve, but it takes on a unique shape when practiced with US college students or short-term vision teams. In a recent three-week adventure with a group of college students who were participating in an interim course on Latin American History, we plunged into seeing through memory. During a section of the course focused on the armed conflict in Guatemala, we traveled to the Lake Atitlan region in order to enter into the painful memory of the murder, rape, and beatings of huge numbers of Mayan people caught in the crossfire of guerilla forces and government counter-insurgency troops. We crossed Lake Atitlan in a boat and visited the Catholic church of Santiago, Atitlan. There, we quietly entered a small room where, thirty years ago, three masked men murdered Father Stanley Rother in the middle of the night.

We sat in the room and "entered" the memory of what happened that tragic day of July 28, 1981. The conversation lead us well beyond the story of his death, into the profound way he lived during his thirteen years of serving the Tzutuhil people of Santiago, Atitlan. It is deeply significant to consider the life of a martyr who laid down his life in almost supernatural joy and mind-boggling faith, but stories of that kind of faith are just not the reality where most of us live. In Father Stanley's story, however, we see a real man, seized with suffocating fear. Yet he willingly stayed in the very place where he knew his life would likely be lost. (Henri Nouwen vividly portrays the story of Father Rother in his book *Love in a Fearful Land: A Guatemala Story*.)[170]

Later that same morning we jumped into the back of a pickup truck and visited the Parque de la Paz ("Park of Peace"). At this location on December 2, 1990, thousands of unarmed indigenous people peacefully approached the army base to demand an end to the incessant violence around them. The army opened fire on the assembled crowd, taking aggressive action to quell what they mistakenly thought would become a violent protest. Thirteen people lost their lives. The park is a memory to their lost lives with tombstones scattered where the bodies fell. On the second day of every month, the local Catholic church holds a special mass at the park to preserve the memory of what happened.

The accounts of Father Stanley's life and death and the massacre at Parque de la Paz became especially relevant when we noticed the way the pick-up driver we had hired took such keen interest in our conversations. Our driver told us that he had been in the crowd marching on the base that day. He was 18-years-old at the time, and his uncle was one of the thirteen killed. His passionate recount of that day allowed us to engage in "living history." Through the lens of his vivid memory, we saw with new eyes the current reality of the town of Santiago, Atitlan and its beautiful people.

The next day we journeyed to a town on the opposite side of the lake called San Lucas Tolimon where we met with a Mayan woman known as Chona. Her story became for many of the students the capstone of their entire three-week experience in

Guatemala. Chona shared about her life during the conflict. She recalled the day her husband disappeared—his body was never found. She described in vivid detail the life-threatening risks she took to protect children who had witnessed the murder of their own parents at the hands of army troops.

Chona knew all about the murder of Father Rother because she had been in his church the day of the killing. With deep emotion, she told us how she had personally dabbed up the blood on the floor after Father Rother's murder and put it into a container where it remains to this day, interned behind a plaque in the wall of the church. As our time with Chona ended, we learned that her full name is *Encarnación,* ("Incarnation")—a fitting name for the way she lives her life.

Henri Nouwen writes, "Forgetting the past is like turning our most intimate teacher against us."[171] The process of seeing through memory is the act of greeting an intimate teacher with a holy kiss. In reclaiming the memory of a place, new possibilities for the future open up and inspiration is found for the journey. With servant-leaders in missional communities, we are learning to use a remembering process that brings pain and suffering into vivid focus so that we can in turn dream new dreams for the future and experience the first steps toward healing.

Another "memory visit" brought us to San Salvador, where we met with the late Father Dean Brackley, a Jesuit Priest and chaplain at La UCA (The Universidad Centroamericana José Simeón Cañas). I (Joel) was accompanied on this trip by my friend and colleague Nate Bacon, who is the Central American Director for InnerChange ("a Christian order among the poor") and an ordained Catholic deacon. In addition, Nate and I were blessed to have with us Eliberto Juarez, who is coordinator of the missional community we serve in El Salvador and director of an organization in San Salvador called "Seeds of New Creation."

Father Brackley was one of the priests who came to El Salvador after the murder of six Jesuit priests and two women who assisted them in preparation of meals. The murder occurred on the campus of La UCA on November 16, 1989 and was a watershed moment for the Jesuit mission in El Salvador. Father Brackley was an author and noted authority on the art of discernment in spiritual formation, especially rooted in the work of St. Ignatius. After an illuminating meeting and lunch, Father Brackley prayed a special blessing over Nate and me as we stood in front of a rose garden that was planted on the plot of land where the eight people were murdered.

We entered a small museum on campus dedicated to the memory of these men and other martyrs of the El Salvadoran conflict. Eliberto stopped in one corner of the room in front of a plaque commemorating "la masacre del Mozote" that occurred on December 12, 1981 by the military battalion "Atlacatl." His demeanor changed considerably and a somber cloud seemed to encircle him. I noticed tears welling in the corner of his eyes, so I approached to put my arm around his shoulders in solidarity with the pain of a dear brother—a pain I could not understand. We stood in silence for a few minutes, and then he began crying more deeply and said, *"Se quedaron en confianza que El Señor les iba a proteger* (They stayed, trusting that God was going to protect them)." I did not know what he was referring to as I stood in front of a plaque with the name of a place I'd never heard of, let alone could even pronounce.

When I asked him to share more, he clearly recounted the story of that day. A group of Pentecostal Christians decided not to flee after many threats that all found there would be killed.

They believed that God had told them to stay put and place their confidence in him because he would protect them from all danger. They were all killed—men, women, and children. Eliberto's tears continued to flow and, in much struggle and pain which seemed to burst from a collective Salvadoran soul, he blurted out, *"Donde estaba Dios? Porque no les protegió? Donde estaba?* (Where was God? Why didn't he protect them? Where was He?)."

Nate and I stood there with Eliberto, sensing we were on very holy ground. Through the vivid, painful memory of this precious Salvadoran brother, we were being ushered into the question that was rising from the blood-stained Salvadoran soil. Where was God? Why didn't He protect them? Where was He? We all sat in silence for what seemed like hours before the holy abyss of that question, as if waiting for God to answer. Like Job, we sat in front of a God accused of foul play in a disaster that made no sense, waiting almost arrogantly for God to respond to our seemingly valid lawsuit. We heard nothing but Eliberto's quiet sobs. The silence was deafening.

Eventually we comforted one another with embraces of reassuring presence and took a reverent walk toward the chapel of the university. We went quietly in three different directions upon entering the chapel, still trying to process what we had just seen through the memory of Eliberto's pain. As a preacher, I was drawn to the pulpit to see what it would feel like to preach a sermon on a Sunday morning in that space. As I reached the front and looked back toward the pews, my breath was taken away by what I saw. On the back wall of the chapel were seven or eight huge drawings of naked murder victims.

The pictures were far from the polished images of the saints normally depicted in Catholic worship spaces. An artist had taken a pencil and used it to bring to life the pain and agony of massacre and execution. One picture depicted three naked men lying face down on the floor with their hands tied behind their backs. Another portrayed a fully nude woman, her face grimacing in agonized pain. Another showed a naked couple lying face down on their stomachs, their backs punctured with bullet holes. The painting, however, that captured my gaze in a vice grip was of two women lying face up on either side of a man who was completely naked with his legs spread wide open. His two arms were jutting out in either direction making the unmistakable shape of a cross. I tried to imagine what it would be like preaching a sermon from that pulpit with these images spread across the back wall behind the people to whom I was speaking. I tried to imagine the shock of my children if they were ever to enter that space and see those images of death and torture so graphically displayed.

I was disoriented and disturbed. I sat with my shock for a while before making my way over to Nate, who had approached the drawings. I whispered to ask if he as a Catholic could help me make sense of what these graphic images were doing in a sacred place of worship. Nate explained that the artwork depicted "the crucified ones" of El Salvador. As part of the Body of Christ, they, like the martyrs before them, had spilled their blood for the sake of Christ and the Salvadoran people. Their blood, mingled with the blood of Christ, was part of the new seeds of resurrection in the Body of Christ in El Salvador and beyond. After all, he suggested, cannot the words of Jesus in the celebration of Communion, "Do this in memory of me," also mean, "Offer your own body and blood for the sake of Christ and his kingdom?" The art on the walls, I was learning, was incarnational— representing Jesus present in the martyrs of *this* land. It was a call for us to follow Jesus in the same way.

In the weeks after the trip, I began a correspondence with Nate and I learned more about his unique faith journey. Though he had grown up in a liturgical tradition, he ended up in a charismatic evangelical church, drawn by the free style of the worship. Over time he became more involved in the suffering of immigrants and refugees and the exuberant worship at his church felt disconnected from their pain.

"A worship and theology revolving solely around the victory of Christ and the resurrection rang hollow," he wrote.

> Yet, at the same time, in the midst of hearing painful stories of poverty, suffering, torture, and even death squads, I was feeling the presence of Christ in a way that I had not previously experienced. This didn't square with worship on Sunday morning. Little by little my paradigm began shifting, and Scripture which I had essentially ignored began shining brighter—verses about sharing in the sufferings of Christ, and dying with him in order to rise with him.

Nate found himself drawn more and more to the communion table—the *Eucharist* (literally "thanksgiving"), as it is called in the Catholic Church. For the first time, he saw the centrality of the Eucharist to a life of faith. He wrote:

> In the Eucharist, the Word became flesh. Here also, was not just symbolic theater, but something absolutely real. The one sacrifice of Christ was mysteriously re-presented in the here and now, and we were invited to that ancient and eternal table…All of the worst of the pain, suffering, and death in this world was subsumed in the death of Christ…Here too all of the joys and greatest hopes of all humanity were

caught up in the true victory of Resurrection: Good Friday and Easter Sunday inextricably linked! This was radical optimism bursting forth from the fountain of pain and suffering, by virtue of Christ's redemption! Worship finally re-connected and gave meaning to my friendships and experiences in my immigrant neighborhood. I was nourished by the Word at Table.

Communion is where we remember our Lord, and in doing so, we "re-member" the world that has been so broken. Notice the often repeated verbs in this meal of re-membrance: *took, blessed, broke, gave,* and *said.* These verbs help us see that in communion, Jesus is inviting us to remember that we are the Body of Christ and what happens with Jesus also happens to us. Just as Jesus took, blessed, broke, gave, and said, so too are we "taken" into the hands of a loving God. So too are we "blessed" by that same abundant love. So too are we "broken" in that love and distributed to the world as a sign. And so too are we called to "speak" words that will help the world remember such love.

The process of seeing through our memories and the memories of others, even those we might consider outsiders, is crucial in the process of exploring the geography of grace. If we are going to move into the future of our neighborhoods, cities and countries and participate in the work of transformation, we need to learn how to cultivate a long memory.

16

cruciform community

And I, when I am lifted up from the earth,
will draw all people to myself.
John 12:32

Trust your heart if the seas catch fire, and live by
love though the stars walk backward.
e.e. cummings[172]

THROUGHOUT HIS MINISTRY on the way to the cross, Jesus
imagined a new community. While his disciples imagined
a community of glory and triumph, he called them to a community centered on the cross. "If any want to become my followers, let them deny themselves and take up their cross and
follow me" (Matt. 16:24). When the resurrected Christ appeared to his disciples, the first thing he did was to show them
the wounds of his suffering. Then he immediately constituted

them as a community, saying, "As the Father has sent me, so I send you" (Jn. 20:21). It is a community that de-centers, disrupts, subverts, and re-centers all of humanity. To be precise, this "new" community was not new at all, or it was only new in the sense that it had only rarely taken root in Israel's history. One could say of Israel what G. K. Chesterton said of the Christian faith, "Christianity has not been tried and found wanting; it has been found difficult and not tried."[173] Jesus was not inventing a new community as much as he was inviting and empowering his disciples to become the kind of community that God had been calling forth from the beginning. What does such a "cruciform" community, shaped profoundly by the cross of Christ, look like? How does it function? What is its mission? What sustains it? In an attempt to explore these questions, we want to highlight three aspects of a cruciform community, revealed in and through Jesus.

AN EFFULGENT COMMUNITY

The Westminster Confession teaches that God created humanity out of the effulgence of his glory. The word effulgence comes from the Latin word *ex*, "out of, from" + *fulgere*, "to shine."[174] It literally means "to shine forth." Effulgence suggests the image of light that cannot be contained. Such is the nature of the Son, who is the "effulgence" of God—"The Son who is the effulgence of God's splendor and the stamp of God's very being."[175] The Gospel of John says, he is "the light [that] shines in the darkness, and the darkness did not overcome it" (1:5).

The community of the cross is like the moon reflecting the sun's light—it is the uncontainable and uncontrollable light of the Father's glory that shines in and through the Son. A cruciform community in mission is not overwhelmed by the darkness of this world. But without a deep awareness of *effulgence,* or "the light that shines in darkness" that is not overcome, mission becomes needy and the cross becomes impossibly heavy to bear. Worse yet, mission becomes a tool of oppression and an act of violence.

Needy mission feeds off the needs of others in a twisted effort to fill up what is lacking with regard to our own afflictions as opposed to Christ's afflictions.[176] Mission that is moved and motivated by need binds itself to the needs of others in ways that can only be described as a complicated form of self-hatred.

Today, much has been written about "asset-based" mission that celebrates the assets of vulnerable communities and builds on them. Asset-based mission refuses to bind itself to the needs of the community—and this is a great step forward for mission. It guards us from building ministries around need. It reminds us of the abundance of the Father who sets us free from the demon of need. Effulgence—basking in that light that cannot be quenched—not only keeps us from obsessing on the needs of others, it also keeps us from obsessing about our own needs. To put it more accurately, it allows us to enter our needs without being defined by them.

For asset-based ministry to have meaning and for it to be grounded in the effulgence of God's glory, it must be liberated from the secret passions that fuel our appetites and keep us feeding off one another, particularly feeding off the misery of others. Let's face it, ministry at the margins is a breeding ground for those of us who need a steady diet of misery—for those of us who need to be needed. For most of our ministry careers, we have both harbored this sad secret and we (Joel and Kris) are both working through the shame of it. We have found ourselves at times feeding off the pain of others like parasites.

Kris has serially used the African-American culture in particular and Joel the Latino culture and needy people in general
to articulate the pain that we could not, or would not, articulate for ourselves. We have secretly hoped that we might receive
their courage by some kind of spiritual osmosis. We have felt
safe in the arms of another's need as long as we didn't have to
articulate or confess our own. We have sought out needy people
and bound ourselves to their need, feeding off of it and seeking out needy people, only to create mutually defeating relationships. If our host ever outgrew their need (or ours), we would
dismiss each other or worse yet, subtly undermine attempts at
health to keep the relationship functioning out of need. This cycle is why need-based ministry is a complicated form of self-hatred. We bind ourselves to that which we hate in ourselves and
congratulate ourselves for doing so. God did not create humanity out of need, nor did God bind God's love for us to our need
for God. God's life-giving light, God's effulgence, frees us from
a parasitic, needy love.

Perhaps the most dramatic example in Scripture of God's
abundant, effulgent love is found in the parable of the prodigal
son. In this familiar story we encounter what Kenneth Bailey
calls the "Gospel within the Gospel."[177] Bailey spent years living
and laboring among Middle Eastern peasants, trying to understand this parable in its Middle Eastern cultural context. He offers a brilliant and insightful retelling, and when we adjust our
theological and cultural lenses through Bailey's guidance, we
see that this parable is not at all the story of a prodigal son. This
is the story of the prodigal father.

As we mentioned previously, the word "prodigal" means
reckless, extravagant and wasteful spending.[178] When told in its
cultural context, the father emerges as the reckless, extravagant,

and wasteful one—it is the story of a father's scandalously shameful display of grace.[179] The wild boy and his older brother are simply props to make this point. If we replay the story in slow motion, we see how the father repeatedly shames himself throughout the story and how his display of irresponsible and scandalous grace leaves the hearers of the story deeply offended.

First, the father shames himself when he acquiesces to his youngest son's request for his inheritance. In the North American cultural context, which emphasizes freedom and rights, we miss the significance of the son's request. In Middle Eastern culture, to request an inheritance from one's father while he lives is tantamount to wishing your father dead.[180] That the request comes from the youngest son only magnifies the scandal. The only thing worse is the father's willingness to grant the son's request. The father's action, Bailey argues, is what shocked and offended Jesus' audience. Bailey discovered that it still shocks and offends the Middle Eastern peasant today. The father brings shame on himself for not standing up to the son's insulting request, but he also shames his entire village. They take on his shame because one of their leading citizens has lost face and, with it, his authority as a man of great standing.[181] Individual shame becomes community shame in a culture whose strength is derived from the dignity of its elders.

The father shames himself a second time in front of his village when he rushes to meet his son who, after having exhausted himself on his wild binge, returns to seek refuge in his father's house. Bailey reminds us that the son's arrival home would have stirred the village, and they presumably would have told the father his son was on his way home.[182] Those who listened to Jesus tell this story would have formed a mental picture in which the whole village came to witness the meeting between the father and the son to see if the father would redeem his authority. However, the community would turn its head in shame as the father makes a fool of himself yet again.

No head of a household worth his manhood would go out to meet his son, let alone *run* to meet him. Worse yet, he throws himself upon his son with such effusive affection that again his authority and that of the community is completely undermined. No dignified man would kneel to his son's transgressions. No man would cut short his son's explanation in order to give his own cloak, ring, and sandals to such a scoundrel. This scene is more shameful than the first. Bailey suggests this is very likely the return of an unrepentant son who is coming home to take further advantage of his father's reckless generosity.[183] Before the son returns, he hatches a plan and prepares a speech that will feign repentance before an idiotic father. Nothing in the text, argues Bailey, suggests a repentant son.[184] Again, the community turns its head in shame.

The father shames himself a third time by throwing a party for his son. The father asks for a fatted calf, which would have fed about one hundred people. In Middle Eastern village culture, the whole community would have been expected to attend such a feast. Refusal would have been an offense. And so the whole village is pulled further into the delusions of a father who refuses to save face and deal with his incorrigible son in the privacy of his own home. This party is not only a shameful party, it is a party for *shame itself*. By now, even the most calloused and wasteful of sons would have been embarrassed, not for himself, but for the outlandish behavior of his father. There was music and dancing at this party, but it is probable that the father is the only one enjoying himself. The heart of the community turned inward as the Father's heart was poured out.

The final act of shame was when the father "came out" for the second time in this story, but this time to meet his oldest son.[185] He does this in full view of the villagers who were likely trying hard to look as if they were enjoying themselves. While the music plays, the oldest son comes in from the fields to discover, to his surprise, a huge party. A young servant tells him about his brother who has come home. True to form, the eldest son is filled with rage at his father's idiocy. Jealously burns as he hears of his younger brother's cock-n-bull stories. He refuses to enter the party, but stands outside and waits.

As Bailey points out, such an act was itself a grave offense in Middle Eastern culture, where the oldest son would have been expected to participate and help host such a party.[186] The oldest son's public defiance spreads throughout the party until word finally reaches the father, who is still shamelessly preoccupied with his youngest son's return.

The party stops. All eyes turn toward the father. We can imagine the guests whispering to one another, "What will he do now? Will he finally demand some dignity and tell his oldest son to show some respect?" But the oldest son stands resolute and we with him. The party, as well as the story, now takes its most awkward turn. The whole community looks on. Even the youngest son, by this time, can hardly watch his old man completely strip himself of all dignity. Heads fall as the father rushes out to meet his oldest son, shaming himself yet again in front of the whole world.

The poetic structure of this story is what scholars call a parabolic ballad (Type D).[187] Bailey argues that Jesus' audience would have been familiar with this form and, therefore, would have noticed that something was missing in the story:[188] Jesus does not tell his hearers the last line of the story. The end of

the parable is missing. It is what Jesus fails to say in the story—
the missing conclusion—that fully and finally sticks in his listeners' minds. Like the original audience, we are left to wonder
if the eldest son ever goes into the party. The technique is genius. Suddenly, we are the eldest son, standing face to face with
God's prodigal grace. We are scandalized by such extravagance
and not at all sure we want to attend such an awkward party, let
alone befriend such a shameless, prodigal God. It takes courage
to celebrate such extravagant grace and build communities that
reflect it.

A KENOTIC COMMUNITY

Kenosis comes from the Greek word *kénōsis* which means "emptying."[189] When applied to Jesus, it expresses God's self-emptying nature inherent in the incarnation. The classic text for this
is Philippians 2:5-8:

> Let the same mind be in you that was in Christ Jesus,
> who, though he was in the form
>   of God,
> did not regard equality with
>   God
> as something to be exploited,
> but *emptied* himself,
>   taking the form of a slave,
>   being born in human likeness.
> And being found in human form
>   he humbled himself
>   and became obedient to the
>   point of death—
> even death on a cross (*italics added*).

This text was one of the earliest hymns of the church, used to instruct and lead the community of faith in "the way" of Jesus. If the way of the Father is effulgence, the way of the Son is kenosis. It is only because of the effulgent love of the Father that Jesus does not need to grasp or exploit his equality with the Father. Because of this love, when he takes on skin and bones, Jesus can empty himself or "pour out" his omnipotent, omnipresent, and even his omniscient attributes that he enjoys in the form of God.

A critical and controversial word in this passage is the word "though." The New Revised Standard Version that we quoted above reads, "though he was in the form of God . . . " Other translations say, "Although he existed in the form of God . . . " The word "though," or "although," creates an artificial tension between Jesus and his divine nature, as if to say *in spite of the fact* that Jesus is God he decided to empty himself. We are concerned with this translation on theological grounds, and note that linguistic scholars (which we are not) allow for other interpretations. We prefer the American Standard Version, the New International Version, The Message, as well as the King James Version in this instance. All of them offer a very different interpretation. In essence, they all imply that *because* Jesus was in the form of God, he emptied himself. From *although* to *because* changes everything. The emptying of Jesus was not in spite of his divine nature. Rather, it was *because* of his divine nature that he emptied himself. Self-emptying is the very nature of God. And we are empowered to do the same.

Because of God's abundant love, a cruciform community is called to pour itself out like Jesus, so that it might express God's abundant love—to abandon and give up any compulsion to grasp or hold onto that which the Father gives so abundantly, freely, and without ceasing. Grasping kills the kenotic life. The poet William Blake put it this way:

He who bends to himself a joy,
Doth the winged life destroy.
But He who kisses the joy as it flies
Lives in eternity's sunrise.[190]

Every attempt to grasp, hold, and control ruins the very thing that gives us life. Kris has tried to teach his own children what he calls "the hardest prayer in life." To illustrate, they begin with their hands reverently folded together and held high on their chests in proper Sunday school fashion. Then they slowly release them to an open position with palms up. That's the prayer. His young boys usually respond by telling him how easy it is to pray this prayer. "It is easy for you now," Kris says, "But it gets harder the older you get." Anyone who has ever tried to live with open hands and palms up knows how difficult this can be.

Jacob knew the difficulty of this prayer. His very name means "heel grabber." He was always grasping to get what he feared would never be given. He grasped at the heel of his brother in the womb, hoping to be the oldest and enjoy the benefits and blessings of the oldest. Even in his mother's womb, he feared that he would get the short end of the stick if he didn't take matters into his own hands. Later, he grasped at his brother's birthright, and still later for his father's blessing, and yet again when he wrestled with God in the desert, of whom he would not let go without first getting his blessing. He got it, but it cost him dearly and he walked with a limp for the rest of his life. Ironically, it was Jacob, the deceiving heel grabber, who God renamed *Israel*.

The movement from Jacob to Israel is the counterintuitive movement of letting go, and it is entirely dependent on the fullness of God's love. We can let go of God's love and our ideas of that love with the confidence that God's love will not let go of us. Kenosis preserves our relationship with God. God remains creator and we the created. God holds us in the palm of his hand so that our hands might be free enough to serve others.

What is at stake here is power. Kenosis empties us of all illusions of power. The self-emptying nature of Jesus on the cross invites us to give up trying to manipulate, coerce, or control God's goodness and trust and it reminds us that it will be forever available to us in abundance. The self-emptying life allows us to come alongside vulnerable people with our own vulnerability. We cease to be a threat to the powerless because we have given up any need to grasp at power.

J. R. R. Tolkien explores the issue of power in his trilogy *The Lord of the Rings* where the ring itself is the symbol of power.[191] Apart from the overwhelmingly complex and dramatic layering of his epic, the basic storyline is simple: The ring must be returned to the evil kingdom of Mordor, where it had been made, and destroyed there if Middle Earth is to be saved. As it turns out, only one lowly and insignificant hobbit named Frodo can deliver the ring, but not without the help of his hobbit friends and a host of others, not the least of whom is the pathetic creature named Gollum. Frodo's sole purpose is to give the ring away—to return it to the place where Mordor will consume it and itself in the process.

Tolkien offers a profound insight into the nature of power—that in order to be properly stewarded, it must be given away. Every attempt to seize power transforms it into a demon that seizes us instead. When we grab for it, it grabs us. In the end, even Frodo can't give it up. Gollum, that rascally beast, quite literally bites the hand that feeds him and devours the ring himself. With the ring in his mouth, Gollum falls into the molten fire of Mount Doom where not only Gollum and the ring are devoured, but Mordor itself implodes in a bad case of cosmic indigestion. Several things are worth considering here.

First, authentic power has a kenotic or "letting go" quality to it. Power becomes death-dealing when we hoard it. It is only life-giving when we give it away, especially to the powerless. Such a gift is why Jesus emptied himself of his power, and in doing so, taught us to live with our hands open to the love of God. He served humanity by generating power through relationships and then giving that power away. Remember that he always asked people what they wanted from him, and only after they articulated their own needs did he do what they asked. This, by definition, is what it means to give away power.

Ultimately, Jesus established his authority on earth as God by becoming completely powerless on the cross. Our friend Lowell Bakke teaches that it is only as a result of becoming powerless on the cross that Jesus is able to say, "All authority in heaven and on earth has been given to me" (Matt. 28:18). This power and authority is then granted to the Church with the express purpose of giving it away to those who are rejected.

Secondly, Gollum, the enemy, is enlisted in the service of redemption, and redemption could not have happened without his part in the story. Jesus likewise seemed to understand the important role Satan would play in the plan of redemption. He tells Satan to get behind him but he does not dismiss or destroy him altogether. How else do we explain Judas or the thorn in Paul's flesh, which is itself a "messenger of Satan" that God chooses to use for good? Somehow the power of God includes and is even perfected in and through evil. This mystery is too deep for us to grasp, and that is why we can only acknowledge it with reverence.

Thirdly, power consumes itself with itself in the end. Revelation 17 says as much when one day the great Beast of Satan will express hate for his own servant, "the whore of Babylon." In the final dance of death, the Beast will devour and consume itself. Death consumes itself when it is fully and finally revealed by the cross of Jesus Christ.

Kenosis—emptying, letting go—is a way of life for the cruciform community of Jesus. There is nothing morbid or morose about it. It is simply emptying ourselves of anything that is not ourselves. And even then it is emptying ourselves of the need to grasp, hold control, and coerce life. The kenotic life lives freely in the gratuitous love of God.

A Perichoretic Community

Perichorisis is the theological term used to describe the "mutually indwelling" nature of God. Each person of the Trinity mutually inhabits the other. This mutual interpenetration preserves "the individuality of each person . . . while insisting that each person shares in the life of the other two."[192] As Augustine might say, the effulgent overflow of *love* and the kenotic self-emptying of the *beloved* creates room for *loving* mutuality. Love, beloved, loving— each member of the Trinity is present to the other in ways that are mutually-affirming and always life giving. What emerges here is the picture of God as community—but if God exists as community, it is a particular kind of community. It is the kind of community that enjoys unity while preserving diversity. In our increasingly globalized world where every kindred tribe and nation lives next door to each other, such a community is desperately needed.

Our interest in *perichorisis* focuses on the way mutually-affirming love is experienced and expressed in mission. In this sense, our interests lie primarily in how we experience the Trinity rather than how God experiences God's self within the Trinity.

There is much talk these days about the explosive nature of

radical religious fundamentalism—whether Christian, Muslim, or Jewish—and about the ability of these religious factions to peacefully coexist. From a distance, one can hardly tell the difference between these communities who live at each other's throats. There is also much talk about nationalism and its rush toward violence to protect or expand itself. In many cases, nationalism, or the line that separates, one group of people from another, is fueled by ethnic identity. Taken as a whole, we do not need to search far for examples of disunity in the world.

In his book *War is the Force That Gives Us Meaning*, Chris Hedges cites historian Will Durant who claims there have only been twenty-nine years in all of human history in which wars didn't rage somewhere in the world.[193] In the last century alone, more people have been killed in war (over 100 million) than in all of history combined.[194] How can we possibly expect anything different in the future? What possible influence can Christianity have on this powder keg, especially when Christianity has been used to justify so much of the violence to date? If Phillip Jenkins is right in his predictions, Christianity will enjoy a new boom in the twenty-first century, adding to the two billion Christians worldwide that we already have (that's a one-third of the "market share" of the world).[195] If Jenkins is right that the next Christendom is the new "global Christianity," that is, more Southern than Northern, more Eastern than Western, and more black and brown than white, what does this mean for the world?[196] If the new "global Christianity" is the coming of what Buhlmann calls the Third Church (referencing the third world), and this Third Church will be increasingly marked by its conservative fundamentalist tendency to define themselves over and against all other groups, what kind of gospel will we unleash on the world?[197] With the Christian community divided among Orthodox, Catholic, and thousands upon thousands of Protestant denominations, what kind of unity can we possibly we hope for? If, as Denise Levertov says, we are "living on the rim of the raging cauldron" what possibility is there for peace?[198] What kind of gospel will see us through?

The closer Jesus came to the cross, the more he revealed what was in his heart. Perhaps this is one of the gifts of mortality. Death has a way of refining and revealing our hearts. In the 17th chapter of John, Jesus asks his Father to unify his disciples. He prays this prayer on behalf of his disciples and on behalf of those who would come to faith through the witness of the disciples. He prays "that they may all be one. As you, Father, are in me and I am in you, may they also be in us, so that the world may believe that you have sent me" (17:21). As if searching for just the right words, Jesus goes on in verses 22-24, repeating himself, offering new variations on the same theme.

> The glory that you have given me I have given them, so that they may be one, as we are one, I in them and you in me, that they may become completely one, so that the world may know that you have sent me and have loved them even as you have loved me. Father, I desire that those also, whom you have given me, may be with me where I am, to see my glory, which you have given me because you loved me before the foundation of the world.

Jesus' prayer for unity is a *perichoritic* prayer—a prayer that seeks unity, but not at the expense of honoring the uniqueness of the other. It is obviously a prayer that is still in the process of being answered, at best.

We must confess that it is not clear if we are moving closer or further away from realizing the heart of Jesus' prayer.

Jenkins's gushing optimism about the global Christian movement raises some concern for us in this regard—it is laced with the kind of triumphal belief in all things big, as if the growth of Christianity alone is good. We find such triumphalism disconcerting and perhaps even part of the problem. Not all growth is good growth and not all growth leads to unity. It is reminiscent of what we call the mustard seed syndrome that afflicts so much of the church—the unexamined belief that God delights in bigness and that somehow the growth of the Church automatically equals blessing to the world. As a result, we often project our desires onto the gospel and squeeze into the text an interpretation that satisfies those desires—*eisegesis* as opposed to *exegesis* (reading *into* vs. *out of* the text). Consider the parable of the mustard seed.

In a super-sized, big box culture where size matters, the parable of the mustard seed is often interpreted with the assumption that this parable is about the Church—the conclusion is that God wants the Church to be big. The story is familiar. What starts as a small seed becomes the largest of trees. If growth is Jesus' main point, he chose a poor metaphor for it, and this is perhaps proof that Jesus was a certainly more carpenter than farmer. The farmers in the crowd would have been shocked by this story. It simply makes no sense. Robert Capon points out the fact that the mustard tree is a weed no farmer wants in his garden.[199] It may start off as a small seed but even at full height, it only stands six feet tall. It could hardly compete for splendor with the cedars of Lebanon that filled Solomon's temple. If Jesus is after size, he picked the wrong shrub. And this is the point he is trying to make. He probably did know after all that the mustard tree is a "shrub"—a weed that farmers spent their days trying to eliminate because these weeds became homes for birds that in turn ate the good seeds of the garden that the farmer spends his whole life cultivating. If the kingdom of heaven is like a mustard seed, then who would want it?

Jesus presses on with another parable. "The kingdom of heaven is like yeast that a woman took and mixed in with three measures of flour until all of it was leavened" (Matt. 13:33). This one sentence capstone of Jesus' teaching is the stone that Israel rejected, and so do we—for good reason. Yeast is a mold that was considered unclean in Hebrew culture. With Jesus using a weed and a mold to illustrate the kingdom, what is he suggesting? Could it be that the kingdom of God is the very thing that our culture, our ideologies, and our theologies have conditioned us to reject? Could it be that the weeds and molds that we have systematically tried to get rid of are the very things that reveal the presence of God and are the keys to genuine community and unity? These texts invite us to move toward a kind of unity that makes room for the "other," particularly the "other" that we are most conditioned to reject—including people from faith traditions other than our own.

The unity and diversity of God expressed through *perichorisis*, or this mutually inhabiting nature, has a whimsical and playful side. Whatever else *perichorisis* means theologically, its literal translation may hold the greatest gift. *Perichorisis* stems from the Greek *peri* which means "around" and *choresis* which means "to dance." The literal meaning of *perichorisis* is "to dance around," and this is precisely the nature of the Spirit. If the person of the Spirit is anything, She is the member of the Trinity who dances. As T.S. Eliot said, at the center of the universe—or the sacred center of life—is "the still point of a turning world."[200] At the still point of the turning world "there the dance is."[201] There, at the still point around which the world

turns, "the darkness shall be light and the stillness the dancing."[202] It is the dance of the Spirit that sustains—that marks the
movement of the cruciform community. It is this eternal dance
to which we are called.

The movie *Little Miss Sunshine* is one of the best pictures of
grace in recent years.[203] It is the quirky story of an incredibly
odd but endearing family who is committed to seeing its youngest member, Olive, compete in the Little Miss Sunshine youth
beauty pageant.

Olive, a seven-year-old with a slight weight problem, comes
from a pathetically dysfunctional, but endearing family. Olive's
father, Richard, is a motivational speaker whose career is in
the toilet, much like his marriage. Richard's wife, Sheryl, is los-
ing patience with her husband's absurd dream of being a motivational speaker. They are out of money when Richard loses
a book deal that he thought was in the bag. Their oldest son,
Dwayne, is a teenager devoted to Nietzsche's philosophy of
meaninglessness, which mirrors his view of his family. Olive's
grandfather is a foulmouthed, but likable drug addict who enjoys racy movies. He is the one who has been preparing Olive
for the pageant, and he is the only one who seems to understand
Olive's secret desire to be crowned Miss America one day—to be
noticed and beautiful, to be the apple of somebody's eye, to be
queen. Finally, there is Uncle Frank. Uncle Frank is one of the
leading Proust scholars in the country, who recently lost his gay
lover as well as a prestigious literary grant. Uncle Frank is stay-
ing with Olive's family after being released from the hospital for
a suicide attempt.

These six misfits pile into a VW van that looks and runs like
the lives they lead. Their mission is to drive Olive hundreds of
miles to a pageant where she can compete for the crown. On

the way to the pageant, the characters are revealed and so are their dysfunctions. The father loses the book deal, Uncle Frank sees his lover with another man, Grandpa dies from too much heroin, and Dwayne has a breakdown. The dysfunctions, which seemed so remote at the beginning of the journey, become our own dysfunctions by the time we arrive at the pageant. And when we arrive, this is no longer just Olive's pageant.

The problem, of course, is that Olive has no business being in this pageant. She hasn't the talent, training, beauty, or charisma to compete. Her family has been too busy obsessing about their own lives to notice this fact until it is much too late. The weight of this reality finally hits home when Olive is preparing for the final talent competition. She is completely outclassed by the other girls throughout the pageant and is clearly out of her league. It finally dawns on the father and the rest of the family that Olive is going to make a fool of herself in front of the entire competition. In preparing to plead their case with Olive and rescue her from catastrophic failure, the mother makes an uncharacteristic stand. She stands with her daughter and defends her daughter's right to live her dream. Borrowing her mother's courage, Olive prepares to display to the world the dance that her grandfather taught her before he died. What happens next is priceless.

Olive steps out on stage. The family nervously awaits disaster, and they don't have to wait long. Olive launches into what can only be described as a quasi-striptease to the Rick James song "Super Freak." Mayhem ensues. The family looks on powerlessly as Olive unwittingly makes a fool of herself and them too. But Olive is unfazed. And she dances. She dances without pretense or concern for what is happening around her. She dances without fear or judgment. She just dances. And her dance is as bad as it is real. The pageant director tries to shut down the bawdy routine, but Olive dances on. The MC steps in to pull her off stage, but Olive doesn't stop and several people in the audience leave the room embarrassed and completely offended. Finally, the father acts. He jumps up on stage to rescue his daughter from her own humiliation as well as his own. He prepares to move her off stage when an epiphany hits him like a ton of bricks. He pauses in recognition of what's happening. He sees the freedom of this awkward dance and he finally gives in. He throws aside his own shame and joins his daughter's dance and so does the rest of the family. They dance their awkward heads off to Super Freak. They accept who they are and dance on the grave of their own shame and fear. They dance.

In the demonic grip of fear and shame, the Spirit calls. Stripped of all pretension and polish on the stage of life, the Spirit comes. Between the calling and the coming of the Spirit, there is dancing. And we do not dance alone. That is the Gospel. We are a community of dancers because God is the God of dance. The Spirit, who defends us against the divisive voice of our accuser and sets us free to be one with God, also invites us onto the dance floor of life. There we dance in the *effulgent* (light giving), *kenotic* (surrendering), and *perichoretic* (intertwining) love of God, inviting the world to do the same. Such is the super-freakish nature of a cruciform community.

AT THE CENTER OF IT ALL

At the center of it all is joy. Joy is what sustains the cruciform community of Jesus who is the "joy of man's desiring." It is not doom and gloom. It does not have a morbid preoccupation with death. It is unbelievably buoyant and light. The following poem by Jack Gilbert entitled "A Brief for the Defense," makes the

point beautifully, especially for those of us who find ourselves
serving in hard places:

> Sorrow everywhere. Slaughter everywhere. If babies
> Are not starving someplace, they are starving
> Somewhere else. With flies in their nostrils.
> But we enjoy our lives because that's what God wants.
> Otherwise the mornings before summer dawn would
>   not
> Be made so fine. The Bengal tiger would not
> Be fashioned so miraculously well. The poor women
> At the fountain are laughing together between
> The suffering they have known and the awfulness
> In their future, smiling and laughing while
>   somebody
> In the village is very sick. There is laughter
> Every day in the terrible streets of Calcutta,
> And the women laugh in the cages of Bombay.
> If we deny our happiness, resist our satisfaction,
> We lessen the importance of their deprivation.
> We must risk delight. Not enjoyment. We must have
> The stubbornness to accept our gladness in the
>   ruthless
> Furnace of this world. To make injustice the only
> Measure of our attention is to praise the Devil.
> If the locomotive of the Lord runs us down,
> We should give thanks that the end had magnitude.
> We must admit there will be music despite
>   everything.[204]

It is easy to slip over the edge into life-killing despair, or at
least cynicism. Righteous anger that once fueled our passion for
justice becomes the kind of anger that poisons the soul. Inspired

ideas become disincarnated from real people and real places. Unintended violence is done to those we love. What begins as a heartfelt prayer to God becomes a veiled praise to the Devil. Like the proverbial frog bathing in the pot, we don't know we've reached the boiling point until we're cooked. Gilbert's poem is a tonic for this.

Gilbert's verse calls forth from us a much-needed confession. We admit how often we have "praised the Devil" by making injustice the only measure of our attention. We admit how often we have failed to "risk delight." We are deeply saddened at how often we lessen the importance of those who are deprived by denying our own happiness.

The reality is that we are embarrassed to admit just how much gladness we have covered up the last several years. In truth, we have walked through some dark waters. But all in all, we have tasted joy more than we have a right to and much more often than we have let on. We have not wanted to flaunt this, especially with our friends who serve on the front lines and have known personal pain at levels that we simply cannot fathom. We have been much afraid that our gladness would be interpreted as a sellout to those whose lives are marked by catastrophic failure.

We are learning to see that not all the world is an open wound. We bear witness to this in our own lives. It is not only for our sake, but for the sake of those we serve that the Gospel invites us to "risk delight" in the face of absurdity. We pray for God to raise up leaders who can laugh without denying the horrendous evils that accost them and their communities. We pray for leaders who know the kind of joy that dignifies those who live without it. We pray for leaders who have the stubbornness to accept their gladness in the ruthless furnace of the world.

Because such gladness, such joy, is at the center of it all.

—section four—
ascending

The streets of the city shall be
full of boys and girls playing.
Zechariah 8:5

God is a comedian playing
to an audience too afraid to laugh.
Voltaire[205]

17
seeing a new thing

I am about to do a new thing; now it springs forth,
do you not see it?
Isaiah 43:19

It takes grace to see grace.
Karl Barth[206]

THE FOLLOWING STORY may seem far-fetched to some of our readers. Given that it happened many years ago, perhaps we can be forgiven if we have misplaced a few details, but anyone who has worked with urban kids who are unaccustomed to spending time communing with nature will know that our story is far from fiction. It is more likely that we are underselling the facts to maintain some degree of authenticity.

Several years ago when I (Kris) worked with urban kids in Portland, Oregon, my friend Ron and I took a group of middle school kids to Mt. Hood for the day. Mt. Hood stands 11,000 feet high and is only 50 miles southeast of Portland. The mountain is an iconic feature of the region and provides a majestic backdrop to the cityscape on a clear day. Clouds frequently camouflage the mountain, but when the sun is out the mountain is spectacular and hard to miss. The infrequency of clear skies makes it all the more visually demanding when you can see it.

It is a short drive to Mt Hood from Portland, and while the winding roads and lowland hills are thick with trees that make it hard to see the mountain at times, there are plenty of stretches where the mountain is clearly visible. There is nothing quite like rounding a bend in the road, and suddenly there it is—11,000 feet of mountain staring you in the face. It is imposing, intimidating, and breathtaking. In typical youth program fashion, we packed a fifteen passenger van with twenty kids from urban Portland, all of whom had never been to Mt. Hood and (as we discovered) had never seen it. To be more precise, they weren't able to see it.

It was a beautiful, clear spring day and the mountain was in full glory. About 45 minutes into the drive, we had entered the national park and were nearing Timberline Lodge at the base of the mountain where we would spend the day. We rounded a bend and the mountain jumped out like a 3-D picture in full relief. Spectacular! Ron instinctively called out to the kids who were stuffed cheek to jowl in the back of the van, "There it is!" There was no response. We attributed this to the fact that the kids were completely engrossed in spirited conversation of the kind that is common to urban middle school kids. We rounded another bend in the road and were greeted once again with an amazing view of the mountain. Ron called out again to the kids,

"Look at that!" One of the kids acknowledged Ron and asked, "Look at what?" Ron pointed to the mountain straight ahead and said, "That!" Ron's animated voice caught the attention of the other youth, who repeated almost in unison, "Look at what?" As will often happen with leaders who become exasperated with the antics of the kids they serve, Ron became slightly irritated. He said, with some conviction in his voice, "Look at the mountain, you knot-heads!"

"What mountain?" replied one of the kids. "Where?" replied another. "Right there!" said Ron who was now visibly frustrated and had rather hastily pulled the van onto a turnout in the road. He stopped the van and said, "Look out the window, the mountain is right there!" Again, the kids shouted, "Where? I want to see it! I want to see it!" Ron ordered all of us to get out of the van and stand facing the mountain that only he and I could see. He told the kids to look at the first row of trees across the road and asked if they could see the trees. "Yes," they replied in unison, "We see the trees." He said, "Now lift your eyes a little higher. Can you see a small hill just beyond the first set of trees?" "Yes," they replied in unison, "We see the hill." Ron said, "Great. Now lift your eyes again and look beyond that hill . . . look a little higher . . . can you see . . ." Before he could finish the question, the whole group started pointing and shouting in utter amazement, shocked at what they saw. "There it is, there it is . . . look at the mountain . . . I can see it!" Ron and I looked at each other in equal amazement, shrugged our shoulders, shook our heads and then laughed.

God speaks through the prophet Isaiah and says, "I am about to do a new thing; now it springs forth, do you not see it?" (43:19). As it turns out, seeing a "new thing" is not so easy, whether it's seeing an 11,000 foot mountain for the first time, or seeing the resurrected Christ for the first time. This is always a work of grace, and we can only handle so much of it at once. Seeing things as they actually are usually takes time. How else are we to explain the fact that no one—*no one!*—recognized the resurrected Jesus at first sight? Seeing the resurrection requires a second look, another glance. It takes a while for our eyes to adjust to the light of the resurrection, and then all of life looks radically different. In this sense, seeing a "new thing" is not so much seeing something that did not exist before, but seeing an old thing in a new way through a new lens. Such is the miracle of gospel sight—to see what has always been there in such a radically new way that it becomes a new thing.

We love Robert Barron's take on all this business about sight in *And Now I See: A Theology of Transformation*. Barron writes,

> Christianity is, above all, a way of seeing. Everything else in Christian life flows from and circles around the transformation of vision. Christians see differently, and that is why their prayer, their worship, their action, their whole way of being in the world, has a distinctive accent and flavor.[207]

Unfortunately, Barron's ideal has not always been the reality for many of us who call ourselves Christian. Seeing as a Christian is not necessarily the same as seeing Christianly. Learning to see Christianly, (especially for Christians) very often takes time and dedicated practice. Most of us are like the blind man in the Gospel of Mark who is led "by the hand out of the village" by Jesus, who then touches his eyes with saliva. At first the man sees only trees, but after a second touch from Jesus he "saw everything clearly" (8:23-25).

Interestingly, the second touch that allows us to see life through the reality of the resurrection of Christ is different for each person. Consider Mary Magdalene at the tomb. At first the resurrected Jesus addresses her in a general way, calling her "woman." Upon hearing this, she doesn't recognize him. She thinks Jesus is a gardener (Jn. 20:15). But when Jesus calls her by her name, "Mary," she recognizes Jesus and runs to embrace him. Thomas needs to touch the wounds of Jesus before he can see. In touching the wounds, Thomas's eyes are opened and he declares that Jesus is "my Lord and my God" (Jn. 20:28).

For Peter, it is just the opposite. Instead of Peter touching the wound of Jesus, Jesus touches Peter's wound. Jesus puts his finger on the wound through a series of questions that mirror Peter's denial of him. After Jesus repeats his question a third time, the text says that Peter "felt hurt" (Jn. 21:17). We are witnessing a kind of divine wounding of grace. In touching Peter's wound, Jesus not only restores Peter, but forever changes the way Peter sees that most tragic day in his story.

For Cleopas and his friend on the road to Emmaus, it is only after Jesus presides over the meal that they recognize the stranger who has been with them throughout the day. By reenacting the last supper, Jesus helps them remember, and "their eyes were opened and they recognized him" (Lk. 24:31). And Saul (Paul), the murderous persecutor of the early Church, finds himself on yet another path to sight. Jesus blinds Saul so that he might see. After hearing the voice of Jesus, "though his eyes were open, he could see nothing" (Acts 9:8). It requires a fearful Ananias to lay hands on Paul, and "something like scales fell from his eyes" (Acts 9:18). Each person's path to sight is a unique process.

Grace gives sight to the one who is blind and blinds the one who sees. It works both ways. In John 9, after healing the blind man and dealing with the controversy it generated among the Pharisees, Jesus summarized his ministry this way, "I came into this world for judgment so that those who do not see may see, and those who do see may become blind" (9:39). This is a confusing verse at first glance because it sounds uncharacteristically harsh and judgmental, but a closer look reveals that Jesus is making something more like a non-judgment. He turns the tables of their tit-for-tat, *quid pro quo* thinking into a lesson on the radical nature of grace. The entire story of the blind man in John 9 is set against the backdrop of sin and judgment. The unexamined assumption for all of the characters in the story is that the man is blind because he is under God's judgment—someone had sinned, the only question in their minds was who. Was it the blind man? His parents? Who messed up? Jesus refuses to be drawn into the rivalries surrounding the blame game. And yet they insist on knowing God's judgment. In the end, Jesus gives them the "judgment" of God, which is grace—a grace that works in two directions. *If you're blind (and know it), I will give you sight so that you can see. If you think you see (but are blind), I will blind you so that you can learn to see again.* God's grace falls on both. Either way, it takes grace to see grace.

18

the new normal

As they were coming down the mountain, he ordered them to tell no one about what they had seen,
until after the Son of Man had risen from the dead.
Mark 9:9

It is as we forgive and are forgiven
that we come to see what really is.
James Alison[208]

T HE GOSPEL NOT only empowers us to see, but to see from a
particular vantage point. It invites us to see from *within* the
reality of the resurrection. It is from within this reality that all
of life comes into focus. It is a place that re-describes the world,
as Walter Brueggemann might say. When we talk about seeing
from within the reality of the resurrection, we are not talking
about the kind of vision that comes from studying something

as though we are on the outside looking in. We are reaching for something different. We are talking about finding ourselves on the *inside* of a reality that is unlike any other. It is a reality that excludes no one nor defines itself over and against any other reality. It is a place so radically other than anything we've ever known that it is as if we need a whole new language to describe it. We find ourselves on the inside of something that describes us, and the world around us, in a way that makes everything more real. It calls us, and all things into true being. It is not a place from which we look out on everything else, as if other things were outside and separate. It fact, it is not really a separate place at all. It is more like an un-place. It simply *is*.

Seeing from within this reality and straining to convey how it re-describes everything, including our perception of God, is the extremely difficult task of evangelism. Studying this from the outside looking in is a little like trying to imagine breathing underwater, or seeing a whole school of people who look human but who are breathing easily and freely underwater. We stand dumbfounded. Breathing underwater not only appears to be possible but quite *normal* for those who find themselves on the inside of this reality. It's the normalcy that is the key. We are talking about a way of seeing God and the world that moves us from impossibility to possibility to normalcy.

Of course, the normalcy we are talking about inside the resurrection has little or nothing to do with cool supernatural tricks like breathing underwater (simply a metaphor here!) or superhuman capacity for moral achievement or perfection. We'll say something more about resurrection normalcy in a moment, but first we must pause to mention one other thing. There is nothing quite so dangerous as trying to occupy this place prematurely or falsely.

To illustrate this danger we turn to the Gospel of Mark. Throughout this gospel, Jesus repeatedly tells his disciples not to mention his identity too soon. Theologians often refer to this as the "messianic secret." After Peter confesses that Jesus is the Messiah in Mark 8, Jesus tells Peter and the disciples not to say anything to anyone. And after the transfiguration of Jesus on the mountain in Mark 9, Jesus strictly warns Peter, James, and John not to say anything *until after the resurrection* (Mk. 9:9). What a strange remark! Why is it okay to speak of Jesus after the resurrection and not before? What will they see after the resurrection that they cannot see before?

One thing we know for certain is that when Peter, James, and John saw Jesus transfigured on the mountain, Jesus had not yet been crucified. Had the disciples become evangelists on the basis of their limited vision on the mountaintop, they would have run the risk of proclaiming a false gospel in the valley. And so Jesus tells his disciples not to speak until after they have witnessed the resurrection. Jesus asks them to wait until they have seen for themselves, like Job (Job 42:5), what it means to pass through death and come out safe on the other side. He tells them not to speak until after they have seen on Jesus' resurrected body the very marks of death that he triumphs over. Then and only then will they have the authority to speak, but not before. Then and only then, will they see things as they really are— most especially, death itself.

We have a hunch that one of the primary reasons there is so little transformative authority in the Church today is because there is so little transformative vision. So much of what passes for authoritative speech is not wrong so much as it is formed prematurely in a kind of blindness devoid of the paschal mystery. So, Jesus implores his disciples to wait.

O Death, Where is Thy Sting?

Eventually the disciples do witness the resurrection. Their eyes are opened, and ours too. Perhaps the biggest and most radical change we see when looking at life from within the reality of the resurrection is that death is not really the enemy we had thought. Death is not the end of the road. Much to our surprise (and it is a delightful surprise!), death is the gateway to life itself. It opens more doors than it closes. Death is but one more of God's beautiful servants.

This is the gigantic surprise of the gospel that can only be seen from within the resurrection. It is the great impossibility that is normalized by the death and resurrection of Jesus. Our minds do not easily grasp this reality because we have a vested interest in relating to death as the ultimate enemy. It is the only way we have known. We need the help of poet-prophets who subvert the calculating mind and who speak to the heart where truth can be more easily digested. Hear the words of German poet Rainer Maria Rilke in "Letter to Countess Margot Sizzo-Noris-Crouy":

> So long as we stand in opposition to Death we will disfigure it. . . . Death is our Friend, our closest friend, perhaps the only friend who can never be misled by our ploys and vacillations. And I do not mean that in the sentimental, romantic sense of distrusting or renouncing life. Death is our friend precisely because it brings us into absolute and passionate presence with all that is here, that is natural, that is love .[209]

When we live inside of the resurrection, even death is reclaimed as friend. Again, to be clear we are not talking of death in its fallen state that holds us hostage and devastates and dehumanizes us all. We are speaking here of death in its state of grace as a natural part of life. Because Jesus has freed us from death as a principality we are not only empowered to set others free from its grip, and defend the defenseless against it, we are also free to accept death in its most natural state and befriend it.

Again, what was impossible before the cross, not only becomes possible but normal in the resurrection. From inside the resurrection it is quite normal, even pedestrian, to make friends with death. It is exactly what we Christians are supposed to do. We make friends with our enemies and in befriending our enemies we come to see them quite differently.

THE GIFT OF THE ENEMY

The Holocaust of the Old Testament was Babylon's invasion of Jerusalem and the southern kingdom of Israel in 587 B.C. Of all the military campaigns and defeats that Israel suffered in its history, this one was arguably the worst and the most humiliating. The Jews were convinced that evil itself had destroyed the holy city of Jerusalem—raped her women, killed her children, and left her poor to fend for themselves. The conquerors drove the leaders of Jerusalem, unaccustomed to hard labor, on a six-hundred-mile eastward trek to the banks of the Chebar River in Babylon where, utterly defeated, they wept. There, the Babylonian tormentors mocked and jeered their captives. They taunted the Jews to sing the songs of Zion. The Psalmist responded bitterly in 137:4, "How can we sing the Lord's song in a foreign land?"

What makes this question so haunting is that the Jews were not merely in a foreign land—they were in the land of their enemy. As a result of a brutal military defeat, the Jews had no homeland, no priest, no temple, and no king. Perhaps worst of all, they had no city to call their own. Jerusalem, the city of their God, the city of peace, was in ruins. All of the ways that Israel had learned to worship God were no longer available to them. They were a humiliated and destroyed people. Perhaps in this context, we begin to understand the searing closing lines of Psalm 137:9, in which the psalmist cries out, "Happy shall they be who take your little ones and dash them against the rock!" Hardly a measured and compassionate pastoral response.

Soon after the Jews were marched into Babylon at the point of a spear, Jeremiah prophesied (25:9-12) that it would be seventy long years before the Israelites would see their beloved city again. They would descend into the bowels of Babylon, the city of pride and the center of all that is evil. It would be seventy years before the Israelites would limp back to Jerusalem. We don't know for sure, but one of those who limped back to Jerusalem after the long captivity may have been the prophet Zechariah. Confronted by the devastation of his city, Zechariah was inspired by the Spirit. He "saw" a new Jerusalem—a Jerusalem that would embody all God's hopes and dreams for his people, where one day "the city shall be full boys and girls playing in its streets" (Zech. 8:5). It is a beautiful and poetic vision that has inspired more than a handful of sermons from inner-city pulpits and given hope to many generations of urban dwellers—beginning with Zechariah's own. Zechariah was beginning to see through the eyes of Easter.

For our purposes, the important thing to note about Zechariah's vision is where it originated. Zechariah's vision for the New Jerusalem was nurtured *in Babylon*. Babylon and Jerusalem stand as archetypes throughout Scripture. Babylon represents the enemy of God—she is all that stands against Jerusalem. So the irony here is as bitter as it is amazing:

Zechariah's vision for the New Jerusalem—the Jerusalem that one day would be the full expression of God's shalom for humanity—comes out of Babylon itself. How can this be? How can the home of death and destruction be the ground from which God's sustaining vision for his people springs? How does the enemy of God help the people of God see?

Once again we turn to John Howard Yoder who writes, "God is working in the world, and it is the task of the Church to know how he is working." That is to say, "Behold, here is Christ. This is where God is at work!"[210] It is one thing to discern the work of God in Jerusalem where we are prepared to see God. It is quite another to discern the work of God in Babylon in the face of our enemy. Both Jeremiah and Zechariah are teaching us a hard but liberating truth—biblically speaking, vision for life originates in the context of death. Nothing could be more counter-intuitive.

The Jewish-philosopher-turned-Catholic-mystic Simone Weil observed that there are two things that awaken us to God: beauty and affliction.[211] When we stop to consider the reciprocal relationship between the two, we realize that one is the source of the other. The greatest beauties in life are sometimes (always?) the source of our deepest afflictions. We need to look no further than marriage or children to know the truth of this. The reverse is also true. Our deepest afflictions are sometimes (always?) the source of our greatest beauties. It is essentially a question of vision—do we have eyes to see beauty in affliction and vice-versa?

We must tread lightly here, but if we are honest, even our worst nightmares have been the crucible of God's grace in our lives. We are talking about the gift of our enemies and the mystery they enfold. Knowing the scandal of this teaching, Jesus teases us with a riddle and uses a metaphor, "The stone the builders rejected has become the cornerstone."[212] This statement, of course, is self-referential, but we can't help but wonder if Jesus is also referring to a larger principle of life. Our deepest afflictions—the ones we spend our lives running from and systematically rejecting, are, if we let them be, the cornerstones that give our lives meaning, hold our lives together, and ultimately complete us. The stone we reject is the stone that completes and perfects us if we let it.

Babylon was, without a doubt, Israel's deepest affliction and greatest source of shame. It was the cornerstone that Israel rejected. This is why God spoke through the prophet Jeremiah, "Seek the peace of the city and pray for it, for in its welfare you will find your own" (29:5). James Alison puts it this way, "We love our enemies because when we don't they are given free rental space in our souls and we become our enemies."[213] The six hundred mile walk to Babylon was more than a much-needed workout for the aristocracy of Israel who had grown fat and lazy in their abuse of the poor. Their transplant from the rooftop gardens of Jerusalem to the hanging gardens of Babylon was not just a lesson in horticulture. Somehow, Babylon held the key to unlock the fullness of God's love for God's people. Can we see it? Herein lies the gift of Babylon—the gift of our enemy.

Perhaps it is no surprise to discover that the very name "Babylon" embodies a profound secret. Babylon, not only means what it sounds like—babble or confusion—it also means "gateway of God."[214] It is our enemy who can reveal and even unfold the nature of God's love within us.

We confess that we are drawn to the poetics of this teaching, but we must also confess that the practical reality is a strong cup of coffee. It is one thing to suggest that an enemy holds the secret to our redemption—that somehow God clothes himself as my enemy, or as what Mother Teresa called "the distressing disguise" of another.[215] It is quite another thing to suggest that our sin and the sin of our enemies are servants of God's love and that this somehow completes and perfects God's love. But this is precisely what we are saying.

So let us now return to the question of whether death is friend or foe, and we look to Jesus to show us the way. Paul uses strange language when describing Jesus' relationship with death. Quoting an early creedal hymn, he says Jesus became "obedient to the point of death, even death on a cross" (Phil. 2:8). Jesus' triumph over death has less to do with its elimination and more to do with its transformation—or to be more precise, our transformation. To put it quite practically, we are all going to physically die, all of us. No exceptions. The deaths of our bodies and souls are a natural part of life. The only question that remains is how we will experience death. Will we make peace with our finitude, or will we follow the path of Dylan Thomas who wrote, "Do not go gentle into that good night . . . Rage, rage against the dying of the light"?[216]

As Swiss-born psychiatrist Elizabeth Kubler-Ross revealed in her landmark book *On Death and Dying*, there is something of an art to dying well, moving through cycles of denial, anger, bargaining, emptiness, and finally acceptance.[217] The beauty of death is that in the end, it's the one test of life that we all pass—some with flying colors, others by the skin of our teeth; but we all pass. If the resurrection means anything, it means that Jesus not only rises from the grave to show us how to live, but he rises from the grave to show us how to die. It is this second part that catches all of us by surprise and turns out to be the most liberating (albeit much harder) lesson.

If all this sounds like we are advocating for a passive acceptance of violence, brutality, and the dehumanizing forms of death that plague humanity, we have not been clear. We work with and serve leaders in contexts of brutal violence. We are not suggesting that we quietly accept such evil. We are not suggesting that we remain inside the cycle of violence or stand idly by the side of the road while innocent victims are destroyed. We are not romanticizing death in any of its many unnatural and fallen forms. We are, however, suggesting that until we come to see death from within the reality of the resurrection, we will not be free from it. In fact, the irony is that until we come to see death Christianly, we will be ruled by and enslaved to it. We will not be able to distinguish that part of death that is friend from that part of death that is foe. This is critical to understand because it is at the core of the resurrection and also the point of Jesus' cryptic teaching, "For those who want to save their life will lose it, and those who lose their life for my sake, and for the sake of the gospel, will save it" (Mk. 8:35). This teaching shows up in all four Gospels. In John's Gospel, it is tied to the question of sight. The Greeks wished "to see Jesus," and Jesus responds by saying, "Unless a grain of wheat falls into the earth and dies, it remains just a single grain; but if it dies, it bears much fruit" (Jn. 12:24). Death is not the enemy we thought it was.

Until we see from within the resurrection, we will not be able to distinguish that part of death which is natural to the rhythm of life from that part of death which is not. We will not know what to accept and what to resist. More importantly, we will not know how to engage death in any form without being consumed by it. We have said it before, but a death-denying gospel is a death-dealing gospel. To see all of life, particularly death, from within the reality of the resurrection is to see how thoroughly we have been constituted by death and how often our very attempts to eradicate it only further entrench us in it, like Chinese handcuffs.

So how do we escape the grip of death? Here is the secret—we don't. That is the first lesson of the resurrection, and perhaps the most liberating one. Consider again Thomas who put his finger into the wounds of the resurrected Jesus. The resurrected body of Christ is a wounded body—it bears the wounds of death just as the Lamb who shows up in Revelation as a "lamb who was slain" (Rev. 5:6). We can't have one without the other. The wounds of our salvation are preserved in Christ. Why? The theological and pastoral implications of this are huge: The resurrected Christ has the power to hold within his body the wounds of this world. In the same way, the resurrected Christ has the power to hold death itself without being consumed by it. This is the power of the resurrection and the new normal it established. It overcomes death, particularly in its most evil forms, not by eliminating it, but by embracing it, making friends with it and ultimately transforming it. This is why we can declare, "Where, O death, is your sting?" (1 Cor. 15:55).

To speak more sacramentally, we are describing the baptismal journey which, as we've already discussed, is the process of dying and rising. We pass through the chaotic waters of death that we might be raised into new life. In a sense, baptism is the cross before the cross. The baptismal journey is Noah's journey—floating over the chaos of judgment on a flimsy boat, cracks stuffed with pitch. It is Moses's journey—marching through the sea on dry ground and seeing the dead armies of Pharaoh on the shore in the morning light. It is Joshua's journey—guiding the people through a flood-crested river without the reassuring presence of his beloved mentor, nor the benefit of a visible miracle parting the waters before they stepped in. It is Jonah's journey—thrown overboard and entombed in the belly of the whale for three days. It is Jesus' journey and it is ours as well. It is a journey that transforms the way we see.

In baptism something dies, but we must be clear about what dies. What dies in baptism is *all that is not,* so that *all that is* can rise. What Thomas Merton calls the essential "true self" does not die, for that would make God like all other gods who demand human sacrifice. What dies in baptism and is buried with Christ is the "false self" with all its illusions. It is buried with Christ so that the true self that has always existed in Christ since the foundations of the earth can rise. In baptism, God simply asks us to die to things that *are not* so that we can live to things *that are.*

To illustrate our point, consider the familiar story of Moses who asked to see God face to face. God responds to Moses, "You cannot see my face; for no one shall see me [my face] and live" (Ex. 33:20). This must have been confusing to Moses, who likely remembered that Jacob saw God's face and lived. In fact, later in Deuteronomy it is said of Moses, "Never since has there arisen a prophet in Israel like Moses, whom the LORD knew face to face" (Deut. 34:10). Can we see God face to face and live, or not? Perhaps it helps to remember that when Jacob saw God face to face, something did in fact die. In a sense, Jacob died and was resurrected with a new name given to him by God. God named him Israel. And what about Moses? Well, in his case we see an exquisite display of God's sense of theological humor. God puts Moses in the cleft of the rock and shows him his back *(achor),* which can figuratively mean his "backside" or "hindparts." To speak in plain contemporary idiom, God "moons" Moses, and the cosmic mooning of God makes Moses' face shine with such glory that he had to veil his face when he went back to his people

(Ex. 34:33), because they would otherwise presumably die.

In short, whenever we see God face to face, something does die, and what dies is all that is false so that all that is true might rise. The *essential us* lives eternally in Christ. All that is not is eternally buried. Baptismal death strips us of our false selves so our true selves might live.

In the end, baptism is death before death, the cross before the cross. In other words, baptism is all about learning how to die and what to die to, so that we know how to live and what to live for.

PARTICIPATING IN CREATION

We mentioned earlier that seeing from within the resurrection is the very essence of creation itself. In this sense, creation is not an event that happened in the past, but something that exists in the heart of God. Creation is God's way of being. So, it is always happening, if we have the eyes to see it. When Thomas touches the wounds of the risen Christ and sees Jesus as "Lord and God," we catch another glimpse of this reality at work and we hear Jesus' invite his disciples (and us) to participate in the ongoing act of creation.

In John's account of the story, the risen Jesus reveals himself to his disciples, and we can imagine that it is "the first day of the week," which is to say that it is the first day of creation—the new creation in Christ. Notice that Jesus' disciples are hiding, locked inside a room—locked within the prison of fear, only able to see the world through that fear. Up to that point, they had not encountered the risen Christ and could only see what fear allowed them to see—a world filled with enemies. The world is a dangerous place when seen through that dark lens, and God is a dangerous God.

The text says that while they were locked inside the room, trembling in fear, "Jesus came and stood among them and said, 'Peace be with you'" (Jn. 20:19). We pause here to notice that the first word of the resurrected Jesus to his disciples is "Peace." Peace is always God's first word to a frightened creation. As we pointed out earlier in Chapter 14, Jesus declares peace three times in this passage, as if to say that peace is not only the first word of the resurrection, but it is also the middle and the last word as well. It is the summary of all that God is about. In a word, the resurrection finally and fully declares shalom—all is well. The resurrection is proof to humanity that Jesus' prayer on the cross was answered, "Father forgive them, for they know not what they do." The resurrected Christ confirms God's forgiveness to a fearful and violent humanity. When seen through the lens of fear, God's expansive, abundant love is easily mistaken for wrath, but when seen from within the power of resurrection all is disclosed to be radically otherwise.

Having declared peace, Jesus then commissions the disciples to do the same. He says, "As the Father has sent me, so I send you." Here Jesus is asking the disciples to imitate his declaration of peace, and then Jesus does what God always does with creation: He breathes on them, empowering them with the Spirit to be instruments of peace in the world. The poetry of this scene is stunning. Once again we encounter the mystery of God's breath.

What gentleness!

What power!

The image is rich and the text invites us to remember the Spirit (breath) hovering in Genesis, brooding over creation, calling forth life. We remember God breathing the breath of life into the dust of humanity. We remember God's name—Yahweh—the Breathing One, and we also remember the last creative

breath Jesus took on the cross that moves in the depths of darkness for three days. Like the vision in Ezekiel, the breath of God
sweeps over the valley of dry bones, and eventually our eyes are
opened so that we can begin to live fully into the resurrection.

To relax into the mystery of God's breath is to know ourselves as God's beloved. It is to know we are forgiven. And here
again we are confronted with another impossibility that is made
normal by the resurrection. We discover that God is not only
at work recreating us in Christ, but that God is inviting us to
participate in creation itself. He is offering us authority to author life, conferred on us by Jesus himself. As Jesus stood among
his disciples, he breathed on them and said, "Receive the Holy
Spirit." The text is quite clear. Jesus invites us to receive the
breath of life so that we might breathe the breath of life into
others.

Here is how it works: After he breathes on the disciples, Jesus
tells them, "If you forgive the sins of any they are forgiven; if
you retain the sins of any, they are retained" (Jn. 20:21-23). The
whole point of Jesus' breathing is to remind the disciples that
they have been forgiven and to empower his disciples to imitate
him. Once again we return to the words of James Alison, "It is
as we forgive and are forgiven that we come to see what really
is."[218] *What really is,* is this: To live inside of the resurrection is
to know ourselves as forgiven; and to know ourselves as forgiv-
en is to forgive; and to forgive is to participate in the ongoing
work of creation itself. Creation is both accessed and advanced
through the receiving and giving of forgiveness.

As Alison points out, in the most traditional and foundational theology of the Church, forgiveness precedes confession. It
is only in being forgiven that we come to know the true nature
of our sin. We know the truth of this intuitively. Who has ever

understood their sin apart from having first received forgiveness? It is forgiveness that reveals our sin for what it is. It is only after Peter receives the forgiveness of Jesus that he sees the devastating truth of his denial. Practically speaking, it makes no sense to point out the sin of the world and demand a confession from "sinners" before they have come to know themselves as forgiven. Again, this is why Jesus says, "Father forgive them, for they do not know what they are doing." This is the way of God. It is in and through the power of forgiveness that creation unfolds and discovers itself. It is in and through the power of forgiveness that we declare peace—*shalom!*

It is quite possible that Jesus is teaching us that creation is not just an event that happened in the past, any more than the fall of humanity is an event that happened a long time ago. Perhaps creation is the ongoing, contemporaneous act of God that is always happening, everywhere, in all places, and we are invited to participate in this miracle. It is our birth rite. Forgiveness is our way inside creation. It is how we access and participate in creation. To live is to forgive. It is the way of God. This is the new normal that the resurrection makes possible. On the other hand, withholding or refusing forgiveness is not merely refusing to participate in creation, it is an active participation in the fall. When we withhold forgiveness we retain not only the sins of those we refuse to forgive, we retain all that comes with an unforgiving heart, which is the undoing of creation itself.

We would like to offer two concrete examples of what it means to see from within the reality of the resurrection and participate in the ongoing work of creation.

Several years ago an eight-year-old boy named J.D., the firstborn son of close friends, died of a brain aneurism. One minute J.D. was playing with his cousins and the next he fell

unconscious and died soon after. It was a parent's worst night-
mare and the whole community of friends and family reeled in
shock. The grief was unbearable.

After the memorial service, a smaller group of friends and
family arrived at the graveside where J.D. was to be buried.
There is a haunting finality about seeing a coffin lowered into
the ground and dirt scattered over the dead body of a loved
one—especially when that loved one is a child. Attending the
service there was a little boy, a friend and classmate of J.D.'s.
Like J.D., he was eight years old. I remember the boy because he
stood alone, watching his friend being lowered into the ground.
The boy's father had excused himself to have a smoke and calm
his nerves. The absence of the father made the presence of the
boy stand out even more. I remember how alone he seemed, and
yet I couldn't seem to move. I just watched as the little boy stood
there by himself, alone and confused, and like the rest of us utterly disoriented. And that's when I noticed J.D.'s father walk to
the other side of the grave where the boy stood. It was not at all
clear where he was going or what he was up to. Even though it
seemed slightly out of place and a little awkward, he walked over
to the boy on the other side of the grave, quietly came alongside
the boy who was lost in his own grief and put his arm around
him. The boy responded in kind. They just stood there, arm in
arm, a sonless father and a fatherless son holding each other as
they watched dirt being scattered over the casket.

This image is not simply the image of two grief-stricken people holding onto each other for dear life. It is the image of hope.
It is the power of the resurrection. J.D.'s father saw something
that the rest of us could not. What he saw compelled him to
move, to take action. What held those two together was not simply their grief, but a kind of abundant goodness hovering over

us all that is calling us all into a deeper and more true existence. As we (Kris and Joel) write this, we are both fathers of eight-year old boys. Neither of us wants our vision of God's abundant goodness tested like this, but if it is, we pray that we too are firmly held by such goodness.

Tita Evertz is another example of someone who is learning to see from within the reality of the resurrection and to partici-pate in the ongoing work of creation. Tita is one of the people in our network in Guatemala featured in the movie *Reparando*, which tells stories of hope in Guatemala City. In the movie, the camera focuses on Tita as she gazes out over the squatter settle-ment known as *La Limonada,* a community of 60,000 people living on both sides of a deep ravine with a river of raw sewage running down the middle. Tita has spent almost two decades directing a ministry that serves the residents of *La Limonada* and operates two schools for the children there. The ravine and its inhabitants are disdained by many residents of Guatemala City—it is considered the "Nazareth" of the city from which no good thing could possibly emerge.

In this scene, Tita looks out over one of the schools in the middle of the ravine and reflects on the *La Limonada* that she has come to love. She considers the "Nazareth" that most peo-ple see when they look down into the valley strewn with cinder block homes and twisted rebar. Deep emotion bubbles to the surface from a soul seasoned by years of graceful seeing:

> I have learned that God's heart breaks when he
> sees us under oppression and in darkness. When it
> comes to *La Limonada*, I think there are people that
> see it like a cup filled with evil and darkness. But I
> see it like a place where God is very tangible. I can
> touch God and feel how he is here. It is a beautiful

place. I can sit at the edge of *La Limonada* and all I smell is hope.[219]

Tita Evertz has the gift of vision. She doesn't live in denial, blinded to the reality of the mind-numbing poverty and relentless violence surrounding her at every angle. Quite the contrary, she serves the people of *La Limonada* in deep solidarity with their pain and suffering, but she is able to see from within the reality of the resurrection. She has been given the gift of seeing a "new thing" in *La Limonada*, and her behavior toward this place has been radically affected as a result.

Tita is learning to see through the eyes of Easter. We too sit with Tita Evertz on the edge of the world and smell the sweet fragrance of hope. A clear vision of the future radically alters the way we are able to live in the present. The promised New Jerusalem of Revelation 21 is coming down out of the sky into the concrete reality of our present existence. It is the movement from abstraction to concreteness (what a wonderful image the city presents), and that practical future informs the way we live in the present: *"I am about to do a new thing; now it springs forth, do you not see it?"*

19

the god who sees

So she named the Lord who spoke to her,
"You are *El-Roi.*"
Genesis 16:13

If you wish to see, listen.
St. Bernard Clairvaux[220]

A s we approach the end of our journey into the geography of grace, we would like to return to where we began.
In the first chapter, we explored the biblical narrative of the unnamed concubine in Judges 19. Here in the penultimate chapter we will return to one of those strange narratives from the
Old Testament, another "text of terror." It is the story of another
concubine that bookends the story of Judges 19. The similarities
are haunting.

In Genesis 16, we read the story of Hagar, an Egyptian

household servant to Sarai. Sarai has grown impatient with God who has been slow to fulfill his promise of many descendants for Abram (called Abraham in subsequent chapters of Genesis), so she takes matters into her own hands and Abram goes along with it. The text says that Abram "listened to the voice of Sarai" (16:2), which implies that Abram is not listening to the voice of God.

This is something that plagued Abram throughout his life. Several times his story, Abram hides behind his wife to protect himself rather than trusting God. In fact, even after God's promise, he cuts a deal with Sarai when they leave Haran. The text is painfully clear regarding his cowardice, and he admits as much, "And when God caused me to wander from my father's house, I said to her [Sarah], 'This is the kindness you must do me: at every place to which we come, say of me, He is my brother'" (Gen. 20:13). Abraham gave Sarah to men of power to save his hide at least twice. If you leave behind the sanitized Sunday School version and ask anybody in our network to read this story, they will understand what's happening immediately. Harsh as it may sound, Abraham pimps Sarah on several occasions to protect himself and his growing fortune. This is partly how Abraham grew rich.

As Sarai grows increasingly impatient, Hagar becomes a pawn in Sarai's hands and is offered to Abram in a manner that, in effect, turns her into a sex slave, not unlike the nameless concubine in Judges 19. Ironically, Hagar is a servant from the very place that Israel will one day find herself in slavery.

It is important to remember that throughout the story, Hagar is acted upon, against her will, over and over again. She is acted upon by Sarai and then by Abram. After Hagar conceives her son, Sarai grows jealous and resentful; Hagar then flees to the desert—ready to die. The angel of the Lord arrives on the scene and does what no one else has done for Hagar—the angel uses Hagar's name. It is an important detail. In the simple act of naming her, Hagar becomes a real person. Hagar is never addressed by name in the story except by God. She is always talked about in the third person and she is treated like disposable property by those with power and privilege. To be talked about in third person is to be objectified and marginalized, like the indigenous peoples of Guatemala, Eastern European orphans, prostitutes, and the street youth of a thousand world cities. Eventually it is to inhabit a nameless identity, like the incarcerated gang members who respond only to nicknames, having abandoned many, many years ago the names given to them by their parents.

God, in the form of an angel, comes to Hagar with a beautiful question—"Where have you come from and where are you going?" God asks Hagar to tell her story. It is a beautiful example of empowerment. The divine messenger may have a clear idea where she is coming from and what she has gone through, but the angel chooses to ask her a beautiful question. Consider the humility of God who empowers this hurting, broken slave woman so that she might be able to use her own voice to tell her story.

The biblical text is rich with detail about Hagar's dilemma. Consider the comparison between Sarai and Hagar. Sarai is married, rich, free, and a Hebrew, but in spite of these inherent advantages, she is barren. Hagar, in turn, is single, poor, a slave, and African, but in spite of all these disadvantages, she is fertile. When reading Scripture from above—from a position of privilege and power—the temptation is to demonize Hagar by saying she must have found herself in this circumstance through some fault of her own that is not revealed to us in Scripture. Conversely, we want to say that Sarai was blessed for some reason that is unique to her moral character. But, the text does not allow us to do this. We are called to see things for what they are, not what we wish them to be in order to preserve our moral categories. The text invites us to ask if it is possible that the Hagars of this world are often more fertile ground for the gospel than the Sarais of this world? Both are blessed by God, but notice who is fertile and who is not. Notice where the larger miracle lies. Once we can accept this, we can make sense of the rest of the story.

When Hagar encounters the angel in the wilderness, the angel gives Hagar's son a name, Ishmael. *Ishmael* means "God hears."[221] It is remarkable to note that Hagar is the first woman outside the Garden of Eden who is visited by a heavenly messenger. She is also the first woman to receive a direct promise of descendants as opposed to having such revelations mediated through a man. After receiving the name Ishmael for her son, she does the unimaginable—she, an African sex slave, names God. She calls him *El-Roi,* the "God who sees."[222] It is the first instance in scripture of humanity naming God—a full six chapters before Abraham does the same.

If we pay attention to the original wording, there is a rich interplay between Ishmael and *El-Roi.* The God Who Hears (Ishmael) is also the God Who Sees (*El-Roi*). It is as if, in being heard by God, Hagar can finally see. This is a beautiful story that should be dusted off and put to use in our ministries with those who have been crushed by life. Not unlike Judges 19, there are many people who in this story find their own.

In the "desert region" of Guatemala there is a men's prison with a surprising group of residents. In what used to be the dining hall, a ragtag group of girlfriends, wives, sisters, and mothers of a hated group of Central American gang members sleep under and on top of cement slab tables. One of the chaplains in our network visits this prison on a regular basis. After an altercation in their previous "home," the only option the prison system could find for the women was a converted dining hall in this out-of-the way facility.

The chaplain began receiving requests from the gang members with whom he worked to please go and check on their "girls" for fear of their safety. After one visit, he could not stay away and made a plan to take the three-hour ride every other week. On one of those trips he invited me (Joel) to tag along, and I will never forget what I saw and experienced that day.

We entered the men's prison and had to pass down a long corridor lined with shirtless, tattooed men looking out from locked cells. We came to a locked gate, and from the hallway could see several bed sheets hanging from the ceiling, visually blocking the former dining hall, now home to a couple dozen women—most of them guilty only by association to the incarcerated men they called brothers, boyfriends, or husbands.

We were allowed to enter and meet with the women and after a couple hours of small talk, we began a conversation centered in Hagar. The women quickly made personal application to the story. They could relate to being unnamed and used as property by people in positions of authority and power over them. They knew what it felt like to live in "deserts" of loneliness caused by insidious rejection and marginalization. In Hagar's story, they found their own and they were captivated by surprise and wonder when they learned that Hagar was the first to name God.

A few weeks after our visit, the chaplain was able to complete the first phase of a prison remodeling project to build a cement block wall that physically separated the women from the men. Upon completion of that wall, the idea emerged to paint a mural and a discussion ensued as to what the women wanted to paint. They unanimously decided on the story of Hagar from Genesis 16 with the words, *"El Dios Que Me Ve"* ("The God Who Sees Me") as the focal point.

As relationships with these amazing women have continued, it has become obvious that these present-day Hagars have captured an ability to see the great *El-Roi* in a profound and unique manner. Ironically, the institutional church in Latin America often marginalizes the very people, like these women, and places that can provide the vision and sight the church so desperately needs.

What is it about Hagar that allows her to see God this way so much sooner than Abraham, especially in light of the fact that it is Abraham in Genesis 15 who is first to receive the promise from God? There are radical implications for mission when we understand that the Hagars of this world often catch sight of the scandalous nature of grace long before the Abrahams do. Again, it is a matter of geography. In other words, incarcerated gang members can arrive at some prophetic insights before the institutional church ever does. Street kids can point us to a Jesus that others of us cannot see. Families in extreme poverty understand what it means to have a relationship of daily submission and surrender to God, far beyond what the rest of us can ever grasp. Thus, we are learning to exercise humility and look to the Hagars—those labeled the least, the last, and the lost of the world—for insight and direction.

God is teaching us that the first people to "get it" usually are not those of us inside the church. Quite the opposite, Hagar's story calls us to move out of our churches with the deep

conviction that God is at work outside of our services and programs. This is not about making poor people feel better by asking patronizing questions so they gain a sense of importance.
No, this is much more profound—we believe that the next prophetic voices for the church are going to be the Hagar's of our
world—and the unnamed, dismembered concubines of our
communities.

Of course, it is important to remember that Abraham eventually "gets it" in Genesis 22, six chapters after Hagar names
God. Abraham is preparing to sacrifice his son Isaac—a ram is
caught in the thicket, and Isaac's life is spared. God's provision
of the ram redefines Abraham's vision of God. In Genesis 22:14,
Abraham names Mount Moriah *Jehovah Ra'ah* ("God will be
seen"). This text is often translated *Jehovah Jirah* and there are
valid reasons for this, but it is actually *Jehovah Ra'ah*, or to be
more precise, *YHWH Ra'ah*, a variant of *El-Roi*—the God who
will be seen.[223] Abraham eventually sees what Hagar sees, and
that new set of lenses changes everything.

20

community of desire

Take delight in the LORD,
and he will give you the desires of your heart.
Psalm 37:4

We dance under the banner of God's desire.
Robert Farrar Capon[224]

COMMUNITY IS THE litmus test of life. Kurtz and Ketcham, in their immensely helpful book *Spirituality of Imperfection* remind us, "We find ourselves only by the practice of locating ourselves within community."[225] It is in and through community that we come to know who we are.

A literary group in England called the Inklings met together each week for decades at the Eagle and Child pub in Oxford. It included the likes of C. S. Lewis, J. R. R. Tolkien, Charles Williams and others who would read each other's unfinished manuscripts, offer spirited critique and discussion, and share more than a little laughter and life. Then, tragedy—Williams died suddenly in 1945. Williams' death devastated Lewis, who called him "my dearest friend." In his attempt to find some small comfort, Lewis mentioned to Tolkien at one of their gatherings that perhaps the loss of their good friend Williams would at least be compensated by a deeper friendship between the two of them. Lewis reasoned that with Williams gone, perhaps he and Tolkien would have more time to invest in their friendship and could relate more deeply as a result. And yet Lewis discovered quite the opposite was true—with Williams gone, Lewis's ability to connect with Tolkien did not grow, but actually suffered. Lewis noticed that Williams brought out dimensions of Tolkien's personality that Lewis couldn't, and vice versa. With Williams gone, Tolkien and Lewis knew less of each other, not more.

This is a poignant image of community's counterintuitive way. We get more of each other through the broad richness of community than without it. Certain people draw out unique dimensions of our personality and character that only comes to life when activated by their presence with others. Apart from the group, that aspect of who we are is lost or diminished. This same principle holds true even in marriage. Community, when it functions healthfully, calls forth dimensions of our spouses' personality and character that are otherwise unavailable to us. In a dominant culture that tends to idolize a form of romantic love that can't possibly meet all our needs for community, we often miss this counterintuitive gift.

The calculus of authentic community is this—the more diverse the constellation of our friendships, the more full-bodied we become as individuals. In the end, we are a reflection of our communities, and it is in and through community that we come to know ourselves most deeply.

Perhaps this explains the renewed interest in an authentic experience of community among people of faith where the virtues of individualism and romance have been strained to their breaking point. This hunger has produced many new forms of community life among followers of Christ. Within the Protestant context, there are new monastic movements and the rise of the emergent church. We see a similar hunger within the Catholic context. And, to a large extent, even the secular "third space" movement tries to find ways of socializing that are not defined by work or home. Starbucks Coffee is perhaps the best example of a business that has understood the need for a third space and new forms of socialization in our culture. Given the influence that all these forces exert, we think it is important to pay attention. Whether or not we support them, our interest here is not to evaluate these movements but to understand what they mean for God's mission in the world. Where is the Spirit is moving in this regard?

A Brief Excursion

Before we go any further, we would like to offer two disclaimers and a few reminders of our method. First, we are not experts in these movements—they are not "our" movements in the sense that we did not grow up in them, nor have we been directly shaped by them. We serve in other contexts (typically devoid of Starbucks shops), and they have caught our attention only out of the corner of our eye. Our urban neighborhoods are generally the last stop for the movements we are describing— many of which originate in nonurban, more affluent worlds. As missional people, our movement has been primarily to be "the

Church scattered," whereas these are often movements toward "the Church gathered."

Secondly, it is hard to assess the shifts we are experiencing within the Church and society today while being caught up in the middle of it ourselves. It is not at all clear how we fit or how history will judge our contributions.

That said, we think it is important to ask how *doing theology from below* is connected to the larger movement of the Spirit within the Church today. It is a critical question that has practical implications for the leaders we serve. Clearly, the Church is growing worldwide in an astonishing variety of forms, and it is growing most among the urban poor who live outside North America and Europe. The church is rapidly expanding in almost all places except its traditional home base for the last 1,500 years. The face of Christianity is radically changing from white, Northern, and Western to brown, Southern, and Eastern. It is becoming an urban faith, which is a huge shift from its rural and suburban identity of the 20th century. The current movements among the emergent church and the new monastic movements, whether Protestant or Catholic, must be seen in light of this larger backdrop.

One practical implication of all this is that doing "theology from below" must be done in dialogue with "movements from above." To use a meteorological analogy, a local weather forecast relies on an understanding of the prevailing jetstream and shifting barometric pressure fronts. At an even larger level, it helps to know something about La Niña or El Niño patterns and the effects of global climate change. The further removed from the local context a weatherman, or theologian, is the more abstract meterological science, or applied theology becomes, but that shouldn't prevent us from trying to discern our larger context—because the implications can be huge.

As for our method, we want to remind our readers that we hold firm to Martin Kahler's insight that "mission is the mother of theology."[226] It is in and through mission that we as the body of Christ reflect most meaningfully on what it means to be the body of Christ in a given context. This is what we tried to convey on our short tour of the book of Acts in Chapter 10 "Unbounded Spirit." The Spirit is doing something "out there" that mirrors what the Spirit is doing "in here." Finding the connection is the work of discernment, and we take heart in Jesus' promise to send us the Spirit who will guide us into all truth.

A missional approach to discernment saves us from what James Alison calls the "problem of theory," which is the "need to get the formula right before we put it into practice."[227] Theory begins with the assumption that we have privileged information about how life is supposed to be, and that our job is to make life conform to that image. This approach is an addiction of the modern age and has caused great harm in our contexts. We have watched and even participated as the institutional Church, with its sometimes privileged theologies (the way things ought to be), neglect or even push away reality (the way things actually are).

This is why we are exploring what it means to read Scripture anthropologically, which locates its reading within the lived experience of those who wrote it and the lived experience of those of us who read it, rather than starting from a privileged set of abstract theological assumptions about how life is supposed to be. In other words, we are allowing anthropology (the reality of human life) to converse with our theology.

Many critics inform us of the dangers of this approach. They warn that it will lead to heretical forms of eisegesis instead of

God-inspired exegesis, as we impose our experience and ideas into the text rather than letting God tell us what is true. Our response to this challenge is twofold.

First, we throw up the white flag. We are guilty as charged. We are constantly imposing our ideas on the text, as every reader of Scripture throughout the ages has always done. We are part of a cloud of witnesses in that regard.

And secondly, as it turns out, perhaps this is not the devilish thing that it is made out to be—it is conversely quite orthodox. It seems God is not actually threatened by our ideas or experience in the least, if Scripture is any witness. A plain reading of Scripture reveals it to be not the blueprint we might have presumed, but an invitation to a conversation that God has longed to have with humanity from the beginning. To read Scripture anthropologically from below, from within the lived experience of real people living real lives, is to find a starting place for real dialogue not only with God, but with each other. Nothing could be more orthodox.

By starting anthropologically, we are finding a freedom in the direction of humility—a profoundly liberating experience. An anthropological reading of Scripture in community says, *Here are my thoughts, but since my thoughts are not necessarily God's thoughts, then I'd like to know your thoughts on this as well. Perhaps God will reveal God's self as we talk together.* To begin our reading of the text theologically (from above) is to begin with the assumption that we have a sense of what is true before we start. This quite naturally leads to competition and rivalistic tendencies. It becomes an all-out contest to see who gets to speak for God and inform the rest of the world how things are supposed to be.

Let's assume for a moment that this approach is right.

Consider the consequences—it will eventually lead to violence between competing factions, each of whom believes they speak for God and therefore must defend their position as their rightful act of obedience. It could be argued that reading Scripture from above is inherently violent, and at the very least we can observe this often happening in history. Is not this approach far more risky than reading the text anthropologically with appropriate humility? We all choose our risks, and we have chosen to live with all the many challenges that come with genuine dialogue with the Word and the world.

We share this because the movements that we see breaking forth from the Church worldwide have incredible potential to lead us to a place of deeper shalom—the kind of shalom that helps heal a deeply fractured and divided world. We also recognize these movements have the potential to deepen the divisions that already plague the Church and grieve the heart of God. These are not theoretical concerns. Our world is a tinder-box of competing ideologies and theologies, and if they are sparked in the wrong way there could be dire consequences for many people—most of whom unwittingly live with categories and assumptions that have been generated in North America and exported to the world. We (Kris and Joel) have a foot in both worlds, and sense a moral obligation to reflect deeply at this time in history. We do not intend to inflate the importance of our kind of work, but doing theology from below is a service to more than just a handful of poor folk in hard places. It may perhaps provide a way forward in times of deep uncertainty. For this reason, we invite many others, as we ourselves have been invited, on the journey into the geography of grace.

End of the Excursion

What follows are a few thoughts regarding our ongoing experience of "community" that we think honors the movement of the Spirit as well as the deep hunger of our culture for meaningful connection with others. It has been our experience that doing theology from below tends to call forth what we have begun to call a *community of desire*, and we are indebted to the work of anthropologist René Girard and theologian James Alison for helping us understand what we are experiencing on the ground regarding community.[228]

A community of desire understands and honors the very essence of what it means to be human—that we are created in and through desire. Like many saints throughout the history of the Church, and in conjunction with modern medical and social science research, Girard has argued convincingly that humanity is constituted in and through desire. Girard puts forth a simple but profound truth: In a process he calls mimesis, our ability to imitate the desire of others is what makes us human; as he says, "We desire according to the desire of others."[229]

There has always been a minority within the Church tradition that has understood and affirmed the role of desire in becoming human. For example, many of the mystics have seen the gift of desire as humanity's elemental source of inspiration. St. Ignatius was particularly aware of this. Unfortunately, the majority position within mainstream Christianity has tended to demonize desire as the source of temptation and sin—even the root of the original fall of humanity. While it is true that misplaced and displaced desire has caused great problems for all, desire itself is not the problem. As it turns out, it is the denial and repression of desire that is dangerous.

The Psalmist puts it this way, "Take delight in the LORD,

and he will give you the desires of your heart" (Psalm 37:4). The Psalmist is teaching us what Girard and science is only beginning to understand—we must learn to borrow our desires, not from others in rivalry and conflict, but from the Other in whom there is no rivalry. By imitating God who exists in ever unfolding trinitarian desire (positive mimesis by which the Son imitates the Father, and the Father imitates the Son through the delight of the Spirit), we discover that it is quite possible to borrow our desires from others without doing so rivalistically. Nonrivalistic relationship is the wellspring of all genuine community. It is the very essence of God's kingdom as revealed to us by Jesus. It is the essence of shalom.

It would be helpful here to further unpack Girard's mimetic theory to reveal how it leads to the formation of communities of desire. Unlike most conventional thinking about the function of desire, Girard maintains, as we've seen, that we borrow our desires from the desires of others rather than possessing our own innate desires unique to us. Girard claims that the idea of the individual as an autonomous being with its own innate desires is largely an invention of Western culture. Girard suggests rather that the individual is socially constructed, resulting in our experiencing desires that do not originate within ourselves.

For this reason the "I" or "self" is not the unique snowflake that God created from the beginning of time, as is often taught in Sunday school. That sort of "I" does not exist. Rather, the "I" or "self" that exists is a constellation of all the others from whom we have borrowed desires over time. Girard goes on to suggest that we don't borrow our desires from just anyone, but from those whom we perceive to have a greater sense of self than we possess. Because we see these models as somehow greater than us, we begin to want what they want and come to adopt their desires as our own. It is the social other who tells us who we are; or as Alison puts it, "It is always the eyes of the other who let me know who I am."[230] When we realize that we are not ruled by our own desires, but rather by the desires of others, this discovery is usually met with great resistance and some shame.

The modern advertising industry has understood the mimetic process to perfection. They have learned how to entice us to buy a product, not with the value of the product itself, but by inspiring us with models that we want to be like or we somehow connect with. We see something in the model that we want for ourselves; therefore we want what the model wants, but the object of our desire is not the object itself. Rather, it is actually a mirrored "desire" for the object that we seek to possess. The trick, of course, is that we convince ourselves we actually want the object, and that the desire is uniquely ours. In order to preserve our sense of autonomy we will go to great lengths to deny this dynamic. We will even feel ashamed to admit that our real desire is not for the object but is in fact for the person who inspired our desire for the object. The bottom line, according to Girard, is that we often fall into rivalry with the one who inspired our desire for the object in the first place.

Perhaps the clearest example of this is what is played out in every nursery everywhere, where Kid A enters the room and sees Kid B playing with a toy. Kid A sees several other toys on the ground that he could play with, but for some strange reason he simply has to have the toy that Kid B is playing with. Conflict ensues.[231] This is mimetic desire in a nutshell, and it is one of the truly great insights of our age that has huge implications in our work.

Our central point here is that we are profoundly social

beings, at levels that we have only recently discovered or have been willing to admit. In fact, science has confirmed Girard's theory of mimesis, with the discovery of mirror neurons in 1996. Mirror neurons make it possible for us to imitate behavior, learn language, and create memories. They explain why babies within moments of birth are imitating behavior. They explain why humans can get so worked up by simply watching other people. Mirror neurons are an integral part of God's biological hardwiring that makes us human.

In a sense, this entire text has been an attempt at positive mimesis. We have borrowed the desires of those we serve and from a God who loves the people we serve, and we have made those desires our own. At the end of the day, our work is to nurture communities of desire. This is what we are after, or to put it more accurately, this is what is after us—the community of God's own desire. As we borrow our desires from God and learn to imitate Christ, we inspire others to do the same. This is why the writer of Hebrews can say, "Remember your leaders, those who spoke the word of God to you; consider the outcome of their way of life, and imitate their faith" (13:7). Understanding that the locus of desire is outside of ourselves is the key to nurturing communities that give life.

A community of desire that is formed by doing theology from below and exploring the geography of grace has many more characteristics than what we can outline in this text. Thus, we have chosen to highlight just five of the most salient features of such a community that we think are important for today's context.

The Least. A community of desire that is formed in and through the desire of God calls forth ways of being together that honor those who have been labeled the least, last, and lost. There

is always room at the table for those who have been formerly
excluded, particularly the "least of these." By ordering things
this way, it becomes clear that, when functioning well, a community does not exist for itself. When the vulnerable are given
the place of honor, it reminds us all that genuine community is
not a "transactional" process. In other words, there is no "pay
to play" expectation. The terms of acceptance are not dependent
on our ability to offer anything other than ourselves. Humanity
is the price of admission, nothing else. What is important in
such a community is that people recognize that they belong before they are asked to believe. There is no requirement to believe
this or that before achieving a sense of belonging.

John the Baptist sends his disciples to Jesus to ask whether or
not he is truly the Messiah because of this. Jesus instructs the
men to return to John, telling him about what they have seen
and heard: "The blind receive their sight, the lame walk, the
lepers are cleansed, the deaf hear, the dead are raised, the poor
have good news brought to them." (Lk. 7:22). Undoubtedly John
is confused that all of those things were happening without anyone having to "repent and believe" anything in particular prior
to Jesus releasing his healing power. Perhaps knowing that John
would be wondering about this, Jesus concludes his words to
John's disciples by saying, "Blessed is anyone who takes no offense (literally, 'be scandalized') at me" (Lk. 7:23).

The key here is that a community centered around "the least"
is a community centered in God. Jesus said, "Just as you did it to
one of the least of these who are members of my family, you did
it to me" (Matt. 25:40).

Imperfection. A community of desire that borrows its desires from God is a community of imperfection. This is counterintuitive and perhaps even a little disorienting at first, but

idealized communities are toxic and disastrous in the long run—especially when working with the vulnerable. Communities born of a spirituality of perfection only affirm success, and in so doing they drive unwanted behavior underground. Such a spirituality creates an underworld of shame where illicit behavior and thinking flourish. The shadow sides of life are not tolerated and therefore take on a kind of power that eventually threatens the very existence of healthy community.

In comparison, communities of imperfection embrace a spirituality of imperfection. Such spirituality admits with the poet Emerson, "There is a crack in everything God has made,"[232] and with songwriter Leonard Cohen in his refrain, "That's how the light gets in."[233] Our friends Wil and Diane Boegel, living in the mountains above beautiful Lake Atitlan in the Guatemalan highlands, caught the essence of this spirituality in the name they gave to their ministry center. They chose the name "Opal House," because an opal gets its beauty from the internal cracks through which light is reflected and refracted. It is *because* of the cracks that the opal becomes a beautiful gemstone. Communities of imperfection are not governed by external rules of morality, but they understand that morality is governed by the deeper law of mercy that sits at the heart of God.

Peace. A community of desire recognizes that peace is the final frontier of faith. It is the summary of all that God's kingdom is about. Doing theology from below and exploring the geography of God's grace tends to bring about peace. Not the kind of peace born from might—a version of peace that must constantly be policed—but rather a peace that is born out of weakness against which there is no power. A community of peace understands the mechanism of violence and knows how to unplug from it, thus avoiding rivalistic tendencies that lead to violence.

It does not define itself over and against anything. Its identity is not formed and sustained in rivalry with others; rather it is formed and sustained in non-rivalistic ways that call forth and promote peace. In the end, a peacemaking community not only exposes violence for what it is, a work of the evil one, but absorbs it just as Christ did on the cross.

Unity. A community of desire *sees* unity in all things and *seeks* unity in all things. We are not speaking of a unity that demands conformity, rather we are speaking of a unity that honors and celebrates diversity. Theology from below produces a way of seeing the gospel that is not threatened by the other. Our brand loyalty to Christianity is not threatened by the existence of other faith traditions within the Christian family or outside of it. The unity we taste is not bland or compromising—it is centered so deep that we are coming to recognize a kind of kinship that had been formerly unavailable.

Gathered and Scattered. We feel compelled here also to say something about gathered communities (the local church) and scattered communities (mission and outreach). Both are necessary, but there is a difference. One is primarily a community that gathers to worship, the other is primarily a community that exits to serve. These two different communities have been referred to as "modalities" (gathered) and "sodalities" (scattered).[234] Because of the intense nature of the work of sodalities, they tend to produce incredibly intense forms of community. By comparison, modalities provide a place for everyday people to gather once a week for worship, but the lives of such congregants are typically so jam-packed that, at least in a North American context, the community is rather bland by comparison. This has led to a kind of unhealthy rivalry between missional communities and local churches. Sometimes local churches feel threatened by the intensity of sodalities, and sodalities sometimes become judgmental of local churches who simply cannot reproduce their intense flavor of fruit. Missional communities are often tempted to replace the church, and local churches are sometimes tempted to dismiss missional communities as rootless idealists. We would dare to envision a healthy synergy of the two, even in the challenging contexts in which we serve.

City as Classroom, Parish, and Playground. Finally, a community of desire changes the way we see the city itself. As we explained in Chapter 2, we are learning to see the city as classroom, parish, and playground. In this manner, the city becomes personified as our teacher, our healer, and the place where shalom is practiced, modeled, and celebrated. Although we have described this particular way of seeing in depth in Chapter 2, we revisit this paradigm to examine the city through the unique lens of a community of desire.

City as classroom for communities of desire. When we first started training leaders, we developed a curriculum that became known as Street Psalms Intensives. We still offer these trainings, but the increasing ability to see the city as our classroom and our teacher has significantly broadened our vision. Paulo Freire, bell hooks, Gerald West, and others are helping us discover how to create learning environments where the roles of teacher and student merge as all explore the desire and delight that the city evokes. We are also learning how to take context seriously, and let it profoundly shape the learning. To that end, as a community of desire we are creating a much broader menu of training than simply our theological intensives. For example, our menu now includes urban immersion tours (described in detail in chapter 3) in which we map the hurt, hope, and heart of the city with small groups of leaders throughout the year. This includes guided exercises that catapult leaders from the fountain of desire they absorb from their communities more deeply back into those communities. We offer international vision trips to local leaders who want to experience God at work in other contexts. When we see the city as a classroom, the possibilities for surfacing and harnessing creative desire are endless. We tap into the carnival of common grace that is the city, and instead of fleeing from it, we learn to embrace it.

City as parish for communities of desire. When we see the city as our parish, we declare all members of the city as vitally important to God. As we said earlier, no one single expression of the Church is enough for our dynamic and diverse cities; that is why we are increasingly seeing and celebrating the whole body of Christ in all its diverse expressions of desire. The great irony of this approach is that the more we honor the unique traditions of others, the more clearly we can see the particular passions and giftedness of our own. In many of the contexts we serve, this approach is initially perceived as a threat, especially when it moves beyond familiar doctrinal boundaries. However, when folks from vastly different traditions and perspectives begin to experience the rich heritage and core desires of one another, something delightful begins to happen. There is a kind of warm recognition of each other's values and desires.

City as playground for communities of desire. Perhaps the most liberating and the most challenging of our discoveries has been to see the city as a playground for desire. Zechariah's vision that "one day the city shall be full of children playing in its streets" (8:5) refuses the view of a dominant culture that is trained to see the city as a perpetual battleground of rival forces. We think the image of playground holds great promise as we seek to disengage from urban rivalries springing from misplaced desire. This is not pie-in-the-sky naiveté or wishful thinking. We know all too well the deeply entrenched, competing interests within our contexts. Refusing to be drawn into the battleground mentality is by far the most challenging part of our work. We find it relatively easy to model new programs and ideas that spark the imagination of others, and we find great joy in this. But, no sooner do we hatch a new idea than we find ourselves protecting it like our own offspring and warding off competition for resources. How easy for the playground to turn testy! But we are determined to resist, and do find that by engaging the city as a playground, we declare that there is a deeper reality to the city than "us versus them." We are affirming that there is enough for all and that scarcity is a creation of our own making, not God's.

One concrete example of a community of desire is the Street Psalms Community itself. It is a community whose story spans 25 years of service, of a handful of friends who found themselves thrown together at various points along the way in the work of loving and serving the urban poor. We discovered that we not only loved the work, but we enjoyed one another. The friendships made the work lighter, even as it ebbed and flowed, funding came and went, good things happened, bad things happened, life happened. Through it all the friendships remained, and even grew, and so did our call to love and serve the urban poor.

These friendships were forged and tempered in the crucible of urban ministry. As it turns out, "friendship" may be the most tangible outcome of all we have accomplished over the years. Friends attracted friends through the joyful and sometimes painful process of learning to love one another.

Also, through a long process of discernment, we found the courage to give some form and shape to what we saw happening among us. Eventually, we took for ourselves a name (or perhaps we were given one): *Street Psalms – A Community of the Incarnation.*

The Street Psalms Community is an "order" of sorts, though that is not language we often use to describe ourselves. It is true that individuals have been ordained by this community to the ministry of Word and Sacrament among the urban poor, and yet most of the participants of the Street Psalms Community are not ordained. We are a dispersed communion of Christ-centered people who are called to nurture life-giving perspectives and practices that sustain those who live and breathe good news in hard places. We practice a shared life of **action, reflection,** and **discernment**—these are our vows. We are committed to the life-long process of becoming like Christ with and for those we serve. Our task is to see God at work in the world and to celebrate what we see God doing.

In a world full of competition and rivalry, we wanted a community that did not introduce yet another competing faction. The Street Psalms Community does not supplant or replace other church or denominational affiliations we have. Rather, it exists to support and honor these commitments, which in some cases do not have the capacity to serve us in our call. In this sense, we are an external-facing, centered community of "one-offs" that is radically inclusive, existing to nurture leaders in their call to love and serve those on the margins.

Our desire to be a community not only comes from our friendship and deep sense of gratitude derived from those friendships, but it also comes from our own woundedness. This is our reality check—the authority of any community lies very close to its wounds. That is why from the outset the Street Psalms Community has worked hard to identify its wounds and pray for the related charisms (gifts) that are foundational to our community.

The Wound	Charism
The wound of blindness	Charism of sight
The wound of voicelessness	Charism of voice
The wound of despair	Charism of joy
The wound of isolation	Charism of community

Even though the Street Psalms community has been in the making for many years it feels like we are still in the first chapter of our story. We make no pretense that our community is better or more unique than any other community that is out there. It is simply our place to practice what it means to be a community of desire in the lowest places of the world and to live out a story whose full meaning will only make sense in the end.

conclusion (or lack thereof)

In the beginning God created
the heavens and the earth.
Genesis 1:1 (NIV)

We shall not cease from exploration, and the end
of our exploring will be to arrive where we started
and know the place for the first time.
T.S. Eliot[235]

IN THESE PAGES we set out to explore the geography of grace. We have tried to map some of the low places in Scripture as well as some of the communities in which we serve in hopes of finding good news. We wanted to test two assumptions, namely that grace flows downhill, and that to find it we must risk being wrong. We trust our readers have discovered some new grace here; and surely we've managed to be wrong in more than a few of our turns.

It should be abundantly clear by now that exploring the geography of grace does not tend to produce final conclusions. We know less than when we started, but what we do know has grown our faith and expanded our hearts. We think this is worth it.

We will at this juncture relax with some pleasure and affirm with Voltaire this fitting insight: "God is a comedian playing to an audience too afraid to laugh."[236] Though feisty Voltaire was hardly an orthodox believer in Christ, and perhaps made this declaration for very different reasons than we now quote it, he sums up the playfulness of the Spirit we are learning to enjoy as we do theology and practice mission in hard places. We pray that we will join the ranks of those slightly maladjusted saints throughout the history of the Church who got the joke.

With every journey there is a parting. It is never easy to end an adventure—especially one like this. So we won't. We'll give the last word to Tolkien who seemed to know a thing or two about adventures and how to end them.

> The road goes ever on and on
> Down from the door where it began
> Now far ahead the road has gone,
> And I must follow if I can,
> Pursuing it with eager feet,
> Until it joins some larger way.
> J. R. R. Tolkien[237]

appendix

1. Born From Below: The Word Made Flesh (Christology)

This intensive explores the meaning of the incarnation among those who have been labeled the least, last, and lost in the world. We consider the mission, message and method of God in the flesh and what that means for the Church.

Missional Question: What is our image of Christ and how does that shape the way we do ministry?

2. In But Not Of: Understanding the Grammar of God (Pneumatology)

We consider mission in the global, urban, and postmodern context from the perspective of "outsiders." We explore the boundary lines of faith and culture and the unbounded Spirit of Jesus.

Missional Question: What is the work of the Spirit in mission and how does that shape the way we live and serve the world?

3. Scandal of God: Loving the Least, Last and Lost (Soteriology)

Here we focus on the meaning of the cross among those who have been crushed by life. This is a journey into the dark side of faith fueled by the gospel of hope in Christ.

Missional Question: What is the meaning of the cross for those who are crushed by life and live lives of terror?

4. Image Is Everything: Finding God's Breath in Man's Dust (Anthropology)

We explore the power of images among the vulnerable and its meaning for mission. We journey into the ministry of imagination and discover how to reclaim the image of God from the world's broken images.

Missional Question: What does it mean to bear the image of God and how does that image call forth the ministry of imagination in a world struggling to become human?

5. It's a Family Affair: Redeeming Our Inheritance (Ecclesiology)

We consider the complex world of the biblical family and its meaning for ministry. We look at the good, bad, and ugly of family systems and how to preach good news that brings healing and hope to hurting families. Ultimately, we consider what it means to be the family of God.

Missional Question: What does it mean for the church to be the family of God in contexts where families have been destroyed?

6. The City of Joy: Welcome to God's Playground (Eschatology)

This intensive is a journey into the heartland of prophetic imagination on behalf of the most vulnerable people and places. We come to see the city as a classroom, parish and playground. Ultimately we consider how the New Jerusalem impacts the way we live in Babylon.

Missional Question: How does the New Jerusalem of our faith impact the way we live and serve in Babylon?

7. In The Belly Of The Beast: Seeking Peace In a Violent World (Ethics)

This intensive explores how to be a peacemaker in a violent world. We consider what it means to work for justice on behalf of the oppressed without forsaking mercy. We ask how we can beat swords into plowshares without perpetuating bitter rivalries.

Missional Question: In light of the previous six intensives— how then shall we live in a violent world?

bibliography

8 Mile, Director Curtis Hanson, Writer Scott Silver, Released in 2002.

Achebe, Chinua. *Things Fall Apart*. London: William Heinemann, 1958.

Adams, Marilyn McCord. *Horrendous Evils and the Goodness of God*. Ithaca: Cornell University Press, 1999.

Alison, James. *Broken Hearts and New Creations*. New York: Continuum, 2010.

_____. *On Being Liked*. New York: Crossroad, 2003.

Arendt, Hannah. *The Human Condition*. Chicago: University of Chicago Press, 1958; reprint, 1989.

Athanasius. *On the Incarnation*. Edited and Translated by Penelope Lawson. New York: Macmillan, 1981.

Augustine. *City of God*. Translated by Henry Bettenson. 1467; Penguin Classics Ed., London: Penguin, 2003.

_____. *Sermo*. 43. *PL* 38.

Bailey, Kenneth E. *Poetry and Peasant and Through Peasant*

Eyes: A Literary- Cultural Approach to the Parables in Luke, Combined Edition. Grand Rapids: Eerdmans, 1993.

Bailie, Gil. *Violence Unveiled: Humanity at the Crossroads*. New York: Crossroad, 1995.

Baker, Frank, ed. *The Works of John Wesley*, vol. 25, Letters I, 1721-1739. Oxford: Clarendon Press, 1980.

Bakke, Raymond J. *A Biblical Word for an Urban World: Messages from the 1999 World Mission Conference*. Valley Forge: Board of International Ministries, 2000.

_____. *A Theology as Big as the City*. Downers Grove: InterVarsity Press, 1997.

_____. *The Urban Christian: Effective Ministry in Today's Urban World*. Downers Grove: InterVarsity Press, 1987.

Baldwin, James. *Go Tell It On The Mountain*. New York: Dell, 1952.

Banks, Coleman. *Rumi: The Big Red Book: The Great Masterpiece Celebrating Mystical Love and Friendship*. New York: HarperCollins, 2010.

Barnes, Craig M. *When God Interrupts: Finding New Life through Unwanted Change*. Downers Grove: InterVarsity Press, 1996.

Barron, Robert. *And Now I See: A Theology of Transformation*. New York: Crossroad, 1998.

Barrows, Anita and Joanna Macy. *A Year with Rilke: Daily Readings from the Best of Rainer Maria Rilke*. New York: HarperOne, 2009.

Baylor University. *American Piety in the 21st Century: New Insights to the Depth and Complexity of Religion in the US (Selected Findings from "The Baylor Religion Survey")*.

Waco: Baylor University, 2007.

Becker, Ernest. *The Denial of Death*. New York: Free Press, 1973; reprint, New York: Free Press Paperbacks, 1997.

Beltran, S.V.D., Benigno P. *The Christology of the Inarticulate: An Inquiry into the Filipino Understanding of Jesus the Christ*. Manila: Divine Word Publications, 1987.

Berkhof, Hendrikus. *Christian Faith: An Introduction to the Study of the Faith*. Translated by Sierd Woudstra. Grand Rapids: Eerdmans, 1979.

Biblesoft. *New Exhaustive Strong's Numbers and Concordance*. CD-ROM Seattle, Wa:, BibleSoft, Inc., 1994.

Blake, William. Edited by John Sampson. *The Poetical Works of William Blake: A New and Verbatim Text from the Manuscript Engraved and Letterpress Originals*. London: Clarendon Press, 1905.

Blasé, John. *Living the Question in John*. Colorado Springs: NavPress, 2005.

Bonhoeffer, Dietrich. *Letters and Papers from Prison*. Minneapolis: Fortress Press, 2010.

Bonhoeffer, Dietrich. *Life Together: the Classis Exploration of Faith in Community*. Translated by John W. Doberstein. New York: HarperCollins, 1954; reprint, San Francisco: HarperCollins, 1993.

Bosch, David J. *Trasnforming Mission: Paradigm Shifts in Theology of Mission*. New York: Orbis Books, 1991.

Boyle, Gregory. *Tattoos on the Heart: The Power of Boundless Compassion*. New York: Free Press, 2011.

Brown, Robert McAfee. *Spirituality and Liberation: Overcoming the Great Fallacy*. Philadelphia: Westminster Press, 1988.

Brueggemann, Walter. "Biblical Authority." *The Christian Century*, January 2001, 14-20.

_____. "The Costly Loss of Lament." *Journal for the Study of the Old Testament*, 26. 1986.

_____. *Deep Memory, Exuberant Hope: Contested Truth in a Post-Christian World*. Minneapolis: Augsburg Fortress, 2000.

_____. *Finally Comes the Poet*. Minneapolis: Augsburg Fortress, 1980.

_____. *The Prophetic Imagination*. Minneapolis: Augsburg Fortress, 2001.

_____. *Theology of the Old Testament: Testimony, Dispute, Advocacy*. Minneapolis: Augsburg Fortress, 1997.

Brunner, Karl, Emil Brunner, and Karl Barth. *Natural Theology: Compromising "Nature and Grace" By Professor Dr. Emil Brunner and the Reply "No!" By Dr. Karl Barth*. London: Centenary, 1946.

Buber, Martin. *Between Man and Man*. London: Routledge and Kegan Paul, 1947.

_____. *I and Thou*. Translated by Walter Kaufmann. New York: Simon and Schuster, 1970.

Buechner, Frederick. *Secrets in the Dark*. San Francisco: HarperCollins, 2006.

Buhlmann, Walbert. *The Coming of the Third Church*. Slough, UK: St. Paul, 1976.

Burridge, Richard A. *Four Gospels, One Jesus: A Symbolic Reading*. Grand Rapids: Eerdmans, 1994.

Capon, Robert Farrar. *Kingdom, Grace, Judgment: Paradox,*

Outrage, and Vindication in the Parables of Jesus. Grand Rapids: Eerdmans, 2002.

_____. *The Third Peacock: The Problem of Good and Evil.* Palmwoods: Winston Press, 1986.

Chesterton, G. K. *Orthodoxy.* New York: John Lane, 1908.

_____. *What's Wrong With The World.* Simon & Brown, 2011.

Christian, Jayakumar. *God of the Empty-Handed: Poverty, Power & the Kingdom of God.* Monrovia: World Vision International, 2005.

Christianity Today Magazine. "The Top 50 Books That Have Shaped Evangelicals." Magazine online. Carol Stream, Ill.: Christianity Today International, October, 2006. http://www.christianitytoday.com/ct/2006/october/23.51.html, accessed on 4/18/2012.

Cone, James H. *A Black Theology of Liberation.* Maryknoll: Orbis, 1986.

_____. *God of the Oppressed.* New York: Seabury, 1975.

Costas, Orlando. *Christ Outside the Gate: Mission Beyond Christendom.* Eugene: Wipf & Stock, 2005.

Cuming, Geoffrey and R. C. D. Jasper. *Prayers of the Eucharist: Early and Reformed.* Collegeville: Liturgical Press, 1987.

cummings, e. e. and George James Firmage. *95 Poems.* New York: Liveright, 1958.

de Mello, Anthony. *One Minute Wisdom.* New York: Doubleday, 1986.

Dodd, Charles H. *The Apostolic Preaching and Its Developments.* New York: Harper, 1954.

Dostoevsky, Fyodor. *The Brothers Karamazov.* Translated by Constance Garnett. New York: Modern Library Edition, 1996.

Du Bois, W. E. B. *The Souls of Black Folk.* Rockville: Manor, 2008.

Durant, Will. *The Foundations of Civilization.* New York: Simon and Schuster, 1936.

Eckart, Meister. *The Essential Sermons, Commentaries, Treatises and Defense.* Translated by Edmond College, O.S.A. and Bernard McGinn. New York: Paulist Press, 1981.

Ehrman, Bart D. *Peter, Paul, and Mary Magdalene: The Followers of Jesus in History and Legend.* NewYork: Oxford University Press, 2006.

Ekblad, Bob. *Reading the Bible with the Damned.* Louisville: Westminster John Knox Press, 2005.

Eliot, T.S. "Burnt Norton," "Dry Salvages" and "East Coker." In *Four Quartets.* New York: Harcourt Brace Jovanovich, 1943. Reprint, 1971.

Ellis, Jr., Carl F. *Beyond Liberation: The Gospel in the Black American Experience.* Downers Grove: InterVarsity Press, 1983.

Ellul, Jacques. *Money and Power.* Translated by LaVonne Neff Lausanne. Switzerland: Presses Bibliques Universitaires, 1979; Reprint, Downers Grove: Intervarsity Press, 1984.

Endo, Shusaku. *Silence.* Tokyo: Monumenta Nipponica, 1969.

Foster, Richard J. *Streams of Living Water: Celebrating the Great Traditions of Christian Faith.* New York: HarperCollins, 1998.

Frank, Arthur W. *The Wounded Story Teller: Body Illness, and*

Ethics. Chicago: University of Chicago Press, 1995.

Freire, Paolo. *Pedagogy of the Oppressed.* Translated by Myra Bergman Ramos. New York: Continuum, 1970.

Friedman, Thomas L. *The World Is Flat: A Brief History Of The Twenty-first Century.* New York: Farrar, Straus and Giroux, 2005.

Garrow, David J. *Bearing the Cross: Martin Luther King, Jr., and the Southern Christian Leadership Conference.* New York: HarperCollins, 1986; reprint, 2002.

Girard, René. *I See Satan Fall Like Lightening.* Maryknoll: Orbis, 2001.

_____. *Violence and the Sacred.* Trans. Patrick Gregory. Paris: Editions Bernard Grasset, 1972; reprint, Baltimore: Johns Hopkins University Press, 1977.

Gilbert, Jack. "A Brief for the Defense." In *Refusing Heaven.* New York: Knopf, 2006.

Gonzalez, Justo L. *The Story of Christianity, Vol. 2.* San Francisco: HarperCollins, 1984.

Green, Graham. *Power and The Glory.* London: Penguin, 1940.

Guder, Darrell L., Editor. *Missional Church: A Vision for the Sending of the Church in North America.* Grand Rapids: Eerdmans, 1998.

Gutiérrez, Gustavo. *On Job: God-Talk and the Suffering of the Innocent.* Trans. Matthew J. O'Connell. New York: Orbis, 1987.

_____. *Teología de la liberación,* Perspectivas (Lima: CEP, 1971

Hall, Douglas John. *The Cross in Our Context: Jesus and the*

Suffering World. Minneapolis: Fortress Press, 2003.

_____. "Despair as the Spiritual Condition of Humankind at the Outset of the Twenty-First Century." *Journal for Preachers*. Advent 2001.

_____. *God And Human Suffering: An Exercise in the Theology of the Cross*. Minneapolis: Fortress Press; Reprint edition, 1987.

Hedges, Chris. *War is a Force that Gives Us Meaning*. New York: Public Affairs, 2002.

_____. *What Every Person Should Know about War*. New York: Simon and Schuster, 2003.

Heschel, Abraham J. *The Prophets: An Introduction,* Vol. 1. New York: Harper and Rowe, 1962.

Hopkins, Gerard Manley. *Gerard Manley Hopkins: The Major Works*. Oxford: Oxford University Press, 2009.

Hunsinger, George. *For the Sake of the World: Karl Barth and the Future of Ecclesial Theology*. Grand Rapids, Michigan: Eerdmans, 2004.

Iranaeus. *Adversus haereses*. 4.20.7.

Jenkins, Philip. *The Next Christendom: The Coming of Global Christianity*. New York: Oxford University Press, 2002.

Jeremias, Joachim. *The Parables of Jesus,* Revised Edition. Translated by S.H. Hooke. London: SCM, 1963.

Julian of Norwich. *The Shewings of Julian of Norwich*. Edited by Georgia Ronan Crampton. Kalamazoo: Medieval Institute Publications, 1994.

Kähler, Martin. *Schriften zur Christologie und Mission*. Munich: Chr. Kaiser Verlag, 1971.

Keating, Thomas. *The Better Part: Stages of Contemplative Living.* New York: Continuum, 2000.

King, Jr., Martin Luther. "Remaining Awake through a Great Revolution" Speech delivered at the National Cathedral, Washington, D.C., March, 31 1968. Accessed January 20, 2007. Available from: http://www.wagingpeace.org/menu/action/urgent-actions/king/index.htm Internet.

Kinnell, Galway. *A New Selected Poems.* Boston: Houghton Mifflin Harcourt; Reprint edition, 2001.

Kraybill, Donald B. *The Upside-Down Kingdom.* Harrisonburg: Herald, 1978.

Kohlenberger, John R. III, James Strong, James A. Swanson. *Strongest Strong's Exhaustive Concordance of the Bible.* Grand Rapids: Zondervan, 2001.

Kubler-Ross, Elizabeth. *On Death and Dying.* New York: Scribner, 1997.

Kurtz, Ernest and Katherine Ketcham. *The Spirituality of Imperfection: Storytelling and the Search for Meaning.* New York: Bantam Books, 1992.

Lamott, Anne. *Traveling Mercies: Some Thoughts on Faith.* New York: Anchor, 1999.

Lapierre, Dominique *City of Joy.* New York: Pressinter, 1985.

Leddy, Mary Jo. *Radical Gratitude.* Maryknoll: Orbis, 2002.

L'Engle, Madeline. *Two Part Invention: The Story of a Marriage.* San Francisco: Harper Collins, 1989.

_____. *Walking on Water: Reflections on Faith and Art.* New York: North Point Press, 1995.

Levertov, Denise. "City Psalm" in *Making Peace.* Edited by

Peggy Rosenthal. San Francisco: Auerhahn Press, 1964; re
print, New York: New Directions, 2006.

Lewis, C. S. *Studies in Medieval and Renaissance Literature*, ed.
W. Hooper. Cambridge: Cambridge University Press, 1954.

_____. *A Grief Observed*. New York: Seabury, 1961.

_____. *Letters to Malcolm: Chiefly on Prayer*. London:
Harvest, 1963. Reprint, 2002.

_____. *The Last Battle*. London: The Bodley Head, 1956.
Reprint, New York: HarperCollins, 1994.

Little Miss Sunshine. Directed by Jonathan Dayton and Valerie
Faris. Big Beach Films, 2006.

Lull, Timothy F., editor. *Martin Luther's Basic Theological
Writings*. Minneapolis: Fortress Press, 1989.

MacDonald, George. *A Book of Strife, in the Form of the Diary of
an Old Soul*. (London: published personally, 1880).

_____. *Unspoken Sermons*. London: Alexander Strahan,
1867; reprint, London: Kessinger, 2004.

Marshall, Bruce. *The World, The Flesh, and Father Smith*. New
York: Houghton Mifflin, 1945.

Marty, Martin E. *A Cry of Absence: Reflections for the Winter of
the Heart*. San Francisco: Harper and Rowe, 1983.

McGrath, Allister E. *Christian Theology: An Introduction*.
Malden: Blackwell Publishers Inc., 1994.

McKinney, George. *Cross the Line: Reclaiming the Inner City for
God*. Nashville: Thomas Nelson Publishers, 1997.

Meadows, Donella H. *The Global Citizen*. May 31, 1990.

Menahoth. 43b-44a.

Middleton, J. Richard and Brian J. Walsh. *The Transforming*

Vision: Shaping a Christian World View. Downers Grove: Intervarsity Press, 1984.

Moltmann, Jürgen. *The Crucified God.* Translated by R.A. Wilson and John Bowden. New York: Harper and Rowe, 1974; reprint, Minneapolis: Fortress Press, 1993.

Morris, David B. *The Culture of Pain.* Berkeley: University of California Press. 1991.

Newbigin, Lesslie. *The Open Secret: An Introduction to the Theology of Mission,* Revised edition. Grand Rapids: Eerdmans, 1995.

Niebuhr, Reinhold. *The Thought of Reinhold Niebuhr.* Edited by Gordon Harland. New York: Oxford University Press, 1960.

Nouwen, Henri J. M. *Love in a Fearful Land: A Guatemala Story.* Maryknoll: Orbis, 2006.

_____. *Turn My Mourning Into Dancing.* Nashville: Thomas Nelson, 2004.

O'Connell Killen, Patricia and Mark Silk. *Religion and Public Life in the Pacific Northwest: The None Zone.* Lanham: Rowman Altamira, 2004.

O'Connor, Flannery. *Everything that Rises Must Converge.* New York: HarperCollins, 1956.

_____. "A Good Man is Hard to Find." In *The Complete Stories.* New York: Noonday Press, 1990.

O'Connor, Kathleen M. *Lamentations and the Tears of the World.* New York: Orbis Books, 2002.

Oleska, Michael J. *Orthodox Alaska: A Theology of Mission.* Crestwood: St. Vladimir's Seminary Press, 1993.

Oliver, Mary. *Red Bird: Poems*. Boston: Beacon Press, 2008.

Oxford English Dictionary. Second Edition. [CD-ROM] Oxford: Oxford University Press, 1992.

Perkins, John. *Let Justice Roll Down*. Ventura: Regal, 2006.

Peterson, Eugene H. *Christ Plays in Ten Thousand Places: A Conversation in Spiritual Theology*. Grand Rapids: Eerdmans, 2005.

Returning Peace Corps Volunteers of Madison Wisconsin. *Unheard Voices: Celebrating Cultures from the Developing World*. 1992.

Robinson, John A. T. *Honest to God*. Fortieth Anniversary Edition. Louisville: Westminster John Knox, 2002.

Rocke, Kris. "The Magnificent Defeat." To [Center for Transforming Mission *Geography of Grace* conference at tendees]. June 2005.

Rohr, Richard. *The Naked Now: Learning to See as the Mystics See*. New York: Crossroad, 2009.

_____. *Things Hidden: Scripture as Spirituality*. Cincinnati: St. Anthony Messenger Press, 2008.

Saloy, Mona Lisa. "Still Laughing to Keep from Crying: Black Humor." Louisiana Folklife Festival booklet. 2001.

Sider, Ronald J. *Rich Christians In An Age of Hunger: Moving from Affluence to Generosity*. Downers Grove: InterVarsity Press, 1977.

Smedes, Lewis B. *Forgive and Forget: Healing the Hurts We Don't Deserve*. San Francisco: Harper and Row, 1984.

Sobrino, Jon. *Christ the Liberator: A View from the Victims*. Translated by Paul Burns. Maryknoll: Orbis, 2001.

Stringfellow, William. *An Ethic for Christians and Other Aliens in a Strange Land*. New York: Word, 1973; reprint, Eugene: Wipf and Stock, 2004.

_____. *Politics of Spirituality*. Philadelphia: Westminster, 1984.

Mother Teresa. *In the Heart of the World: Thoughts, Stories and Prayers*. Novato: New World Library, 1997.

_____. *In My Own Words*. Edited by José Luis González-Bilbao. New York: Random House, 1996.

Tillich, Paul. *Biblical Religion and the Search for Ultimate Reality*. Chicago: University of Chicago, 1955.

Thomas, Dylan. "Do Not Go Gentle Into That Good Night." In *100 Best-Loved Poems*. Editted by Philip Smith. London: Courier Dover, 1995.

Thurman, Howard. *Jesus and the Disinherited*. Boston: Abingdon, 1949.

Tolkien, J.R.R. *Lord of the Rings*. New York: Ballantine Books, 1954-1974.

Trible, Phyllis. *Texts of Terror: Literary-Feminist Readings of Biblical Narratives*. Philadelphia: Fortress Press, 1989.

Twain, Mark. *Adventures of Huckleberry Finn*. New York: Modern Library Edition, 1993.

United Nations Human Settlements Programme (UN-HABITAT). *The Challenge of Slums: Global Report on Human Settlements*. October 6, 2003.

Volf, Miroslav. *Exclusion and Embrace, A Theological Exploration of Identity, Otherness and Reconciliation*. Nashville: Abingdon Press, 1996.

von Loewenich, Walter. *Luther's Theology of the Cross*. Belfast: Christian Journals, 1976.

Wallis, Jim. *Faith Works*. London: SPCK, 2002.

_____. *God's Politics: Why the Right Gets It Wrong and the Left Doesn't Get It*. New York: HarperCollins, 2005.

Webber, Robert E. *Ancient-Future Faith: Rethinking Evangelicalism for a Postmodern World*. Grand Rapids: Baker Books, 2000.

Weil, Simone. *Writings Selected*. Modern Spiritual Masters Series. Edited by Eric O. Springsted. Maryknoll: Orbis, 1998.

Weisel, Elie. *Night*. Translated by Stella Rodway. New York: Hill and Wang, 1960. Reprint, New York: Bantam, 1982.

Welch, Sharon. *Sweet Dreams in America: Making Ethics and Spirituality Work*. New York: Routledge, 1999.

Wilkinson, Tracy. "Censure Dismays Priest's Supporters." Journal online. Los Angeles, California: Los Angeles Times, 2007. Accessed 3 February 2007. Available from http://www.latimes.com/news/printedition/asection/la-fg- sobrino15mar15,1,5099521.story?coll=la-news-a_sec tion; Internet.

Williams, Charles. *Descent Into Hell*. London: Pelligrini and Cudahy, 1949.

Wink, Walter. *The Powers That Be: Theology for a New Millennium*. New York: Doubleday, 1998.

Wright, N.T. *The New Testament and the People of God*. London: SPCK Publishing, 1996.

Yancey, Philip. *Church: Why Bother? My Personal Pilgrimage*. Grand Rapids: Zondervan, 1998.

_____. *Reaching for the Invisible God: What Can We Expect to Find?* Grand Rapids: Zondervan, 2000.

_____. *Soul Survivor: How My Faith Survived the Church.* New York: Doubleday, 2001.

_____. *What's So Amazing About Grace?* Grand Rapids: Zondervan, 1997.

_____. *Where is God When It Hurts?: A Comforting, Healing Guide for Coping With Hard Times.* Grand Rapids: Zondervan, 1997.

Yeats, William Butler and Richard J. Finneran. *The Collected Poems of W. B. Yeats*, 2nd Revised edition. New York: Scribner, 1996.

Yoder, John Howard. *The Politics of Jesus.* Grand Rapids: Eerdmans, 1972. Reprint, 1995.

endnotes

Introduction

1   By the term "grassroots" in this text, we refer to a deep connection with people on the margins of society.

2   Mark Twain, *Adventures of Huckleberry Finn* (New York: Modern Library Edition, 1993), 317.

3   ee cummings and George James Firmage, "dive for dreams," *95 Poems* (New York: Liveright, 1958), Poem #60.

4   Alison constructs a theological anthropology of original sin through the lens of Rene Girard. Alison celebrates the discovery that some theological assumptions concerning original sin turn out to be wrong.

5   "ebel," *The New Interpreter's Dictionary of the Bible*, Volume 1: A-C (Nashville: Abingdon Press, 2006), 6.

6   Phyllis Trible, *Texts of Terror: Literary-Feminist Readings of Biblical Narratives* (Philadelphia: Fortress Press, 1984), 29.

7   *Fides quaerens intellectum*, an echo of Augustine's *crede ut*

intelligas ("Believe so that you may understand;" Sermo 43, PL 38, 237-238).

8   Mark 9:24

9   George Hunsinger, *For the Sake of the World: Karl Barth and the Future of Ecclesial Theology* (Grand Rapids: Eerdmans, 2004), 89.

10   Robert Ekblad, *Reading the Bible with the Damned* (Louisville: Westminster John Knox Press, 2005).

11   Dietrich Bonhoeffer, "After Ten Years," *Letters and Papers from Prison*, Dietrich Bonhoeffer Works, Vol. 8 (Minneapolis: Fortress Press, 2010), 39.

12   Martin Buber, *I and Thou*, 2d ed (Edinburgh: T. & T. Clark, 1958), 25.

13   Paul Tillich, *Biblical Religion and the Search for Ultimate Reality* (Chicago: University of Chicago, 1955), 13.

14   C. S. Lewis, *Letters to Malcolm: Chiefly on Prayer* (London: Harvest, 1963; reprint, 2002), 80.

15   Phyllis Trible, *Texts of Terror: Literary-Feminist Readings of Biblical Narratives* (Philadelphia: Fortress Press, 1984), 2.

16   Kathleen M. O'Connor, *Lamentations and the Tears of the World* (New York: Orbis Books, 2002), 95.

17   T. S. Eliot, "Burnt Norton" in *Four Quartets* (New York: Harcourt Brace Jovanovich, 1943), 14.

Section 1

18   T. S. Eliot, "Dry Salvages" in *Four Quartets* (New York: Harcourt Brace Jovanovich, 1943. Reprint, 1971), 44.

Chapter 1

19   Trible, *Texts of Terror*, 2.

20   Ibid., 76.

21   Ibid., 2.

22   Henri Nouwen, *Love in a Fearful Land: A Guatemalan Story* (Ave Maria Press, 1966), 113.

23   United Nations Human Settlements Programme (UN-HABITAT), *The Challenge of Slums: Global Report on Human Settlements* (October 6, 2003).

24   Martin E. Marty, *A Cry of Absence: Reflections for the Winter of the Heart* (San Francisco: Harper and Rowe, 1983), 87.

25   René Girard, *Violence and the Sacred* (Paris: Editions Bernard Grasset, 1972; Reprint, Baltimore: Johns Hopkins University Press, 1977), 45.

26   Elie Weisel, *Night* (New York: Hill and Wang, 1960; reprint, New York: Bantam, 1982), 76.

27   Gustavo Gutiérrez, *On Job: God-Talk and the Suffering of the Innocent* (New York: Orbis Books, 1987), 13, 51.

28   Ibid., 10.

29   Eugene H. Peterson, *Christ Plays in Ten Thousand Places: A Conversation in Spiritual Theology* (Grand Rapids: William B. Eerdmans, 2005), 104.

30   Ibid., 5.

Chapter 2

31   http://www.tumblr.com/tagged/rumi?before=1313528321,

accessed on 3/28/2012.

32   Richard Rohr, *On the Threshold of Transformation: Daily Meditations for Men* (Loyola Press, 2010), 326.

33   Ekblad, *Reading the Bible with the Damned*, 2-3.

34   Ibid.

35   Romans 3:22-26, Galatians 3:21-29, Ephesians 2:12-22

36   Kenneth E. Bailey, *Poetry and Peasant and Through Peasant Eyes: A Literary-Cultural Approach to the Parables in Luke, Combined Edition* (Grand Rapids: Eerdmans, 1993), 161.

37   Robert McAfee Brown, *Spirituality and Liberation: Overcoming the Great Fallacy* (Philadelphia: Westminster Press, 1988).

38   Eckblad Updates, "Jesus Inside Guatemalan's Violent Gangs," Oct. 2, 2008.

39   http://www.pbs.org/wgbh/pages/frontline/slaves/etc/stats.html, accessed on 3/26/2012.

40   http://www.wpf.org/reproductive_rights_article/facts, accessed on 3/26/2012.

41   http://www.childtrendsdatabank.org/?q=node/196, accessed on 3/26/2012.

42   http://www.forbes.com/2007/06/11/third-world-slums-biz-cx_21cities_ee_0611slums.html, accessed on 3/26/2012.

43   http://www.unhcr.org/4a3b98706.html, accessed on 3/26/2012.

44   http://cnsnews.com/news/article/number-illegal-immigrants-us-steady-112m, accessed on 3/26/2012.

45   http://www.drug-rehabs.org/alcohol-statistics.php, accessed on 3/26/2012.

46   http://www.samhsa.gov/newsroom/advisories/1201185326.aspx, accessed on 3/26/2012.

47   http://bjs.ojp.usdoj.gov/index.cfm?ty=pbdetail&iid=2230, accessed on 3/26/2012.

48   http://bjs.ojp.usdoj.gov/index.cfm?ty=pbdetail&iid=2230, accessed on 3/26/2012.

49   https://www.ncjrs.gov/childabuse/, accessed on 3/26/2012.

50   http://www.pewsocialtrends.org/2011/06/15/a-tale-of-two-fathers/, accessed on 3/26/2012.

51   http://www.who.int/violence_injury_prevention/violence/world_report/en/summary_en.pdf, accessed on 3/26/2012.

52   http://www.painmed.org/patientcenter/facts_on_pain.aspx, accessed on 3/26/2012.

53   This quote is commonly attributed to Robert Farrar Capon, but the authors have been unable to find the source material.

Chapter 3

54   Denise Levertov "City Psalm" in *Making Peace* (San Francisco: Auerhahn Press, 1964; reprint, New York: New Directions, 2006), 48.

55   Ibid., 48.

56   William Butler Yeats, Richard J. Finneran, "The Second Coming" in *The Collected Poems of W. B. Yeats*, 2d rev ed (New York: Scribner, 1996), 186.

57   Ray Bakke, *A Theology As Big As the City* (Downers Grove: IVP Academic, 1997), 12.

58   http://dirt.asla.org/2010/03/25/world-urban-forum-in-rio-focuses-on-sustainable-urban-development/, accessed on 3/26/2012.

59   See *Pedagogy of the Oppressed*, pages 71-86, for discussion of

teacher-student power dynamics.

60   See John Stahl-Wert's work *City as Parish: An Urban, Intercongregational Curriculum for Collaborative Lay Ministry Equipping.*

61   Foster, Richard, *Streams of Living Water: Celebrating the Great Traditions of Christian Faith.* (San Francisco: HarperOne, 2001).

62   G. K. Chesterton, "Oxford From Without" in *All Things Considered* (Sandy: Quiet Vision Publishing, 2004), 54.

63   Mary Oliver, "Messenger" in *Thirst* (Boston: Beacon Press, 2007), 1.

Chapter 4

64   Meister Eckart, *The Essential Sermons, Commentaries, Treatises and Defense*, Trans. Edmond Colllege, O.S.A. and Bernard McGinn (New York: Paulist Press, 1981), 202.

65   David J. Bosch, *Transforming Mission: Paradigm Shifts in Theology of Mission* (New York: Orbis Books, 1991), 340.

66   Wallace Stegner, "The Sense of Place" (1986), *Where the Bluebird Sings to the Lemonade Springs: Living and Writing in the West* (New York, 1992), 201.

Chapter 5

67   Mark Twain, *Adventures of Huckleberry Finn* (New York: Modern Library Edition, 1993), 315-16.

68   e.e. cummings, "Introduction" *Collected Poems 1922-1938* (Book-of-the-Month Club; reprint edition, 1990).

Chapter 6

69   Madeline L 'Engle, *Walking on Water: Reflections on Faith and Art* (New York: North Point Press, 1995), 50.

70   C. S. Lewis, *A Grief Observed* (New York: Seabury Press, 1961), 52.

71   George McKinney, *Cross the Line: Reclaiming the Inner City for God* (Nashville: Thomas Nelson Publishers, 1997), 210-215.

72   Gerard Manley Hopkins, "As Kingfishers Catch Fire" in *Gerard Manley Hopkins: The Major Works* (Oxford: Oxford University Press, 2009), 129.

Chapter 7

73   C. S. Lewis, "Edmund Spencer, 1552-99" in *Studies in Medieval and Renaissance Literature*, ed. W. Hooper (Cambridge: Cambridge University Press, 1954), 137.

74   Dietrich Bonhoeffer, *Life Together: the Classic Exploration of Faith in Community* (New York: HarperCollins, 1954; reprint, San Francisco: HarperCollins, 1993), 113.

75   Benigno P. Beltran, S.V.D., *The Christology of the Inarticulate: an Inquiry into the Filipino Understanding of Jesus the Christ* (Manila: Divine Word Publications, 1987), 26.

76   Ibid., 26.

77   Ibid., 27.

78   Ibid., 28.

79   Ibid., 25.

80   *Oxford English Dictionary*, 2nd ed, s.v. "symbol" [CD-ROM]

(Oxford: Oxford University Press, 1992).

81   C. S. Lewis, *Studies in Medieval and Renaissance Literature*, ed. W. Hooper (Cambridge: Cambridge University Press, 1954), 137.

82   The concept is succinctly described in an essay entitled, "The Anonymous God: American Civil Religion, the Scandal of Particularity, and the first Table of the Torah" by Dr. David L. Adams. (2002).

83   Patricia O'Connell Killen and Mark Silk, *Religion and Public Life in the Pacific Northwest: The None Zone* (Lanham, Maryland: Rowman Altamira, 2004), 9.

84   Ibid., 9.

85   Ibid., 22.

86   Baylor University, *American Piety in the 21st Century: New Insights to the Depth and Complexity of Religion in the US; Selected Findings from "The Baylor Religion Survey"* (Waco: Baylor University, 2007), 4.

87   Ibid., 4.

88   Ibid., 26.

89   Beltran, *The Christology of the Inarticulate: An Inquiry into the Filipino Understanding of Jesus the Christ*, 206.

90   C. S. Lewis, *Letters to Malcolm: Chiefly on Prayer* (London: Houghton Mifflin Harcourt, 2002), 27.

91   Donald B. Kraybill, *The Upside-Down Kingdom* (Pennsylvania: Herald, 1978), 23.

92   Eph. 6:12

93   Fyodor Dostoevsky, *The Brothers Karamazov*, Trans. by

Constance Garnett (New York: Modern Library Edition, 1996), 273-293.

94   Mary Jo Leddy, *Radical Gratitude* (Maryknoll: Orbis, 2002), 57.

95   Matt. 4:6a

96   James Strong, "ballo," n.p., *Strong's Greek Dictionary on CD-ROM.* Accordance, Version: 9.5.7., 2011.

97   http://www.brainyquote.com/quotes/quotes/a/alberteins130982.html, accessed 2/16/2012.

98   Peterson, *Christ Plays in Ten Thousand Places – A Conversation in Spiritual Theology,* 271.

99   James Strong, "doxa," n.p., *Strong's Greek Dictionary on CD-ROM.* Accordance, Version: 9.5.7., 2011.

100   Walter Wink, *The Powers That Be: Theology for a New Millennium* (New York: Doubleday, 1998), 27.

101   Ibid., 272.

102   J. R. R. Tolkien, *The Fellowship of the Ring* (New York: Ballentine Books, 1970), 473.

103   Stringfellow, William. *An Ethic for Christians and Other Aliens in a Strange Land* (New York: Word, 1973; reprint, Eugene: Wipf and Stock, 2004), 28.

104   Eliot, "The Dry Salvages," *Four Quartets,* 44.

105   Walter Brueggeman, *Deep Memory, Exuberant Hope* (Augsburg Fortress Publishers, 2000), 5.

106   Leddy, *Radical Gratitude* (Maryknoll: Orbis, 2005).

Chapter 8

107   Archbishop of Canterbury William Temple, *Feasting on the Word* (Year A, Volume1), 336.

108   James Strong, "ekklesia," n.p., *Strong's Greek Dictionary on CD-ROM*. Accordance, Version: 9.5.7., 2011.

109   Barna Research Group, "Christians are more likely to experience divorce than are non-Christians," 1999-DEC-21, at: http://www.barna.org/, accessed on 3/27/2012.

110   http://www.hiddenhurt.co.uk/religion_and_domestic_violence.html, accessed on 3/27/2012.

111   http://www.pewforum.org/Politics-and-Elections/The-Torture-Debate-A-Closer-Look.aspx, accessed on 3/27/2012.

112   Richard Rohr, *The Naked Now: Learning to See as the Mystics See* (New York: Crossroad, 2009), 25-26.

113   We do not quote Richard Rohr directly here. The ideas are gleaned from Fr. Rohr's public lectures on this topic.

114   Quoted in Philip Yancey, *Church: Why Bother? My Personal Pilgrimage* (Grand Rapids: Zondervan, 1998), 31.

115   Handwritten response to a question posed to gang members in maximum-security prison in Guatemala regarding what they would like Christian leaders to know about their situation.

116   Originally published at http://www.christianitytoday.com/globalconversation/april2010/index.html, accessed on 3/27/2012.

Chapter 9

117   Miroslav Volf, *Exclusion and Embrace, A Theological Exploration of Identity, Otherness and Reconciliation* (Nashville: Abingdon Press, 1996), 147.

118   Ibid., 9.

119   Volf, *Exclusion and Embrace*, 140-147.

120   Volf, *Exclusion and Embrace*, 146.

121   Lewis B. Smedes, *Forgive and Forget: Healing the Hurts We Don't Deserve* (San Francisco: Harper and Row, 1984), 137.

Chapter 10

122   Coleman Banks, *Rumi: The Big Red Book: The Great Masterpiece Celebrating Mystical Love and Friendship* (New York: HarperCollins, 2010), 376.

123   James Strong, "rachaph," n.p., *Strong's Hebrew Dictionary on CD-ROM*. Accordance, Version: 9.5.7., 2011.

124   For discussion of this see Eugene H. Peterson. *Christ Plays In Ten Thousand Places - A Conversation in Spiritual Theology* (Grand Rapids: Eerdmans, 2005), 44-45.

125   Michael J. Oleska, *Orthodox Alaska: A Theology of Mission* (Crestwood: St. Vladimir's Seminary Press, 1993), 18.

126   John Howard Yoder, T*he Politics of Jesus* (Grand Rapids: Eerdmans, 1972; reprint, 1995), 155.

127   Bosch, *Transforming Mission*, 16.

128   Menahoth 43b-44.

129   W. E. B. Du Bois. *The Souls of Black Folk* (Rockville:Manor, 2008), 19.

130   Ray Bakke, *A Theology as Big as the City* (Downers Grove: IVP Academic, 1997), 142-43.

131   Coleman Banks, *Rumi: The Big Red Book: The Great Masterpiece Celebrating Mystical Love and Friendship* (New York: HarperCollins, 2010), 376.

132   Mary Oliver, "Instructions for Living a Life" in *Red Bird: Poems* (Boston: Beacon Press, 2008), 37.

Chapter 11

133   Anthony de Mello, SJ, *One Minute Wisdom* (New York: Doubleday, 1986), 23.

Section 3

134   Madeleine L'Engle, *Two Part Invention: The Story of a Marriage* (San Francisco: Harper Collins, 1989), 229.

Chapter 12

135   James Alison, "From Impossibility to Responsibility" in *Broken Hearts and New Creations* (New York: Continuum, 2010), 5.

136   Images from http://faculty.bbc.edu/rdecker/alex_graffito.htm, accessed 2/16/2012.

137   Alison, "From Impossibility to Responsibility," 4.

138   http://www.tlf.org.za/feast.htm, accessed 2/16/2012

139   Galway Kinnell, *A New Selected Poems* (Boston: Houghton Mifflin Harcourt; Reprint edition, 2001), 94. Also, http://www.poetryfoundation.org/poem/171395, accessed on 3/28/2012.

140   Gregory Boyle, *Tattoos on the Heart: The Power of Boundless Compassion* (New York: Free Press, 2011), 71.

141   Phillip Yancey, *Where is God When It Hurts?: A Comforting, Healing Guide for Coping with Hard Times* (Grand Rapids:

Zondervan, 1997), 8.

142   David B. Morris, *The Culture of Pain* (Berkeley: University of California Press, 1991), 61.

143   Douglas John Hall, "Despair as the Spiritual Condition of Humankind at the Outset of the Twenty-First Century," *Journal for Preachers* (Advent 2001), 3-6.

144   Douglas John Hall, *God And Human Suffering: An Exercise in the Theology of the Cross* (Minneapolis: Fortress Press; Reprint edition, 1987), 43-47.

145   Chris Hedges, *War is a Force that Gives Us Meaning* (New York: Public Affairs, 2002), 13.

146   Ibid., 137.

147   William Stringfellow, *An Ethic For Christians and Other Aliens In A Strange Land* (Waco: Word Books, 1973), 41.

148   Jürgen Moltmann, *The Crucified God*, trans. R.A. Wilson and John Bowden (New York: Harper and Rowe, 1974; reprint, Minneapolis: Fortress Press, 1993), 1.

149   Ibid., 1.

150   Douglas John Hall, *The Cross in Our Context: Jesus and the Suffering World* (Minneapolis: Fortress Press, 2003), 99.

151   Ernest Becker, *The Denial of Death* (New York: Free Press, 1973; reprint, Free Press Paperbacks, 1997), 32.

152   Hendrikus Berkhof, *Christian Faith: An Introduction to the Study of the Faith*, trans. Sierd Woudstra (Grand Rapids: Eerdmans, 1979), 193. In Hall, *The Cross in Our Context*, 100.

153   Walter Brueggemann, "The Costly Loss of Lament," *JSOT* 26

(1986): 60-61.

154   Timothy F. Lull, editor, *Martin Luther's Basic Theological Writings* (Minneapolis: Fortress Press, 1989), 16.

155   Hall, *The Cross In Our Context*, 28.

156   *Oxford English Dictionary*, 2d ed, s.v. "utopia."

157   Frederick Buechner, *Secrets in the Dark* (San Francisco: HarperCollins, 2006), in John Blasé, *Living the Question in John* (Colorado Springs: NavPress, 2005), 43.

158   Ibid., 33.

159   James Strong, "epithumia," n.p., *Strong's Greek Dictionary on CD-ROM*. Accordance, Version: 9.5.7., 2011.

160   Philip Yancey, "God Behind Barbed Wire: How a Nazi-soldier-turned-theologian found hope," in *Christianity Today*, http://www.christianitytoday.com/ct/2005/september/20.120.html, accessed on 4/17/2012.

161   James Strong, "sachaq," n.p., *Strong's Hebrew Dictionary on CD-ROM*. Accordance, Version: 9.5.7., 2011.

162   G. K. Chesterton, *Orthodoxy* (New York: John Lane, 1908), 289.

163   Ibid., 289-299.

164   James Strong, "pneuma," n.p., *Strong's Greek Dictionary on CD-ROM*. Accordance, Version: 9.5.7., 2011.

Chapter 13

165   Paolo Freire, *Pedagogy of the Oppressed*. Translated by Myra Bergman Ramos. (New York: Continuum, 1970), 88.

Chapter 14

166 http://catholicpittsburgh.org/d/node/160, accessed 3/27/12.

167 Richard Rohr, *Things Hidden: Scripture as Spirituality* (Cincinnati: St. Anthony Messenger Press, 2008), 189.

168 Gil Bailie, *Violence Unveiled: Humanity at the Crossroads* (New York: Crossroad, 1995), 14-16.

Chapter 15

169 http://www.malespirituality.org/images/Remember%20in%20 the%20Darkness.pdf, accessed on 3/27/12.

170 Henri Nouwen, *Love in a Fearful Land: A Guatemala Story* (Maryknoll: Orbis, 2006).

171 Henri J. M. Nouwen, *Turn My Mourning Into Dancing* (Nashville: Thomas Nelson, 2004), 59.

Chapter 16

172 e. e. cummings and George James Firmage, "dive for dreams," *95 Poems* (New York: Liveright, 1958), Poem #60

173 G. K. Chesterton, *What's Wrong With The World* (Simon & Brown, 2011), 48.

174 *Oxford English Dictionary*, 2d ed, s.v. "effulgence."

175 Hebrews 1:2-3, *The New English Bible* (NEB).

176 cf. Col. 1:24.

177 Kenneth E. Bailey, *Poetry and Peasant and Through Peasant Eyes: A Literary—Cultural Approach to the Parables in Luke*, comb ed (Grand Rapids: Eerdmans, 1993), 206.

178   Ibid., 161.

179   Ibid., 202.

180   Ibid., 165.

181   Ibid., 167.

182   Ibid., 178.

183   Ibid., 180.

184   Ibid., 176-179.

185   Ibid., 193.

186   Ibid., 194.

187   Ibid., 191.

188   Ibid., 203.

189   James Strong, "kenosis," n.p., *Strong's Greek Dictionary on CD-ROM*. Accordance, Version: 9.5.7., 2011.

190   William Blake, ed. John Sampson, *The Poetical Works of William Blake: A New and Verbatim Text From the Manuscript Engraved and Letterpress Originals* (London: Clarendon Press, 1905), 176.

191   J. R. R. Tolkien, *Lord of the Rings* (New York: Ballantine Books, 1954-1974).

192   Allister E. McGrath, *Christian Theology: An Introduction* (Malden: Blackwell Publishers Inc., 1994), 298.

193   Chris Hedges, *War is a Force that Gives Us Meaning* (New York: PublicAffairs, 2002), 10, quoting Will Durant, *The Foundations of Civilization* (New York: Simon and Schuster, 1936).

194 Wink, *The Powers That Be*, 137.

195 Philip Jenkins, *The Next Christendom: The Coming of Global Christianity* (New York: Oxford University Press, 2002), 2.

196 Ibid., 3.

197 Ibid., quoting Walbert Buhlmann, *The Coming of the Third Church* (Slough, UK: St. Paul, 1976).

198 Denise Levertov, "Protesters" in *Making Peace* (San Francisco: Auerhahn Press, 1964; reprint, New York: New Directions, 2006), 27.

199 Robert Farrar Capon, *Kingdom, Grace, Judgment: Paradox, Outrage, and Vindication in the Parables of Jesus* (Grand Rapids: Eerdmans, 2002), 262.

200 T.S. Eliot,"Burnt Norton" In *Four Quartets* (New York: Harcourt Brace Jovanovich, 1943. Reprint, 1971) 15.

201 Ibid., 15.

202 T.S. Eliot, "East Coker" in *Four Quartets* (New York: Harcourt Brace Jovanovich, 1943. Reprint, 1971), 18.

203 Jonathan Dayton and Valerie Faris, directors, *Little Miss Sunshine* (Big Beach Films, 2006).

204 Jack Gilbert, "A Brief for the Defense" in *Refusing Heaven* (New York: Knopf, 2005), 3.

Section 4

205 http://www.brainyquote.com/quotes/keywords/audience.html, accessed 3/27/12.

Chapter 17

206 This quote is commonly attributed to Karl Barth, but the

authors have been unable to find the source material.

207   Robert Barron, *And Now I See: A Theology of Transformation* (New York: Crossroad, 1998), 1.

Chapter 18

208   James Alison, *On Being Liked* (New York: Crossroad, 2003), 44.

209   Anita Barrows and Joanna Macy, *A Year with Rilke: Daily Readings from the Best of Rainer Maria Rilke* (New York: HarperOne, 2009), 6.

210   John Howard Yoder, *The Politics of Jesus* (Grand Rapids: Eerdmans, 1994), 155.

211   Simone Weil, *Writings Selected*, Modern Spiritual Masters Series (Maryknoll: Orbis, 1998), 59.

212   Psalm 118:22, Matthew 21:42.

213   James Alison, "Love Your Enemy: Within a Divided Self," http://www.jamesalison.co.uk/texts/eng50.html, accessed on 3/27/2012.

214   "Babylon" is the Greek variant of Akkadian Babilu (bāb-ilû, meaning "Gateway of the god(s)," translating Sumerian KA2. DINGIR.RA. *New Interpreter's Dictionary of the Bible*, Volume 1: A-C, 376.

215   Mother Teresa, *In the Heart of the World: Thoughts, Stories and Prayers* (Novato: New World Library, 1997), 23, 33, and 55.

216   Dylan Thomas, "Do Not Go Gentle Into That Good Night" in *100 Best-Loved Poems* (London: Courier Dover, 1995), 93.

217   Elizabeth Kubler-Ross, On Death and Dying (New York: Scribner, 1997).

218   Alison, *On Being Liked*, 44.

219   Scott Owen Moore, Director, *Reparando* (Athentikos, 2010).

Chapter 19

220   St. Bernard Clairvaux: "The rule of St. Benedict begins with the word: Ausculta – listen!" The full quote from St. Bernard of Clairvaux reads, *"If you wish to see, listen; hearing is a step toward vision."* Could not find a primary reference for this anywhere but it is quoted often by others. Probably most recognized in: Megan McKenna, *Keepers of the Story: Oral Traditions in Religion* (New York: Church Publishing Incorporated, 2004), 31.

221   James Strong, "Yishma{e}l," n.p., *Strong's Hebrew Dictionary on CD-ROM*. Accordance, Version: 9.5.7., 2011.

222   James Strong, "El roi," n.p., *Strong's Greek Dictionary on CD-ROM*. Accordance, Version: 9.5.7., 2011.

223   James Strong, "Yehovah Raah," n.p., *Strong's Greek Dictionary on CD-ROM*. Accordance, Version: 9.5.7., 2011.

Chapter 20

224   We can't find the exact quote, however, for a discussion of God's desire we refer to Capon's chapter Into the Divine Complicity in his book *The Third Peacock*: Robert Farrar Capon, *The Third Peacock: The Problem of Good and Evil* (Palmwoods: Winston Press, 1986), 57.

225   Ernest Kurtz and Katherine Ketcham, *The Spirituality of Imperfection: Storytelling and the Search for Meaning* (New York: Bantam Books, 1992), 86.

226   Bosch, *Transforming Mission*, 16.

227   Alison, *On Being Liked*, 20.

228   See Girard's first major work, *Deceit, Desire, and the Novel: Self and Other in Literary Structure*, where he introduces his core idea of memesis—that desire is not innately hardwired into the individual but that we borrow our desires from others, that desire is triangular rather than linear due to its mimetic, imitative nature. Girard's proposition that desire is mimetic lays the foundation for an anthropology that challenges the dominant Western concept of the individual that informs most mainstream theological paradigms.

229   James Alison, "Contemplation in a world of violence: Girard, Merton, Tolle" (Lecture organized by the Thomas Merton Society at Downside Abbey, London, 2001). For a brief discussion of this insight see the forward to Rene Girard, *I See Satan Fall Like Lightning* (Maryknoll: Orbis, 2009).

230   James Alison, "Love Your Enemy: Within a Divided Self," http://www.jamesalison.co.uk/texts/eng50.html, accessed on 3/27/2012.

231   Gil Bailey, *Violence Unveiled: Humanity at the Crossroads* (New York: Crossroad, 1996), 116-117.

232   Ralph Waldo Emerson, T*he Complete Prose Works of Ralph Waldo Emerson* (Kessinger Publishing, 2006), 30. Ralph Waldo Emerson, *The Complete Prose Works of Ralph Waldo Emerson* (Kessinger Publishing, 2006), 30.

233   Leonard Cohen, "Anthem" on *The Future* (Columbia Records, 1992).

234   Ralph D. Winter, "The Two Structures of God's Redemptive Mission," Missiology 2, no. 1 (1974): 121-139.

Conclusion

235   Eliot, *The Four Quartets*, 59

236   http://www.brainyquote.com/quotes/keywords/audience.html, accessed 3/27/12.

237   J.R.R. Tolkien, *Lord of the Rings* (New York: Ballantine Books, 1954-1974), 44.

Kris Rocke

Kris Rocke lives with his wife Lana and their two sons Grant and Mitchell in Tacoma WA. He has served in urban ministry since 1985 and is the founder and director of Center for Transforming Mission. He earned his B.A. in English at Pacific Lutheran University, in Tacoma, WA and his M.Div. at Palmer Theological Seminary in Philadelphia, PA. He recently completed a D.Min. in Transformational Leadership for the Global City from Bakke Graduate University in Seattle, WA. Kris is also an ordained member of the Street Psalms Community and swears he heard God laugh once.

Joel Van Dyke

Joel Van Dyke has lived and served in Guatemala City since 2003 with his wife Marilyn and their children Joel and Sofia. While in Guatemala, he has directed the work of CTM in Latin America as a career missionary with Christian Reformed World Missions. Prior to moving to Central America, he pastored for 15 years at Bethel Temple Community Bible Church in Philadelphia. He obtained his B.A. in Psychology and Social Work from Calvin College in Grand Rapids, MI and his M.Div. with concentration in Urban Mission from Westminster Theological Seminary in Philadelphia. Most recently, he completed a D.Min. in Transformational Leadership for the Global City from Bakke Graduate University in Seattle, WA. Joel is also an ordained member of the Street Psalms Community and a "wannabe" sports fisherman and a baseball enthusiast who loves playing with his son and coaching his son's team in Guatemala.

CPSIA information can be obtained at www.ICGtesting.com
Printed in the USA
LVOW13s1655150913

352504LV00002B/12/P